# THE COMPLETE 5-INGREDIENT COOKBOOK

# THE COMPLETE
# *5-INGREDIENT*
# COOKBOOK

### 175 EASY RECIPES *for* BUSY PEOPLE

DENISE BROWNING

**ROCKRIDGE
PRESS**

Interior and Cover Designer: Tricia Jang
Art Producer: Sara Feinstein
Editor: Gleni Bartels
Production Editor: Jenna Dutton

Photography © 2020 Andrew Purcell, cover, p. ii, vi-vii, x, 10, 17, 40, 48, 66, 76, 94, 100, 124, 130, 148, 156, 184, 198, 204, 210, 222, 240, 254; Jim Franco, p. 9; Trent Lanz / Stocksy United, p. 12; Laura Flippen, p. 14; Marija Vidal, p. 20; Thomas J. Story, p. 24.

Food styling by Carrie Purcell, cover, p. ii, vi-vii, x, 10, 17, 40, 48, 66, 76, 94, 100, 124, 130, 148, 156, 184, 198, 204, 210, 222, 240, 254.

All illustrations used under license from Shutterstock.com.

Author photo courtesy of © Anna Angenend

Cover recipes (clockwise): Tortellini and Caprese Salad Skewers (page 77); Chicken Puttanesca with Orzo (page 157); Very Berry Salad with Candied Walnuts (page 112); Cherry-Almond Cobbler (page 241)

ISBN: Print 978-1-64611-965-3 | eBook 978-1-64611-966-0

R0

*To THE ONE,*
*for His grace and love.*

◇◇◇◇◇◇◇◇

*To my husband, Jared,*
*for his love and*
*invaluable support.*

◇◇◇◇◇◇◇◇

*To Hannah and Chantal—*
*my toughest food critics*
*and my pride and joy.*

# CONTENTS

# INTRODUCTION

I was born and raised in Brazil. I grew up watching my mother, aunts, and most of all my grandma Socorro, always in the kitchen, cooking up a storm. The food they made was simple yet unfailingly delicious and comforting. My years of happily watching them cook awakened my desire to explore and be daring in the kitchen—and oh boy, was I ever! Sometimes I succeeded, and other times I failed horribly. But my mom never discouraged me. Instead, she and I—and whoever else happened to be in the kitchen—would linger there to enjoy her stories and jokes. This boosted my confidence to keep cooking, regardless of the results.

For many years, I dabbled in the kitchen as more of a weekend hobby, since I had a full-time job as a lawyer.

But after I married and moved to the United States, cooking became a daily ritual. It led me to pursue a formal culinary education and to work in catering before starting my family. Then it felt like everything just clicked into place! I am now proud to be a busy mother of two and a professional chef and food blogger who has been juggling motherhood and an outside career for more than a decade.

Like many, at the end of the day—and at the beginning and in the middle of the day—I want to put good food on the table to feed my family, and I have learned, sometimes the hard way, that simplicity works best for everyone concerned. That's why I have worked to develop so many simple, easy recipes for my blog, *Easy and Delish*,

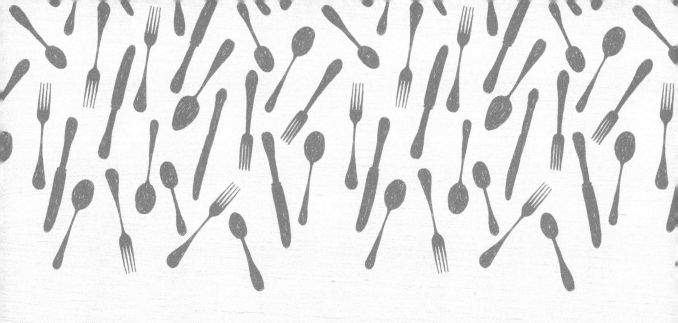

for well-known brands, and for this cookbook—so you won't have to struggle to find effortless, tasty options like I did!

*The Complete 5-Ingredient Cookbook* includes 175 easy, affordable, and delicious recipes that span from breakfast to dinner and everything in between. And while they all use only 5 main ingredients that can be found in any grocery store, I promise they don't skimp on flavor.

You'll learn what you'll need to stock in your pantry, refrigerator, and freezer to ensure recipe success, as well as any essential cooking equipment to have on hand. I've also included meal plans that accommodate different diets and lifestyles to take the guesswork out of your weekly menu-making and shopping lists. Useful preparation and storage tips and simple swaps will help you stretch your ingredients and waste less. All these features will make your life easier, save you both time and money, and hopefully give you some new go-to recipes.

It took me many years to learn what I am sharing with you here. My goal is that you'll come to see how fun and versatile cooking can be. Moreover, I hope this cookbook will be your trusty companion and friend, helping you navigate your time in the kitchen and providing you with joy—both in cooking and in eating.

*Enjoy!*

# 1

## Quality over Quantity

A delicious home-cooked meal produces feelings of warmth, comfort, and connection, but let's face it: getting home-cooked meals on the table on a regular basis can be daunting. In this chapter, I'll help you get your kitchen organized so you can start cooking quick and easy 5-ingredient recipes right away. Together, let's bring the joy of cooking—and the time to enjoy eating—to every single meal!

## THE BENEFITS OF 5-INGREDIENT RECIPES

Say goodbye to long, labor-intensive recipes that require extra trips to the grocery store or so much equipment that you spend the rest of your evening cleaning up. When you base your weekly meal plan on simple, 5-ingredient recipes, you will:

**SAVE TIME AND MONEY.** The fewer ingredients you need, the less time you'll spend at the grocery store. This also has a positive impact on your wallet. In addition, you'll spend less time doing prep work and standing over the stove, which frees you up for the things that really matter.

**PRODUCE LESS WASTE.** With a comprehensive list of 5-ingredient recipes to choose from and a simple weekly meal plan, you can prep your meals ahead of time, using some of the same basic ingredients across different meals, thereby avoiding waste. I've also included "Waste-not" tips with suggestions for using up leftover ingredients.

**HAVE LESS TO CLEAN.** With fewer ingredients to deal with, you will have fewer dishes to clean. At least one quarter of the recipes in this book are adapted for the slow cooker or pressure cooker, and several require only one pan. After all, who wants a full sink to clean after cooking a meal?

## STOCKING YOUR 5-INGREDIENT KITCHEN

All it takes to stock up are a few basic staples and some fresh, frozen, and canned goods available at most grocery stores. Keeping these items on hand will make cooking a breeze.

### BASIC INGREDIENTS

This book emphasizes quality over quantity. Each recipe was created to make the most delicious dish possible using the fewest ingredients, so you can spend more time experiencing the joy and comfort of flavorful home-cooked meals with your family and friends. While each recipe contains no more than 5 main ingredients, basic flavoring staples—such as oil, salt, pepper, and onion—don't count toward the 5-ingredient total in order to save you from bland, unappetizing results.

I've limited the basic ingredients to 8 pantry items (plus water) that provide a flavor foundation across all styles of cooking. You probably have these items on hand already and, if not, stocking up on them should be easy and relatively inexpensive.

The following 8 basic ingredients are used in varying combinations across the recipes:

**ALL-PURPOSE FLOUR:** An important basic ingredient in sweet and savory dishes alike, flour builds structure in cakes, helps bind meatballs, and thickens sauces and gravies.

**BLACK PEPPER:** Pepper provides a touch of heat and depth of flavor to any savory dish.

**CITRUS:** A squeeze of lemon, lime, or orange brings a bright, flavorful zing to many recipes. Citrus also works as a tenderizer, breaking down fibers in marinated meats.

**GARLIC:** This flavor-boosting staple is fundamental to many global cuisines, including Portuguese, Italian, and Indian.

**OIL:** Oil influences the flavor and the texture of a dish. Just think about how hot oil turns your pan-fried chicken a delicious and crispy golden brown.

**ONION:** Another basic ingredient in many cuisines, onions give substance and flavor to many savory dishes.

**SALT:** Salt is one of the most basic flavoring agents in cooking. It brings out the flavors of other ingredients as well as adding a flavor of its own.

**SUGAR:** Indispensable in baking, sugar adds sweetness to cookies, cakes, pies, and other treats.

## IN THE REFRIGERATOR, FREEZER, AND PANTRY

For the sake of convenience and ease, I created these recipes so that many of the ingredients can be used interchangeably or in different combinations to achieve a variety of results. This means that when you keep some very basic items on hand, you will have several quick and easy choices at your fingertips, even if you haven't had time to plan ahead. The ingredients in the following lists are those that appear most frequently in the book.

### Fresh and Perishable

**BACON:** This serves to add flavor or act as a garnish for certain dishes. Thick-cut smoked bacon works well for both purposes.

**DAIRY:** Many recipes call for dairy products such as plain yogurt, cheeses, heavy cream, and cream cheese—especially desserts, breakfast recipes, soups, and stews. In many cases, the dairy products can be replaced with a suitable plant-based substitute of your choice.

**EGGS:** Large eggs are a staple in desserts and some breakfast recipes.

**FRUITS:** Several recipes call for various fruits, but apples, avocados, bananas, berries, peaches, and pears are those that appear most often.

**VEGETABLES:** In addition to basics such as garlic and onion, I use a variety of fresh vegetables: bell peppers, broccoli, carrots, cauliflower, mushrooms, and small potatoes.

## Frozen Goods

**FRUITS:** I like to stock my freezer with various fruits for things like smoothies. Berries, mangos, peaches, and pineapple all appear in multiple recipes.

**MEATBALLS:** Cooked frozen meatballs are a great option when you're short on time. Beef, chicken, turkey, or vegetable meatballs can be used interchangeably in the recipes.

**MEATS:** There are a range of meats used throughout: chicken (mostly thighs), pork (often chops or stew meat), and beef (mainly stew meat), though whatever protein

you have on hand can usually be substituted to give the dish a different spin.

**SEAFOOD:** The recipes from the fish and seafood chapter most frequently call for salmon, cod, or tilapia fillets, or large raw shrimp.

**VEGETABLES:** Frozen vegetables of all kinds are great to have on hand to quickly add nutrients to dishes. I primarily use broccoli, cauliflower, and a frozen blend of onions and bell peppers.

## Canned Goods

**BEANS:** These recipes use black beans, chickpeas, and refried beans. You can always replace black beans with what's on hand, including kidney or pinto beans.

**COCONUT MILKS:** Several varieties of coconut milk products are handy to have. Regular full-fat canned coconut milk is the most versatile and is a great replacement for regular dairy milk in many recipes. Coconut cream is great for desserts, and coconut milk beverage—a smooth version of coconut milk that comes in a carton—is what I recommend for smoothies and breakfast items.

**CORN:** I love corn because it adds sweetness to dishes. Most often, these recipes call for yellow corn, but a few use corn blends, like Southwestern style. Yellow corn and Southwestern-style corn can be used interchangeably.

**DICED TOMATOES:** This is one of the most versatile ingredients you can keep in your pantry. They are a shelf-stable replacement for fresh tomatoes, especially when fresh ones are out of season, and can be pureed to serve as tomato sauce.

---

## GET THE MOST OUT OF THE GROCERY STORE

Below are some of my tried-and-true tips:

- Before planning your shopping list, take a look at your local grocery store flyer for products on sale and any coupons. When available, opt for generic or store-brand products to save even more.
- Stocking up on frozen fruits and vegetables can reduce waste from spoilage and make it easy to always incorporate fruits and vegetables into your diet.
- Embrace Meatless Monday. Sources of protein such as beans and legumes, vegetable meatballs, and eggs can replace meat in a variety of dishes, and they have a longer shelf life.
- Starches like rice and dried pasta are incredibly versatile, have a long shelf life, and are affordable, especially when purchased in bulk.
- Check out the dollar store for staples like spices, oils, vinegars, bottled sauces, and other condiments. They're usually cheaper than a traditional grocery store and the quality is the same.

---

## Dry Goods

**NUTS:** Several recipes call for nuts, including walnuts, pecans, cashews, and pistachios. You can pick just one type to have handy and simply use that as a replacement for any of the others.

**PASTA:** It's always great to have pasta in your pantry for a quick weeknight dinner. Dried spaghetti, lasagna noodles, and orzo are the main types of pasta called for in these recipes.

**RICE:** The two main types of rice used in these recipes are long-grain white rice and Arborio rice. For most recipes, long-grain white rice can be replaced by brown rice (or any other variety you prefer); just be sure to adjust the cooking time according to the package instructions.

## Spices, Herbs, and Flavorings

**BALSAMIC VINEGAR:** Balsamic vinegar can lend color and a sweet, tangy flavor to dishes or can be used as a sauce when reduced.

**BROTH:** The type of broth varies according to the meat you use. However, if you had to choose between beef or chicken broth to keep on hand, go for chicken, as it adds flavor without overpowering the dish. I prefer low-sodium broth but you can use what you have on hand.

**DIJON MUSTARD:** Frequently used throughout these recipes, it adds flavor and a touch of spiciness.

**HERBS:** Fresh herbs, including basil, cilantro, mint, parsley, and rosemary, are used throughout. While I have cross-referenced recipes with fresh herbs in order to minimize waste, you may also either omit them or replace them with dried herbs, if desired. Remember that dried herbs have a long shelf life and are more potent than their fresh counterparts, usually requiring only one-third of the amount of fresh herbs called for.

**SWEETENERS:** Honey and maple syrup are used for drizzling, garnishing, and adding sweetness. They're also suitable replacements for sugar in most recipes. You may keep both on hand or pick one.

**RED PEPPER FLAKES:** While used as an ingredient in many recipes, red pepper flakes can also be added to dishes to give an extra kick! If you like spicy food, I suggest adding ¼ teaspoon of red pepper flakes to sauces, soups, and meat and seafood dishes. On the other hand, if you're not a fan of heat, replace this ingredient with freshly ground black pepper.

**SOY SAUCE OR TAMARI:** Many recipes in this book require soy sauce. Keep in mind that, in order to make a gluten-free recipe, you will need a gluten-free soy sauce or a gluten-free tamari, so be sure to check the labels carefully.

**WHITE WINE:** You may use broth as a substitute for white wine in several recipes, but there are some that depend on it for the best flavor and a lovely acidity. It makes all the difference, especially when cooking seafood and meat stews. A cheap chardonnay or a white cooking wine will do the trick.

# EQUIPMENT AND UTENSILS

All of the recipes in this cookbook use basic kitchen equipment. You probably already have most, if not all, of these items in your kitchen.

**BAKING SHEET AND BAKING DISH:** Have at least one large, rimmed baking sheet and one 9-by-13-inch baking dish (to prepare baked dishes that demand a deeper dish).

**BLENDER OR FOOD PROCESSOR:** Most beverages, sauces, and bisques require either a blender or a food processor. There are several types in different price ranges, but a basic one will do just fine.

**CAKE PANS:** These recipes primarily use a Bundt pan or 8-by-8-inch baking pan. Both are inexpensive and are commonly used to make a variety of cakes, including pound cakes and brownies.

**CUTTING BOARDS AND A SHARP KNIFE:** It's highly recommended that you use two cutting boards, one for raw meat and fish and another for fresh vegetables and breads. You can use cutting boards made of wood or another nonporous material. Be sure that your chef's knife is sharp for easier and safer cutting.

**MIXER:** A simple electric hand mixer will make mixing cake batters, whisking egg whites, or whipping heavy cream so much faster. If you don't have one, make sure you have at least a good kitchen whisk and a sturdy wooden spoon to do those tasks by hand.

**NONSTICK STOCKPOT OR DUTCH OVEN:** These are important and versatile pieces of equipment, perfect for making all your soups and stews.

**SKILLETS:** A large cast-iron skillet, a grill pan, and a nonstick skillet will all come in handy when making these recipes, but if you have to pick one, go with a cast-iron or oven-safe skillet, since you can use it to prepare meals in the oven and on the stovetop.

**SLOW COOKER AND ELECTRIC PRESSURE COOKER:** One-quarter of these recipes have been adapted to make cooking quicker or more hands-off. A 6-quart capacity or larger is good for either appliance, but if necessary, a large soup pot, your stovetop, and maybe a bit more time are all you need.

# HOW TO USE THIS BOOK

All of these recipes were created to be simple and easy to follow. Each contains only 5 main ingredients, though some recipes also include a few other basic ingredients (see page 2) to enhance their flavor. Each recipe comes with labels that provide a quick reference for different lifestyle and dietary needs, including: **Appliance** (electric pressure cooker or slow cooker), **Dairy-Free, Gluten-Free, Nut-Free, Quick** (30 minutes or less to make, including prep time), **Vegan,** and **Vegetarian**. In addition, recipes also include helpful tips:

- **Prep tip**: These tips show you how to prepare an ingredient or make your prep time more efficient.

- **Variation tip**: These tips give suggestions for adding or substituting ingredients to give a different flavor spin or a variation in cooking method.

- **Appliance tip:** This indicates that the recipe uses a slow cooker or electric pressure cooker, or that the recipe contains alternative instructions adapted for them.

- **Storage tip:** These tips detail the proper storage of any extra ingredients or leftovers.

- **Make-ahead tip:** These provide instructions on how to prepare and store a dish or its components in advance.

- **Waste-not tip:** These give suggestions on how to use leftover ingredients, like jarred sauces or fresh herbs, cross-referencing other recipes that use or could include that ingredient.

This cookbook is meant to be as complete as possible, guiding you to prep and cook more efficiently, while saving you time and money. In the next chapter, I'll help you take these ideas a step further with sample meal plans and ready-made shopping lists, so you can be on your way to making and enjoying mouthwatering home-cooked meals in no time.

SHOPPING LIST

- ~~EGGS~~
- MILK
- BUTTER
- CHEESE
- ~~BREAD~~
- SOUR CREAM
- PASTA SAUCE
- BANANAS
- APPLES
- RASPBERRIES
- ICE CREAM
- ~~HOT DOGS~~
- COFFEE

# 2

## Time-Saving Techniques and Sample Meal Plans

This chapter provides essential tips on prepping like a pro, gives simple ingredient substitutions, and shares valuable information about freezing meals. It also features several meal plans with convenient ready-made shopping lists to suit different diets and lifestyles. The goal is to make the entire process approachable and stress-free—and to provide you with surefire time-saving techniques you can rely on.

## PREP LIKE A PRO

Prepping properly ahead of time is crucial in order to remove stress from the cooking process. Following these tips will make cooking a snap, especially when you find yourself pressed for time.

### READ, REVIEW, AND PLAN

While it might seem unnecessary, reading the complete recipe in advance can actually save you time and energy. You'll find out crucial details, such as how long you'll need to prep and cook a dish, what equipment you'll need, the ingredients required, and the order in which the ingredients are used. This helps you determine when to start cooking (on the weekend or during the week) or whether you'll need to make a trip to the grocery store beforehand. So please heed a friendly bit of advice: read, review, and plan!

### MISE EN PLACE

*Mise en place* translates to "putting in place," and it simply means that most of your ingredients should be ready to cook before you start. This can mean that your vegetables are chopped, your spices are measured, and so on. It's also helpful to keep your ingredients lined up in the order they appear in the recipe (which you'll know because you read the whole thing!).

### COOK EXTRA AMOUNTS

This is the basic tenet of meal prepping: Save yourself time by cooking extra that can be used later. For example, you can roast two chickens at once, eat one for dinner, and save the second to transform into other dishes. The same goes for starches like rice and pastas. Cooking extra amounts makes meal prep more efficient, saving you time during the week when you are busy.

# THE FREEZER IS YOUR FRIEND

Freezing meals is a great way to set yourself up for success in advance. You can freeze leftovers to eat as is or use them as components for different dishes. While a lot of these recipes come with tips on how long to store and freeze leftovers, I also want to give you the information you need in order to properly freeze a wide variety of meals and ingredients.

Keep in mind that some foods shouldn't be frozen, as it ruins their texture. These items include anything deep-fried; creamy sauces; mayonnaise, sour cream, and cream cheese; cooked egg whites and hard-boiled eggs; meringue, flan, and gelatin; and fully cooked rice and pastas. You can freeze starches if partially cooked; otherwise, they can easily become overcooked when reheated.

**How to Freeze and Thaw Meals:**

**Step 1:** Prep and cook the dish as stated in the recipe.

**Step 2:** Cool foods properly and quickly to preserve both nutrients and flavors. You can 1) Let the food cool for about 30 minutes at room temperature before transferring to the refrigerator to cool completely before freezing or 2) cool the dish by placing the food container in a large bowl of ice.

**Step 3:** Store in freezer-friendly containers. Use freezer bags when you can to save space, making sure to squeeze out as much air from the bag as possible.

**Step 4:** Make sure to label all your meals with the expiration date, which is usually 2 to 3 months from freezing. (Some exceptions are noted below.)

**Step 5:** Always thaw frozen meals in the refrigerator, allowing at least 4 to 5 hours per pound of food.

**How Long Will It Last?**

- **Cooked meats:** 2 to 3 months
- **Cooked poultry and seafood:** 3 to 6 months
- **Soups and stews:** 2 to 3 months
- **Bread and cakes:** 2 to 6 months
- **Blanched vegetables:** up to 12 months
- **Eggs (out of the shell only):** up to 12 months
- **Fruit:** up to 12 months
- **Ice cream:** 4 months

## COOK MORE ONE-POT AND ONE-PAN MEALS

I've created a bunch of one-pot dishes for this book, including One-Pan Chipotle Chicken Thighs with Guacamole Salsa (page 152) and One-Pan Bratwurst and Vegetables (page 167). These meals save you time by allowing you to cook an entire meal all at once with less time spent washing dishes afterward. You'll usually have leftovers, which is great since these types of meals tend to freeze well.

## PREP EXTRA FOUNDATIONAL INGREDIENTS

Whenever I'm making something that calls for garlic, onions, or other frequently used ingredients, I always prep a little extra. Then, depending on my meal planning, I can either use it later in the week or freeze the surplus for use at a later date.

## CLEAN AS YOU GO

This is something that I learned in culinary school. Cleaning as you go helps to declutter your workspace during the prepping process, especially when cooking in tight quarters. It also leaves less mess to deal with when you finish. A good way to save yourself some time is to put dirty bowls, pans, and cooking utensils to soak in water while the food is cooking or while you're eating. This helps loosen soiled bits and makes the task of cleaning easier and quicker.

## SIMPLE SWAPS

One of the beauties of cooking is its flexibility! In many of these recipes, you can easily swap out ingredients for others that are already in your pantry, refrigerator, or freezer. Here are a few simple substitutions that you can make:

**Broccoli**: Cauliflower usually makes a suitable swap for broccoli and vice versa.

**Coconut cream**: Replace coconut cream with heavy cream.

**Coconut milk**: Replace coconut milk with whole milk, or with half-and-half for savory recipes where the coconut flavor is mild or gets overpowered by other ingredients.

**Fresh garlic and onion:** While not suitable for all recipes, in some cases you can replace these with their dried counterparts. Use it to introduce flavor without wetness or texture as you would with other seasonings. You can replace 1 clove of garlic with ⅛ teaspoon of garlic powder, and 1 medium onion with 1 tablespoon of onion powder. For dried minced onion, 1 tablespoon equals ¼ cup of minced raw onion.

**Fresh herbs**: Replace fresh herbs with dried versions most of the time. But, as mentioned, use one-third of the amount because they're more concentrated and potent. For example, if a recipe calls for 1 tablespoon (i.e., 3 teaspoons) of fresh rosemary, you would need only 1 teaspoon of dried rosemary.

**Heavy cream**: Coconut cream or Greek yogurt diluted with a touch of milk are both great replacements, depending on the recipe.

**Lemon juice**: You can replace lemon juice with lime juice or with red wine vinegar in soups and stews.

**White wine**: You can replace wine with whatever broth works best in your recipe. When it comes to seafood, if you're not using wine, try squeezing in a touch of lemon or lime juice for acidity that will maximize flavor.

# SIMPLE AS 1, 2, 3

Cooking doesn't have to be complicated. These recipes beg to be experimented with, and once you feel comfortable, I encourage you to do so. Tweak them to suit your own individual taste or family preferences, put leftovers to good use, and add exciting new ingredients. It's almost like a math equation. You can use the same few ingredients as the base for a wide variety of meals. Below I take a recipe from the book and show you how simple it is to create a new dish with some easy ingredient trades.

For example, let's say you bought some chicken thighs and already have pesto in your pantry:

Chicken + Pesto + Tomatoes = One-Pan Roasted Chicken Thighs with Pesto and Cherry Tomatoes (page 155)

Chicken + Pesto + Tomatoes + Bread = Italian-inspired chicken salad sandwiches

Chicken + Pesto + Tomatoes + Fettuccini = pesto chicken fettuccini

Or say black beans were on sale, and you have sweet potatoes that you need to use:

Black Beans + Sweet Potatoes + Tortillas + Guacamole = Sweet Potato and Black Bean Crispy Tacos (page 143)

Black Beans + Sweet Potatoes + Quinoa + Enchilada Sauce = a sweet and spicy black-bean bowl

Black Beans + Sweet Potatoes + Onions + Chicken Broth = a smoky black bean and sweet potato soup

And it also works for your sweet tooth!

Peaches + Granola + Cardamom + Brown Sugar + Butter = Peach-Cardamom Crumble (page 242)

Peaches + Granola + Greek Yogurt + Honey = a sweet and crunchy parfait

Peaches + Brown Sugar + Butter + Biscuits = a peaches-and-browned-butter cobbler

# THE MEAL PLANS

One of the best ways to save both time and money is to prep and plan your meals in advance. To give you a helping hand, I've included five different meal plans in this section to fit different schedules and dietary needs.

VEGETARIAN    LOW CARB    GLUTEN-FREE    **QUICK & EASY**    GLOBAL FEAST

Each plan lists meal suggestions for all seven days of the week, with four meals per day: simple breakfasts, lunches, dinners, and a snack. They feature recipes found in this cookbook, as well as suggestions for using leftovers from previous meals in order to minimize food waste.

But that's not all! Each meal plan comes with prep tips and a shopping list to make your weekly meal prep a breeze.

Although each of the meal plans addresses different needs, I make the following suggestions for all:

- If you love variety, you can cook every one of the listed recipes, but if convenience comes first, pick one-third to one-half of the suggested recipes and make extra to repeat the meals on alternate days.

- Either cook everything ahead on the weekend and store for reheating during the week, or prep some items such as grains, meats, and vegetables and store them for cooking on the day that you plan to serve the meal.

- Cut down on your shopping by making substitutions, or simply picking one type of cheese, sweetener, bottled sauce, fresh herb, or bread, and using that as appropriate for all of the recipes.

## VEGETARIAN PLAN

*The beauty of this meal plan is there isn't much prepping involved. Most of the recipes use either frozen foods, convenient canned items, or dry pantry items that have a long shelf life and can be used later in other recipes.*

## Prep Ahead

Here are a few things to prep ahead for the week:

- **Chop the vegetables:** Slice the tomatoes and cucumbers for the Fresh Veggie Sandwich with Chipotle Aioli (page 118); slice the tomatoes for the Caprese Salad with Peppery Balsamic Reduction (page 110); slice the kalamata olives and red onions for the Individual Pita Pizzas with Red Onion and Kalamata Olives (page 134); chop the tomatoes, onions, and cilantro for the Guacamole Dip (page 68); also, chop the onion and mince the garlic for the vegetarian stews. You can also cut celery into sticks for the guacamole dip and Roasted Red Pepper Hummus (page 69). Keep the veggies in the refrigerator if using within 2 days or freeze them in freezer bags with labels to use later in the week. Please note: Cucumbers do NOT freeze well! But you can preslice them and refrigerate them in an airtight container to use within 2 days.

- **Core and slice the fruit:** For maximum freshness, you may choose to core and slice the apples and pear right before assembling the Pear and Apple "Nachos" with Peanut Butter and Cacao Nibs (page 86) and Crunchy "Parfait" Toast with Apples, Peanut Butter, and Honey (page 57). Alternatively, you could prep them ahead to use later on. In the latter case, core and slice the apples and pear, and soak the slices in a mixture of 1 quart of chilled water and 3 tablespoons of lemon juice to prevent browning. Then drain them and place the slices in a single layer on a baking sheet lined with parchment paper. Freeze until solid and pack in freezer bags, removing as much air as possible from the bag before sealing. Before using them, either thaw them in the refrigerator or let them sit at room temperature for 15 to 30 minutes, or until thawed.

- **Pre-slice the fresh mozzarella cheese:** If desired, you can preslice the fresh mozzarella (to use within 3 days) for the Caprese Salad.

- **Make the stews:** Stews such as the Vegetable Meatballs and Cauliflower Korma (page 128), the Pressure Cooker Cauliflower Chickpea Vindaloo (page 126), and the Chickpea and Potato Curry (page 127) can be made on the weekend and refrigerated if they are to be consumed within 3 or 4 days. Do not freeze stews made with dairy because they may separate or become grainy when reheated.

- **Cook the waffles:** You can make waffles on the weekend and freeze them for later use. To do this, let them cool, then place them onto a parchment paper–lined baking sheet, and freeze them until they are fully frozen. Transfer them to freezer-safe bags, where they will keep for 3 months.

| | BREAKFAST 1 | LUNCH | DINNER | SNACK |
|---|---|---|---|---|
| MON | Overnight Chia Pudding with Peanut Butter and Banana (page 54) | Caprese Salad with Peppery Balsamic Reduction (page 110) | Chickpea and Potato Curry (page 127) | Refreshing Pineapple-Mint Juice (page 43) |
| TUE | Crunchy "Parfait" Toast with Apples, Peanut Butter, and Honey (page 57) | Use leftover caprese salad to make sandwiches | Individual Pita Pizzas with Red Onion and Kalamata Olives (page 134) | Pear and Apple "Nachos" with Peanut Butter and Cacao Nibs (page 86) |
| WED | Tropical Fruit Smoothie (page 45) | Fresh Veggie Sandwich with Chipotle Aioli (page 118) | Vegetable Meatballs and Cauliflower Korma (page 128) | Roasted Red Pepper Hummus (page 69) with celery sticks |
| THU | Green Goodness Smoothie (page 47) | Use leftover pita bread and chickpea and potato curry to make sandwiches | Refried Beans and Kale Enchiladas with a Kick (page 146) | Honey and Ricotta Dip with Figs and Granola (page 70) |
| FRI | Mango, Lime, and Chia Smoothie (page 46) | Very Berry Salad with Candied Walnuts (page 112) | Use leftover korma to make pita sandwiches | Guacamole Dip (page 68) with celery sticks |
| SAT | Oven-Baked Buttermilk Blueberry Pancakes (page 58) | Sweet Potato and Black Bean Crispy Tacos (page 143) | Pressure Cooker Cauliflower Chickpea Vindaloo (page 126) | Use leftover honey and ricotta dip to eat with celery sticks |
| SUN | Chai Latte Waffles with Maple Syrup (page 59) | Butternut Squash and Roasted Corn Quesadillas (page 142) | Fire-Roasted Margherita Pizza (page 133) | Spread leftover hummus on toast and top with sliced avocado |

## Shopping List

### CANNED AND BOTTLED ITEMS

- ☐ Chickpeas, 4 (15-ounce) cans
- ☐ Coconut milk,
  1 (13.5-ounce) can
- ☐ Fire-roasted crushed tomatoes,
  1 (15-ounce) can
- ☐ Fire-roasted red bell peppers,
  1 (16-ounce) jar
- ☐ Kalamata olives, 1 (9.5- or
  10-ounce) jar

- ☐ Korma curry sauce,
  1 (15-ounce) jar
- ☐ Salsa, medium, 1 (16-ounce) jar
- ☐ Salsa, mild (8 ounces)
- ☐ Vegetarian refried black beans,
  2 (16-ounce) cans
- ☐ Vindaloo sauce,
  2 (10-ounce) jars

### DAIRY AND EGGS

- ☐ Cheddar cheese, shredded,
  1 (16-ounce) bag
- ☐ Cream cheese (4 ounces)
- ☐ Greek yogurt (8 ounces)
- ☐ Milk, whole (1 quart)
- ☐ Mozzarella cheese, fresh
  (1 pound)
- ☐ Mozzarella cheese pearls
  (8 ounces)

- ☐ Mozzarella cheese, shredded,
  1 (8-ounce) bag
- ☐ Part-skim ricotta (4 ounces)
- ☐ Pepper Jack cheese, shredded,
  1 (8-ounce) bag
- ☐ Queso fresco or feta cheese
  (8 ounces)

### FROZEN FOODS

- ☐ Butternut squash chunks,
  1 (10-ounce) bag
- ☐ Cauliflower florets,
  3 (12-ounce) bags
- ☐ Mango chunks,
  2 (10-ounce) bags
- ☐ Pineapple chunks,
  1 (16-ounce) bag

- ☐ Sweet potato chunks,
  1 (16-ounce) bag and
  1 (10-ounce) bag
- ☐ Vegetable meatballs,
  2 (12-ounce) bags

## PANTRY ITEMS

- ☐ Balsamic vinaigrette salad dressing
- ☐ Balsamic vinegar
- ☐ Bittersweet chocolate chips (optional)
- ☐ Buttermilk pancake mix
- ☐ Cacao nibs
- ☐ Candied walnuts
- ☐ Chia seeds
- ☐ Chipotle aioli
- ☐ Granola
- ☐ Honey
- ☐ Maple syrup
- ☐ Olive oil
- ☐ Peanut butter
- ☐ Pepper
- ☐ Pure vanilla extract
- ☐ Red curry paste
- ☐ Red pepper flakes
- ☐ Salt
- ☐ Tahini paste
- ☐ Vegetable oil

## PRODUCE

- ☐ Apples (2)
- ☐ Avocados (3)
- ☐ Baby spinach, 1 (8-ounce) bag
- ☐ Bananas (5)
- ☐ Basil (1 bunch)
- ☐ Blueberries, 1 pint
- ☐ Broccoli slaw, 1 (9- or 10-ounce) bag
- ☐ Celery (1 small bunch)
- ☐ Chopped kale, 1 (16-ounce) bag
- ☐ Cilantro, fresh (1 bunch)
- ☐ Cucumbers (3)
- ☐ Garlic (3 heads)
- ☐ Jalapeño (1)
- ☐ Kiwis (4)
- ☐ Lemon (1)
- ☐ Limes (5)
- ☐ Mint, fresh (1 bunch)
- ☐ Mixed greens, 1 (8-ounce) bag
- ☐ Pear (1)
- ☐ Raspberries (½ pint)
- ☐ Red onion (1)
- ☐ Tomatoes (7)
- ☐ Yellow onions (3)

## OTHER

- ☐ Coconut milk beverage, 2 (32-ounce) cartons
- ☐ Corn tortillas, 1 (10-count) bag
- ☐ Dried Mission figs, 1 (7-ounce) bag
- ☐ Flour tortillas, 8- or 10-inch, 1 (10-count) bag
- ☐ Guacamole, 1 (8-ounce) container
- ☐ Pita bread, 1 (8-count) bag
- ☐ Refrigerated pizza dough (1)
- ☐ Sliced bread (1 loaf)

# LOW-CARB PLAN

*This meal plan requires the fewest prepping tasks. Many of the ingredients used in the recipes, especially the meats, already come presliced. Cutting vegetables is the biggest task for the week, as you'll see. This plan calls for a few substitutions in the recipes to make them low carb, so keep an eye out for deviations.*

## Prep Ahead

- **Chop the vegetables:** Chop the onion, bell pepper, and parsley, and also mince garlic for the Eggs in Chunky Tomato Sauce (page 65); chop the kale and mince garlic for the Avocado and Kale Gazpacho (page 96); chop the garlic and onion for the Creamy Tomato Bisque (page 99); chop the onion, cilantro, and tomato for the Guacamole Dip (page 68); and cut celery into sticks. Also chop the garlic and cilantro for the Lime and Cilantro Aioli (page 212). Keep prepped vegetables and herbs in the refrigerator if using within 2 days or freeze them in freezer bags with labels to use later in the week.

- **Grate the cauliflower:** You can prep the cauliflower for the Sunny-Side-Up Eggs with Cauliflower Hash Browns and Salsa Verde (page 60) ahead. Grate the cauliflower, squeeze out excess water, and freeze in a freezer bag, removing as much air as possible. Thaw it in the refrigerator before using.

- **Chop the bacon:** Chop the bacon for the Cheesy Bacon and Spinach Frittata (page 64) and refrigerate in a plastic bag, removing as much air as possible.

|  | BREAKFAST | LUNCH | DINNER | SNACK |
|---|---|---|---|---|
| **MON** | Breakfast Tacos with Eggs and Avocado (with low-carb tortillas) (page 63) | Pizza-dilla with Guacamole Salsa (with low-carb tortillas) (page 81) | One-Pan Chipotle Chicken Thighs with Guacamole Salsa (page 152) | Roasted Cashew Nuts with Honey and Rosemary (use sugar-free maple syrup or honey) (page 87) |
| **TUE** | Sparkling Strawberry-Mint Juice (with keto sweetener) (page 42) | Avocado and Kale Gazpacho (page 96) | A green salad topped with leftover Chipotle Chicken Thighs with Guacamole Salsa for dressing | Homemade Frizz Coffee (with keto sweetener) (page 52) |
| **WED** | Eggs in Chunky Tomato Sauce (page 65) | Smoked Salmon Wrap with Capers and Cream Cheese (with low-carb tortillas) (page 120) | Pan-Grilled Pork Chops with Pico de Gallo (page 170) | Guacamole Dip (page 68) with celery sticks |
| **THU** | Mozzarella, Avocado, and Spinach Quesadillas (with low-carb tortillas) (page 62) | Creamy Tomato Bisque (page 99) | Roasted Cauliflower Steak with Harissa (page 131) | Sparkling Strawberry-Mint Juice (with keto sweetener) (page 42) |
| **FRI** | Protein-Packed Raspberry and Dark Chocolate Smoothie Bowls (with keto sweetener) (page 53) | Very Berry Salad with plain walnuts and lemon vinaigrette (page 112) | A green salad topped with sliced leftover pork chops and dressed with leftover pico de gallo | Roasted Cashew Nuts with Honey and Rosemary |
| **SAT** | Sunny-Side-Up Eggs with Cauliflower Hash Browns and Salsa Verde (page 60) | Top a green salad with leftover smoked salmon and dress with lemon vinaigrette | Pan-Seared Pork Chops with Sweet Teriyaki Sauce (with sugar-free honey or maple syrup) (page 173) | Coconut Yogurt Parfait with Mixed Berries and Almond Granola (with a keto sweetener and almonds instead of granola) (page 90) |
| **SUN** | Cheesy Bacon and Spinach Frittata (page 64) | Bacon and Avocado Grilled Cheese Sandwich (with low-carb bread) (page 121) | Zucchini Noodles with Pesto Sauce (page 137) | Celery sticks with Lime and Cilantro Aioli (page 212) |

## Shopping List

### CANNED AND BOTTLED ITEMS

- ☐ Diced tomatoes, 1 (28-ounce) can
- ☐ Guacamole salsa, 1 (15.7-ounce) jar
- ☐ Harissa paste, 1 (8-ounce) jar
- ☐ Pesto (12 ounces)
- ☐ Salsa verde, 1 (7-ounce) can
- ☐ Teriyaki sauce, 1 (10-ounce) bottle
- ☐ Whole peeled tomatoes, 1 (28-ounce) can

### DAIRY AND EGGS

- ☐ Butter (6 tablespoons)
- ☐ Cheddar cheese, shredded (2 ounces)
- ☐ Cream cheese, chive and onion flavor (4 ounces)
- ☐ Eggs (1½ dozen)
- ☐ Half-and-half (½ pint)
- ☐ Heavy cream (½ pint)
- ☐ Keto coconut yogurt (8 ounces)
- ☐ Mozzarella cheese, shredded (16 ounces)
- ☐ Parmesan cheese, shaved (2 ounces)
- ☐ Pepper Jack cheese, sliced (16 slices)

### FROZEN FOODS

- ☐ Mixed berries (1 pound)
- ☐ Raspberries (1 pound)
- ☐ Spiralized zucchini (zoodles), 4 (12-ounce) packages
- ☐ Strawberries, 1 (16-ounce) bag

### MEAT

- ☐ Chicken, 4 bone-in, skin-on thighs
- ☐ Pepperoni slices (20 slices)
- ☐ Pork, 4 to 6 bone-in, center-cut chops (about 3 pounds)
- ☐ Pork, 4 boneless, center-cut chops
- ☐ Smoked bacon (18 slices)
- ☐ Smoked salmon, sliced (8 ounces)

## PANTRY ITEMS

- ☐ Almonds (1 cup)
- ☐ Balsamic vinaigrette salad dressing
- ☐ Capers
- ☐ Carbonated water
- ☐ Cashews (2½ cups)
- ☐ Chipotle powder
- ☐ Coconut water
- ☐ Dark chocolate
- ☐ Dijon mustard
- ☐ Garlic powder
- ☐ Instant espresso powder
- ☐ Keto chocolate protein powder
- ☐ Keto sweetener (keto honey or keto maple syrup)
- ☐ Low-sodium vegetable broth
- ☐ Mayonnaise
- ☐ Olive oil
- ☐ Pepper
- ☐ Red pepper flakes
- ☐ Salt
- ☐ Toasted white sesame seeds
- ☐ Vegetable oil
- ☐ Walnuts (⅓ cup)

## PRODUCE

- ☐ Avocados (11)
- ☐ Baby spinach (1 cup)
- ☐ Blueberries (½ pint)
- ☐ Cauliflower, 1 small head and 2 medium heads
- ☐ Chives, fresh (1 bunch) or dried
- ☐ Cilantro, fresh (1 bunch)
- ☐ Garlic (2 heads)
- ☐ Jalapeño (1)
- ☐ Kale (1 bunch)
- ☐ Lemons (8)
- ☐ Limes (2)
- ☐ Mint, fresh (1 bunch)
- ☐ Mixed greens, 2 (8-ounce) bags
- ☐ Parsley, fresh (1 bunch)
- ☐ Raspberries (½ pint)
- ☐ Red bell peppers (2)
- ☐ Rosemary (1 bunch)
- ☐ White onions (2)
- ☐ Yellow onions (2)

## OTHER

- ☐ Corn tortillas (4)
- ☐ Low-carb sliced bread (1 loaf)
- ☐ Low-carb tortillas, 8- or 10-inch, 1 (12-count) bag
- ☐ Pico de gallo (12 ounces)

# GLUTEN-FREE PLAN

*This plan calls for gluten-free bread as a substitute in some recipes and for making sandwiches out of leftovers. As with all allergens, read ingredient labels carefully to makes sure it has been processed in a gluten-free facility.*

## Prep Ahead

- **Chop the vegetables:** Chop the onion and bell pepper and mince the garlic for the Eggs in Chunky Tomato Sauce (page 65); mince the garlic for the Pressure Cooker Creamy Corn Chowder with Bacon (page 103); slice the tomatoes for the Crispy Caprese Ciabatta Sandwich (page 119); mince the garlic for the Chicken Salsa Verde (page 151) and Garlic and Basil Beef (page 180); chop the onion for the Cuban-Style Beef Picadillo (page 177) and the Butter Chicken (page 161).

- **Grate the cauliflower:** Grate the cauliflower for Sunny-Side-Up Eggs with Cauliflower Hash Browns and Salsa Verde (page 60). Squeeze out the excess water and freeze. Thaw in the refrigerator before using.

- **Chop the watermelon:** Cut the watermelon into chunks for the Watermelon and Lime Juice (page 44), plus extra for snacking on during the week. Keep refrigerated and use within 2 days.

- **Chop the chicken:** Cut the chicken into chunks for the Butter Chicken (page 161). Place into an airtight container, and either refrigerate to use within 2 days or freeze to use later on during the week.

- **Make the soups and stews:** The Pressure Cooker Creamy Corn Chowder with Bacon (page 103), Golden Butternut Squash Bisque (page 101), Chicken Salsa Verde (page 151), and Butter Chicken (page 161) can be made on the weekend and refrigerated in airtight containers for up to 3 days.

| | BREAKFAST | LUNCH | DINNER | SNACK |
|---|---|---|---|---|
| MON | Overnight Chia Pudding with Peanut Butter and Banana (page 54) | Pickled Beet and Crumbled Goat Cheese Salad (page 114) | Butter Chicken (page 161) | Watermelon and Lime Juice (page 44) |
| TUE | Breakfast Tacos with Eggs and Avocado (page 63) | Thai Noodle Salad with Peanut Sauce (page 117) | Use leftover butter chicken to make sandwiches | Frozen Peach Iced Tea (page 49) |
| WED | Banana and Mocha Protein Smoothie (page 50) | Pressure Cooker Creamy Corn Chowder with Bacon (page 103) | Chicken Salsa Verde (page 151) | Leftover watermelon with a hint of honey |
| THU | Mango, Lime, and Chia Smoothie (page 46) | Charred Corn Salad with Cotija Cheese (page 111) | Garlic and Basil Beef (page 180) | Refreshing Pineapple-Mint Juice (page 43) |
| FRI | Tropical Fruit Smoothie (page 45) | Golden Butternut Squash Bisque (page 101) | Butternut Squash and Roasted Corn Quesadillas (page 142) | Roasted Red Pepper Hummus (page 69) with celery sticks |
| SAT | Sunny-Side-Up Eggs with Cauliflower Hash Browns and Salsa Verde (page 60) | Pan-Grilled Reuben Sandwich (on gluten-free bread) (page 122) | One-Pan Roasted Chicken Thighs with Pesto with Cherry Tomatoes (page 155) | Churro Pecans with Chocolate Drizzle (page 88) |
| SUN | Eggs in Chunky Tomato Sauce (page 65) | Crispy Caprese Ciabatta Sandwich (on gluten-free bread) (page 119) | Cuban-Style Beef Picadillo (page 177) | Leftover hummus on toast, topped with Cotija or feta cheese |

## Shopping List

### CANNED AND BOTTLED ITEMS

- ☐ Butter chicken sauce, 1 (15-ounce) jar
- ☐ Chickpeas, 2 (15-ounce) cans
- ☐ Cream-style sweet corn, 2 (14.75-ounce) cans
- ☐ Fire-roasted corn blend, 3 (14.75-ounce) cans
- ☐ Fire-roasted red bell peppers, 1 (16-ounce) jar

- ☐ Green olives, 1 (10-ounce) jar
- ☐ Peanut sauce, 1 (12.8-ounce) jar
- ☐ Pesto, 1 (5.6-ounce) jar
- ☐ Pickled beets, 1 (15- to 16-ounce) jar
- ☐ Salsa, mild (8 ounces)
- ☐ Salsa verde (20 ounces)
- ☐ Sauerkraut, 1 (16-ounce) jar
- ☐ Tomato sauce, 2 (8 ounce) cans

### DAIRY AND EGGS

- ☐ Butter (5 tablespoons)
- ☐ Cheddar cheese, shredded (2 ounces)
- ☐ Cotija cheese or feta cheese (2 ounces)
- ☐ Eggs (1 dozen)
- ☐ Goat cheese (2 ounces)
- ☐ Greek yogurt (8 ounces)

- ☐ Milk, whole (half gallon)
- ☐ Mozzarella, sliced (8 slices)
- ☐ Pepper Jack cheese, shredded (2 ounces)
- ☐ Sour cream, 1 (8-ounce) container
- ☐ Swiss cheese, sliced (8 slices)

### FROZEN FOODS

- ☐ Butternut squash chunks (3 pounds)
- ☐ Hash brown potatoes, 1 (16-ounce) bag

- ☐ Mango chunks, 2 (10-ounce) bags
- ☐ Peach slices, 1 (10-ounce) bag
- ☐ Pineapple chunks, 1 (10-ounce) bag

### MEAT

- ☐ Bacon (6 slices)
- ☐ Beef, ground (4 pounds)
- ☐ Chicken, bone-in, skin-on thighs (4 pounds)

- ☐ Chicken, boneless, skinless thighs (2 pounds)
- ☐ Corned beef, sliced (8 slices)

## PANTRY ITEMS

- ☐ Bittersweet chocolate chips
- ☐ Brown sugar
- ☐ Chia seeds
- ☐ Chipotle aioli
- ☐ Chocolate protein powder
- ☐ Ground cinnamon
- ☐ Honey
- ☐ Instant espresso powder
- ☐ Maple syrup
- ☐ Low-sodium chicken broth
- ☐ Low-sodium soy sauce
- ☐ Low-sodium vegetable broth
- ☐ Olive oil
- ☐ Peanut butter
- ☐ Pecan halves (2 cups)
- ☐ Pepper
- ☐ Roasted peanuts (¼ cup)
- ☐ Russian salad dressing
- ☐ Salt
- ☐ Sugar
- ☐ Tahini paste
- ☐ Vegetable oil

## PRODUCE

- ☐ Avocado (1)
- ☐ Bananas (9)
- ☐ Basil, fresh (1 bunch)
- ☐ Bird's-eye chiles (2)
- ☐ Broccoli slaw, 1 (12-ounce) bag
- ☐ Cauliflower (1 small head)
- ☐ Celery (3 to 4 stalks)
- ☐ Cherry tomatoes (12 ounces)
- ☐ Chives, fresh (1 bunch) or dried
- ☐ Garlic (3 heads)
- ☐ Lemon (1)
- ☐ Limes (9)
- ☐ Mint, fresh (1 bunch)
- ☐ Mixed greens, 1 (8-ounce) bag
- ☐ Navel orange (1)
- ☐ Parsley (1 small bunch) (optional)
- ☐ Red bell peppers (2)
- ☐ Red onion (1)
- ☐ Thai basil or basil, fresh (2 bunches)
- ☐ Tomatoes (2)
- ☐ Watermelon (1 medium)
- ☐ White onion (1)
- ☐ Yellow onions (2)

## OTHER

- ☐ Coconut milk beverage, 2 (32-ounce) cartons
- ☐ Corn tortillas (4)
- ☐ Gluten-free flour tortillas, 8- or 10-inch (4)
- ☐ Gluten-free sliced bread, rye or wheat (1 loaf)
- ☐ Pico de gallo (12 ounces)
- ☐ Raisins (¼ cup)
- ☐ Thai rice noodles (6 ounces)
- ☐ Unsweetened iced tea, 1 (12-ounce) bottle

QUICK & EASY PLAN

# QUICK & EASY PLAN

*Each recipe in this quick and easy meal plan can be prepared and cooked in 30 minutes or less. This is a meal plan ideal for those with a busy lifestyle. It delivers a simple and delicious feast every day, without the hassle.*

## Prep Ahead

- **Chop the vegetables:** Mince the garlic for the Quick Paella with Broiled Shrimp (page 188), Spaghetti with Roasted Bell Pepper Sauce and Basil (page 138), Shrimp a la Diabla (page 186), Chicken Puttanesca with Orzo (page 157), and Creamy Chicken Tikka Masala (page 162); chop the onion and mince the garlic for the Pressure Cooker Cauliflower Chickpea Vindaloo (page 126). Put the vegetables for each recipe into a single covered container, making them easy to use later. Keep prepped vegetables in the refrigerator if using within 2 days, or freeze them in freezer bags with labels to use later in the week.

- **Chop the watermelon:** Cut the watermelon into chunks for the Watermelon and Lime Juice (page 44), plus extra to snack on during the week. Keep refrigerated and use within 2 days. If freezing, be aware that watermelon can become mushy when thawed.

- **Cook the meatballs ahead:** Cook meatballs ahead for the Sweet and Spicy BBQ Meatball Sub (page 123), let them cool, and refrigerate in an airtight container for up to 4 days. Reheat before assembling the sandwiches.

- **Cut the chicken:** Cut the chicken into chunks for the Creamy Chicken Tikka Masala (page 162) and Orange Chicken (page 160), put each into an airtight container, and either refrigerate (if using within 2 days) or freeze for later use during the week.

- **Make the stews:** Stews such as the Creamy Chicken Tikka Masala (page 162) can be made ahead and refrigerated in an airtight container if they are to be eaten within 3 days. Do not freeze stews made with dairy because they may separate or become grainy when reheated.

|  | BREAKFAST | LUNCH | DINNER | SNACK |
|---|---|---|---|---|
| MON | Banana and Mocha Protein Smoothie (page 50) | Crispy Caprese Ciabatta Sandwich (page 119) | Quick Paella with Broiled Shrimp (page 188) | Watermelon and Lime Juice (page 44) |
| TUE | Protein-Packed Raspberry and Dark Chocolate Smoothie Bowls (page 53) | Sweet and Spicy BBQ Meatball Sub (page 123) | Orange Chicken (page 160) | Leftover watermelon with a hint of honey |
| WED | Crunchy "Parfait" Toast with Apples, Peanut Butter, and Honey (page 57) | Caprese Salad with Peppery Balsamic Reduction (page 110) | Shrimp a la Diabla (page 186) | Honey and Ricotta Dip with Figs and Granola (page 70) |
| THU | Leftover granola with milk or Greek yogurt | Leftover BBQ meatballs with cooked rice | Leftover shrimp a la diabla on corn tortillas for shrimp tacos | Homemade Frizz Coffee (page 52) |
| FRI | Mozzarella, Avocado, and Spinach Quesadillas (page 62) | Pan-Grilled Reuben Sandwich (page 122) | Creamy Chicken Tikka Masala (page 162) | Leftover honey and ricotta dip with celery sticks |
| SAT | Eggs in Chunky Tomato Sauce (page 65) | A green salad with leftover corned beef and with the Russian dressing and sauerkraut from the Reuben sandwich | Leftover chicken tikka masala on a sub roll | Vietnamese Iced Coffee (page 51) |
| SUN | Breakfast Tacos with Eggs and Avocado (page 63) | Pizza-dilla with Guacamole Salsa (page 81) | Chicken Puttanesca with Orzo (page 157) | Frozen Peach Iced Tea (page 49) |

## Shopping List

**CANNED AND BOTTLED ITEMS**

☐ Chipotle chiles in adobo sauce,
    1 (7-ounce) can

☐ Diced tomatoes,
    1 (14.5-ounce) can

☐ Guacamole salsa,
    1 (15.5-ounce) jar

☐ Puttanesca sauce,
    1 (24-ounce) jar

☐ Sauerkraut, 1 (16-ounce) jar

☐ Sweetened condensed milk,
    1 (14-ounce) can

☐ Tikka Masala curry sauce,
    1 (15-ounce) jar

☐ Tomato puree,
    2 (29-ounce) cans

**DAIRY AND EGGS**

☐ Cream cheese, plain (4 ounces)

☐ Eggs (4)

☐ Greek yogurt (8 ounces)

☐ Half-and-half (½ pint)

☐ Milk (1 quart)

☐ Mozzarella cheese, fresh
    (1 pound)

☐ Mozzarella cheese, shredded
    (8 ounces)

☐ Mozzarella cheese, sliced
    (8 slices)

☐ Part-skim ricotta (4 ounces)

☐ Provolone cheese, sliced
    (6 slices)

**FROZEN FOODS**

☐ Meatballs, Italian-style
    (1 pound)

☐ Peach slices, 1 (10-ounce) bag

☐ Raspberries (1 pound)

**MEAT**

☐ Chicken, boneless, skinless
    thighs (6 pounds)

☐ Corned beef, sliced (8 slices)

☐ Large shrimp, raw (3 pounds)

☐ Pepperoni slices (20 slices)

**PANTRY ITEMS**

☐ Barbecue sauce

☐ Carbonated water

☐ Chocolate protein powder

☐ Coconut water

☐ Cornstarch

☐ Dark chocolate

- ☐ Dark-roast coffee beans
- ☐ Dried orzo pasta
- ☐ Granola
- ☐ Honey
- ☐ Instant espresso powder
- ☐ Low-sodium chicken broth
- ☐ Low-sodium soy sauce
- ☐ Olive oil
- ☐ Orange marmalade
- ☐ Parboiled rice
- ☐ Pepper
- ☐ Peanut butter
- ☐ Red pepper flakes
- ☐ Salt
- ☐ Sugar
- ☐ Vegetable oil

## PRODUCE

- ☐ Apples (2)
- ☐ Avocados (3)
- ☐ Baby spinach (1 cup)
- ☐ Bananas (6)
- ☐ Basil, fresh (2 bunches)
- ☐ Celery (3 or 4 stalks)
- ☐ Garlic (3 heads)
- ☐ Lemon (1)
- ☐ Limes (3)
- ☐ Parsley, fresh (1 bunch) (optional)
- ☐ Red bell peppers (2)
- ☐ Tomatoes (6)
- ☐ Watermelon (1 medium)
- ☐ White onion (1)

## OTHER

- ☐ Ciabatta sandwich rolls (4)
- ☐ Corn tortillas, 1 (10-count) bag
- ☐ Dried Mission figs, 1 (7-ounce) bag
- ☐ Flour tortillas, 8- or 10-inch, 1 (12-count) bag
- ☐ Pico de gallo (4 ounces)
- ☐ Sliced bread, multigrain or rye (1 loaf)
- ☐ Sub rolls (6)
- ☐ Unsweetened iced tea, 1 (12-ounce) bottle

## GLOBAL FEAST PLAN

*Prepare yourself to feast on dishes inspired by various world cuisines, such as Italian, Mexican, and German. All the ingredients are conveniently available at local grocery stores. The prep is minimal, and all the dishes are easy and delish.*

## Prep Ahead

- **Chop the vegetables:** Mince the garlic for the Shrimp Scampi with Orzo (page 187) and chop the bell peppers for the One-Pan Bratwurst and Vegetables (page 167); chop the onion and bell pepper for the Eggs in Chunky Tomato Sauce (page 65) and Chicken Fajitas (page 153). Store the vegetables for each recipe in a single covered container, making them easy to use later. Keep them in the refrigerator if using within 2 days or freeze them in freezer bags with labels to use later in the week.

- **Chop the bacon:** Chop the bacon for the Cheesy Bacon and Spinach Frittata (page 64) and refrigerate in a plastic bag, removing as much air as possible.

- **Cook the meatballs:** Cook the meatballs for the Sweet and Spicy BBQ Meatball Sub (page 123), let them cool, and refrigerate them in an airtight container for up to 4 days. Reheat before assembling the sandwiches.

- **Cut the chicken:** Cut the chicken breast into strips for the Chicken Fajitas (page 153). Place the strips in an airtight container, and either refrigerate (if using within 2 days) or freeze for later use during the week.

- **Prepare the soups:** Cook the Slow Cooker Southwestern Meatball Soup (page 107) and store it in an airtight container in the refrigerator for 3 to 4 days.

- **Cook the waffles:** You can make waffles on the weekend and freeze them for later use. To do this, let the fully cooked waffles cool, then place them onto a parchment paper–lined baking sheet and freeze them until they are completely frozen. Transfer the waffles into freezer-safe bags with a label. They will keep for up to 3 months.

|  | BREAKFAST | LUNCH | DINNER | SNACK |
|---|---|---|---|---|
| **MON** | Chai Latte Waffles with Maple Syrup (page 59) | Slow Cooker Southwestern Meatball Soup (page 107) | Shrimp Scampi with Orzo (page 187) | Refreshing Pineapple-Mint Juice (page 43) |
| **TUE** | Mozzarella, Avocado, and Spinach Quesadillas (page 62) | Sweet and Spicy BBQ Meatball Sub (page 123) | Chicken Fajitas (page 153) | Guacamole Dip (page 68) with celery sticks |
| **WED** | Tropical Fruit Smoothie (page 45) | Leftover shrimp scampi (without orzo) with a crusty bread | One-Pan Bratwurst and Vegetables (page 167) | Toast with leftover guacamole dip |
| **THU** | Breakfast Tacos with Eggs and Avocado (page 63) | Leftover bratwurst on a leftover sub roll | Leftover slow cooker Southwestern meatball soup | Vietnamese Iced Coffee (page 51) |
| **FRI** | Oven-Baked Buttermilk Blueberry Pancakes (page 58) | Fresh Veggie Sandwich with Chipotle Aioli (page 118) | Leftover chicken fajitas on corn tortillas | Roasted Red Pepper Hummus (page 69) with celery sticks |
| **SAT** | Eggs in Chunky Tomato Sauce (page 65) | Leftover BBQ meatballs over rice | Southwestern Chicken Soup (page 105) | Homemade Frizz Coffee (page 52) |
| **SUN** | Cheesy Bacon and Spinach Frittata (page 64) | Top baby spinach with leftover rotisserie chicken, and dressed with leftover chipotle aioli | Fire-Roasted Margherita Pizza (page 133) | Toast topped with hummus and avocado slices |

## Shopping List

### CANNED AND BOTTLED ITEMS

- ☐ Chickpeas, 2 (15-ounce) cans
- ☐ Diced tomatoes with green chiles, 2 (14.5-ounce) cans
- ☐ Fire-roasted red bell peppers, 1 (16-ounce) jar
- ☐ Sweetened condensed milk, 1 (14-ounce) can
- ☐ Tomato salsa, 1 (16-ounce) jar

### DAIRY AND EGGS

- ☐ Cheddar cheese, shredded (3 ounces)
- ☐ Eggs (1 dozen)
- ☐ Half-and-half (½ pint)
- ☐ Heavy cream (½ pint)
- ☐ Mozzarella cheese, shredded (4 ounces)
- ☐ Parmesan cheese, shredded (2 ounces)
- ☐ Provolone cheese, sliced (6 slices)

### FROZEN FOODS

- ☐ Mango chunks, 1 (10-ounce) bag
- ☐ Meatballs, Italian-style (1 pound, 12 ounces)
- ☐ Pineapple chunks, 1 (10-ounce bag)
- ☐ Southwestern vegetable mix, 1 (14-ounce) bag

### MEAT

- ☐ Bratwurst sausages (1 pound)
- ☐ Chicken, boneless, skinless breast (2 pounds)
- ☐ Large shrimp, raw (1¼ pound)
- ☐ Rotisserie chicken, whole (1)
- ☐ Smoked bacon (6 slices)

## PANTRY ITEMS

- ☐ Barbecue sauce
- ☐ Bittersweet chocolate chips (optional)
- ☐ Buttermilk pancake and waffle mix
- ☐ Carbonated water
- ☐ Chai latte powder
- ☐ Chipotle aioli
- ☐ Dark-roast coffee beans
- ☐ Dried orzo pasta
- ☐ Low-sodium chicken broth
- ☐ Maple syrup
- ☐ Olive oil
- ☐ Pepper
- ☐ Pure vanilla extract
- ☐ Red pepper flakes
- ☐ Rice
- ☐ Salt
- ☐ Sugar
- ☐ Tahini paste
- ☐ Vegetable oil

## PRODUCE

- ☐ Avocados (7)
- ☐ Baby spinach, 1 (8-ounce) bag
- ☐ Blueberries (½ pint)
- ☐ Broccoli slaw, 1 (9- or 10-ounce) bag
- ☐ Celery (3 or 4 stalks)
- ☐ Cilantro, fresh (1 bunch)
- ☐ Cucumbers (3)
- ☐ Garlic (2 heads)
- ☐ Jalapeño (1)
- ☐ Lemons (3)
- ☐ Limes (5)
- ☐ Mint, fresh (1 bunch)
- ☐ Parsley, fresh (1 bunch) (optional)
- ☐ Tomatoes (3)
- ☐ White onion (1)
- ☐ Yellow onion, large (1)
- ☐ Yellow potatoes, small (1 pound)

## OTHER

- ☐ Coconut milk beverage (10 ounces)
- ☐ Corn tortillas (4)
- ☐ Fajita seasoning mix, 1 (1-ounce) package
- ☐ Flour tortillas, 8- or 10-inch, 1 (10-count) bag
- ☐ Onion soup mix, 1 (1-ounce) package
- ☐ Pico de gallo (4 ounces)
- ☐ Pizza dough (1)
- ☐ Sliced bread, multigrain (1 loaf)
- ☐ Sub rolls (8)
- ☐ Taco seasoning mix, 2 (1-ounce) packages
- ☐ White wine (½ cup)

*Chai Latte Waffles with Maple Syrup* **59**

# 3

## *Breakfast and Beverages*

# Sparkling Strawberry–Mint Juice

**DAIRY-FREE, GLUTEN-FREE, NUT-FREE, QUICK, VEGETARIAN** .....................................

This healthy homemade soda tastes even better than the fancy store-bought varieties. It's both sweet and tangy, and the bubbles make it festive. Drink it as written, or you can transform it into a drink for entertaining by adding a shot of gin, vodka, cachaça, or tequila.

.........................................................................................

**3 cups frozen strawberries**

**1½ cups carbonated water**

**¼ cup fresh mint leaves**

Juice of 1 lemon

**3 to 4 tablespoons honey**

---

**Serves** 4

**Prep time:** 5 minutes

Combine the strawberries, water, mint, lemon juice, and honey in a blender and blend until smooth. Serve immediately.

**VARIATION TIP:** Substitute agave nectar, maple syrup, or sugar for the honey. Replace the carbonated water with champagne or sparkling wine to make a refreshing cocktail.

**WASTE-NOT TIP:** Use any leftover mint in the Refreshing Pineapple-Mint Juice (page 43) or use as a garnish for the Avocado and Kale Gazpacho (page 96). Add any leftover strawberries to your favorite smoothies.

---

Per serving: Calories: 91; Total fat: <1g; Saturated fat: 0g; Protein: 1g; Carbohydrates: 24g; Sugar: 18g; Fiber: 3g; Sodium: 3mg

# Refreshing Pineapple–Mint Juice

**DAIRY-FREE, GLUTEN-FREE, NUT-FREE, QUICK, VEGAN** ..........................................

This is a tropical juice inspired by the cuisine of my home country, Brazil. It's mildly sweet and sour with a cooling, fresh mint flavor. My family absolutely loves this juice in the morning or on hot days as ice pops. Just pour it into ice pop molds and freeze.

**3 cups frozen
   pineapple chunks**

1½ cups cold water

**¼ cup fresh mint leaves**

Juice of 1 lime

**2 to 3 tablespoons
   maple syrup**

**Serves** 4
**Prep time:** 5 minutes

Combine the pineapple, water, mint, lime juice, and maple syrup in a blender and blend until smooth. Serve immediately.

**VARIATION TIP:** Substitute agave nectar, honey, or sugar for the maple syrup.

**WASTE-NOT TIP:** Use leftover mint to make Sparkling Strawberry-Mint Juice (page 42), Watermelon Salad with Feta, Mint, and Honey-Lime Dressing (page 109), or use it as a garnish for the Avocado and Kale Gazpacho (page 96). Leftover pineapple can replace the mango in the Tropical Fruit Smoothie (page 45), transforming it into a piña colada smoothie.

Per serving: Calories: 90; Total fat: 0g; Saturated fat: 0g; Protein: <1g; Carbohydrates: 21g; Sugar: 17g; Fiber: 2g; Sodium: 1mg

# Watermelon and Lime Juice

**DAIRY-FREE, GLUTEN-FREE, NUT-FREE, QUICK, VEGETARIAN** ....................................

This juice has summer written all over it. To add a fun and festive touch to this drink, dip the rims of the glasses into a small bowl of water, and then dip the rims into a small bowl of coarse sugar, rotating until they're coated.

....................................................................................................

**4 cups chopped watermelon**

2½ cups cold water

2 cups ice cubes

Juice of 2 limes

**3 tablespoons honey**

**Serves** 4
**Prep time:** 5 minutes

Combine the watermelon, water, ice cubes, lime juice, and honey in a blender and blend until smooth. Pour into glasses and serve immediately.

**WASTE-NOT TIP:** Use leftover watermelon to make the Watermelon Salad with Feta, Mint, and Honey-Lime Dressing (page 109).

Per serving: Calories: 99; Total fat: <1g; Saturated fat: 0g; Protein: 1g; Carbohydrates: 25g; Sugar: 23g; Fiber: 1g; Sodium: 3mg

# Tropical Fruit Smoothie

**DAIRY-FREE, GLUTEN-FREE, QUICK, VEGAN** ...............................................

Bring the tropics home with this smoothie. Feel free to experiment by adding other tropical fruits or replacing those in the recipe with what you have on hand. For example, you can substitute frozen papaya, pineapple, or avocado for the mango. You can also substitute fresh fruit for the frozen fruit in this recipe, if you wish.

**3 cups frozen mango chunks**

**1¼ cups coconut milk beverage**

**2 medium bananas, peeled and roughly chopped**

Juice of 1 lime

**2 to 3 tablespoons maple syrup**

---

**Serves** 4
**Prep time:** 5 minutes

Combine the mango, coconut milk, bananas, lime juice, and maple syrup in a blender and blend until smooth. Serve immediately.

**STORAGE TIP:** You can freeze this smoothie in a freezer-safe container for up to 2 months. The night before you plan to serve it, put it in the refrigerator to thaw. Stir well to blend the flavors before serving.

---

Per serving: Calories: 163; Total fat: 2g; Saturated fat: 1g; Protein: 1g; Carbohydrates: 37g; Sugar: 28g; Fiber: 3g; Sodium: 7mg

# Mango, Lime, and Chia Smoothie

**DAIRY-FREE, GLUTEN-FREE, QUICK, VEGAN** ...........................................................

This mango-and-lime smoothie has it all. It's thick, creamy, sweet, tart, and has a great tropical flavor. It contains chia seeds, which are a healthy, plant-based source of protein, fiber, and antioxidants. You can make this smoothie into a more robust meal by turning it into a smoothie bowl topped with pieces of fruit, shredded coconut, and nuts.

.............................................................................................................

**3 cups frozen mango chunks**

**1¼ cups coconut milk beverage**

Juice of 2 limes

**4 tablespoons maple syrup**

**1 tablespoon chia seeds**

---

**Serves** 4
**Prep time:** 5 minutes

Combine the mango, coconut milk, lime juice, and maple syrup in a blender and blend until smooth. Stir in the chia seeds. Pour into four glasses and serve.

**VARIATION TIP:** Substitute frozen pineapple, blueberry, papaya, or avocado for frozen mango. You can replace the maple syrup with agave nectar, honey, or sugar. If desired, use regular milk or any plant-based milk to replace the coconut milk.

**STORAGE TIP:** You can freeze this smoothie in a freezer-safe container for up to 2 months. The night before you plan to serve it, put it in the refrigerator to thaw. Stir well to blend the flavors before serving.

---

Per serving: Calories: 154; Total fat: 3g; Saturated fat: 1g; Protein: 2g; Carbohydrates: 31g; Sugar: 27g; Fiber: 3g; Sodium: 7mg

# Green Goodness Smoothie

GLUTEN-FREE, NUT-FREE, QUICK, VEGETARIAN .................................................

This creamy fruit-and-vegetable smoothie is one of the best sneaky ways to incorporate greens into your diet. While the green color might scream "vegetables," the flavor is mostly fruity, with a zing from the pineapple and kiwi. It makes a great healthy breakfast or on-the-go snack, and it can be made even more refreshing if you add a few ice cubes before blending.

3 cups baby spinach

2 cups milk

½ cup frozen
   pineapple chunks

2 medium bananas, peeled
   and roughly chopped

4 kiwis, peeled
   and chopped

Serves 4
Prep time: 5 minutes

Combine the spinach, milk, pineapple, bananas, and kiwis in a blender and blend until smooth. Serve immediately.

VARIATION TIP: If you'd like to, add 2 to 3 tablespoons of sugar, honey, maple syrup, or agave nectar to this smoothie. Likewise, you can replace the milk with the plant-based milk of your choice.

WASTE-NOT TIP: Add any leftover pineapple chunks to the Tropical Fruit Smoothie (page 45). Use leftover spinach to make the Mozzarella, Avocado, and Spinach Quesadillas (page 62) or the Cheesy Bacon and Spinach Frittata (page 64).

Per serving: Calories: 192; Total fat: 5g; Saturated fat: 3g; Protein: 6g; Carbohydrates: 34g; Sugar: 22g; Fiber: 5g; Sodium: 91mg

# Frozen Peach Iced Tea

**DAIRY-FREE, GLUTEN-FREE, NUT-FREE, QUICK, VEGETARIAN** ....................................

Cool off on hot summer days with this peach iced tea. It's the perfect drink for picnics and pool parties—it's pure Georgia goodness in an ice-cold glass!

**3 cups frozen peach slices**

**1½ cups unsweetened iced tea**

**⅓ cup honey**

Juice of 1 lime

1 to 2 cups ice cubes

**Serves** 4
**Prep time:** 5 minutes

Combine the peaches, iced tea, honey, lime juice, and ice into a blender and blend until smooth. Serve immediately.

**WASTE-NOT TIP:** Add any leftover frozen peaches to your favorite smoothie.

Per serving: Calories: 125; Total fat: 0g; Saturated fat: 0g; Protein: 1g; Carbohydrates: 33g; Sugar: 30g; Fiber: 2g; Sodium: 1mg

# Banana and Mocha Protein Smoothie

.........................................................

This smoothie combines two of my favorite things: chocolate and coffee. It's the best wake-up call in the morning. The bananas make it creamy and, when combined with the protein powder, keep you full until lunchtime. To spice it up a little bit, add a dash of chili powder. It's like having a Mexican mocha smoothie instead of a Mexican hot chocolate.

.....................................................................................................................

**6 large bananas, peeled and halved**

**3 cups milk**

**5 tablespoons honey**

**¼ cup chocolate protein powder**

**1 teaspoon instant espresso powder**

**Serves** 4
**Prep time:** 5 minutes

Combine the bananas, milk, honey, protein powder, and espresso powder in a blender and blend until smooth. Pour into four glasses and serve.

**VARIATION TIP:** You can substitute blueberries, apple, or pear for the banana. If desired, replace the milk with the plant-based milk of your choice.

Per serving: Calories: 420; Total fat: 7g; Saturated fat: 4g; Protein: 17g; Carbohydrates: 78g; Sugar: 55g; Fiber: 5g; Sodium: 116mg

# Vietnamese Iced Coffee

GLUTEN-FREE, NUT-FREE, QUICK, VEGETARIAN ........................................................

This simple and sweet Vietnamese Iced Coffee is sure to make your mornings more cheerful. You can make it on the stovetop, as I do, or prepare 4 cups of coffee using the coffee maker of your choice and proceed directly to step 2. I like to use a darker roast, but any roast will be delicious. In the winter, skip the ice cubes and serve it hot.

4 cups water

½ **cup ground dark-roast coffee beans**

1 to 2 cups ice cubes (optional)

½ **cup sweetened condensed milk**

Serves 4
**Prep time:** 5 minutes
**Cook time:** 15 minutes

1. In a medium saucepan, combine the water and coffee and bring to a boil over high heat for 8 to 10 minutes. Continue to boil for 2 to 4 minutes more. Strain the coffee into a 5-cup glass measuring cup using a mesh strainer.

2. Set out four tall glass mugs and fill each one-third full with ice cubes. Pour 2 tablespoons of sweetened condensed milk into each mug. Stir 1 cup of coffee into each mug. Serve immediately.

**MAKE-AHEAD TIP:** Make one or more batches of coffee ahead of time and freeze it in ice cube trays covered with plastic wrap for up to one month. Thaw enough coffee for the number of servings desired and proceed with the instructions from step 2.

**WASTE-NOT TIP:** Use any leftover sweetened condensed milk to make the Almond Queijadinha (page 225).

Per serving: Calories: 130; Total fat: 3g; Saturated fat: 2g; Protein: 3g; Carbohydrates: 23g; Sugar: 23g; Fiber: 0g; Sodium: 41mg

# Homemade Frizz Coffee

**GLUTEN-FREE, NUT-FREE, QUICK, VEGETARIAN** ........................................................

If you're a fan of both coffee and tongue-tingling seltzer, be forewarned: you'll love this drink! I consider this to be a homemade version of the Italian Frizz Coffee, a sweet and bubbly espresso soda.

........................................................................................................

1 cup water

**4 teaspoons instant espresso powder**

4 tablespoons sugar

2 cups ice cubes, divided

**3 cups carbonated water, chilled**

½ cup half-and-half

---

**Serves** 4
**Prep time:** 5 minutes
**Cook time:** 5 minutes

1. In a small saucepan, bring the water to a boil over high heat. Stir in the coffee until dissolved. Then stir in the sugar.

2. Set out four tall glasses and put ½ cup of ice into each one. Pour ¼ cup of coffee into each glass. Then add ¾ cup of carbonated water into each glass.

3. Lightly mix 2 tablespoons of half-and-half into each glass, making swirls. Serve immediately.

**VARIATION TIP:** For a richer drink, replace the half-and-half with heavy cream. For a cocktail version, mix in half a shot of coffee liqueur, vodka, or Kahlúa.

**WASTE-NOT TIP:** Use any leftover instant espresso powder to make Banana and Mocha Protein Smoothie (page 50). Use the half-and-half as a replacement for milk or heavy cream in creamy soups such as New England Clam Chowder (page 102) and Pressure Cooker Broccoli and Cheddar Soup (page 98).

---

Per serving: Calories: 87; Total fat: 3g; Saturated fat: 2g; Protein: 1g; Carbohydrates: 14g; Sugar: 14g; Fiber: 0g; Sodium: 12mg

# Protein–Packed Raspberry and Dark Chocolate Smoothie Bowls

**QUICK, VEGETARIAN** ..................................................................

These endlessly customizable smoothie bowls make a quick, easy, and healthy breakfast, packed with protein and antioxidants. They work well with any type of fresh or frozen berry you might have on hand, and you can replace the coconut water with regular water or any kind of milk.

..................................................................

**1 pound frozen raspberries**

**¼ cup coconut water**

**3 to 4 tablespoons honey**

**2 tablespoons chocolate protein powder**

**⅓ cup finely chopped dark chocolate**

**Serves** 4
**Prep time:** 10 minutes

1. Combine the raspberries, coconut water, honey, and protein powder in a blender and blend until smooth. If the mixture is too thick, add a small amount of coconut water to thin.

2. Evenly distribute the smoothie among four small bowls. Top one side of each bowl with dark chocolate.

**VARIATION TIP:** Feel free to add extra toppings such as sliced bananas, fresh berries, pomegranate seeds, shredded coconut, or nuts.

**STORAGE TIP:** Store any leftovers in an airtight container in the refrigerator for 2 to 3 days.

Per serving: Calories: 238; Total fat: 6g; Saturated fat: 4g; Protein: 7g; Carbohydrates: 44g; Sugar: 30g; Fiber: 10g; Sodium: 22mg

# Overnight Chia Pudding with Peanut Butter and Banana

**DAIRY-FREE, GLUTEN-FREE, VEGAN** ...........................................................

Other than 30 seconds to heat the peanut butter or the topping, this overnight plant-based breakfast pudding requires no cooking at all. It's a "mix and chill" meal that's as simple as it is versatile: you can serve it for breakfast, as a snack, or even as a healthy dessert.

...........................................................................................................

**2 cups coconut milk beverage**

**⅓ cup chia seeds**

**¼ cup peanut butter, plus 2 tablespoons for topping**

**2 to 3 tablespoons maple syrup, plus 2 tablespoons for topping**

**1 large banana**

---

**Serves** 4

**Prep time:** 10 minutes, plus 1 hour, or overnight, to chill

**Cook time:** 30 seconds

1. In a medium bowl, whisk together the coconut milk, chia seeds, ¼ cup of peanut butter, and 2 to 3 tablespoons of maple syrup until homogeneous. Let the mixture rest at room temperature for about 5 minutes. Then whisk again to remove any clumps.

2. Evenly divide the mixture among four containers, then cover tightly and refrigerate for at least 1 hour, or overnight.

3. Right before serving, slice the banana and arrange the slices on top of each serving of chia pudding. Heat the remaining 2 tablespoons of peanut butter in the microwave for 10 to 30 seconds and drizzle a small amount over the banana slices on each serving.

4. Drizzle the remaining 2 tablespoons of maple syrup evenly over each serving.

**VARIATION TIP:** You can use any type of plant-based milk or regular milk, if you prefer. If desired, replace the maple syrup with agave nectar or honey and the peanut butter with any other nut butter.

---

Per serving: Calories: 326; Total fat: 19g; Saturated fat: 5g; Protein: 10g; Carbohydrates: 34g; Sugar: 19g; Fiber: 9g; Sodium: 121mg

# Blackberry Chia Overnight Oatmeal

**GLUTEN-FREE, NUT-FREE, QUICK, VEGETARIAN** ...............................................

Just mix and pour these ingredients together at night and—*voilà!*—in the morning you'll have a wholesome, nutritious breakfast ready to serve. For a creamier oatmeal, add 2 to 3 tablespoons of Greek yogurt into the oat mixture. For a vegan version, use agave nectar or maple syrup instead of honey, and use a plant-based milk.

..........................................................................................................

**2 cups steel-cut oats**

**2 cups milk**

**3 to 4 tablespoons honey, plus extra to drizzle**

**2 tablespoons chia seeds**

**1 (6-ounce) container of fresh blackberries**

---

**Serves** 4
**Prep time:** 10 minutes, plus overnight to chill

1. In a medium mixing bowl, whisk together the oats, milk, honey, and chia seeds. Divide the mixture evenly among four containers. Cover tightly and refrigerate overnight, or up to 4 to 5 days.

2. Before serving, stir the oat mixture and top with blackberries. Drizzle extra honey over the berries.

**WASTE-NOT TIP:** Use leftover chia seeds in smoothies, mixed into cereal or granola for breakfast, or to make the Overnight Chia Pudding with Peanut Butter and Banana (page 54).

---

Per serving: Calories: 455; Total fat: 11g; Saturated fat: 4g; Protein: 17g; Carbohydrates: 80g; Sugar: 21g; Fiber: 13g; Sodium: 61mg

# Banana Bread Baked Oatmeal

GLUTEN-FREE, NUT-FREE, VEGETARIAN .................................................................

This banana bread baked oatmeal is the epitome of comfort. There's no special preparation—all you have to do is mix and bake! Serve the oatmeal as is, or add chocolate chips or chopped nuts to the mixture before baking. A drizzle of maple syrup on top adds a nice touch of sweetness, too.

.......................................................................................................

Oil, for greasing the pan

**2 overripe bananas**

**2 cups steel-cut oats**

**2 teaspoons ground cinnamon**

**1 teaspoon vanilla extract**

2 tablespoons sugar

**3 cups whole milk**

---

**Serves** 6
**Prep time:** 5 minutes
**Cook time:** 45 minutes

1. Preheat the oven to 375°F. Lightly grease a 9-by-13-inch baking dish with oil before lining it with parchment paper. Set aside.

2. In a large bowl, mash the bananas. Add the oats, cinnamon, vanilla, sugar, and milk and stir until well combined.

3. Pour the mixture into the prepared dish and bake for 40 to 45 minutes, or until set. Let the oatmeal cool at room temperature for at least 10 minutes before serving. You can also refrigerate it and serve it chilled.

**VARIATION TIP:** The cinnamon can be replaced with allspice, pumpkin spice, or apple spice, depending on your preference. You can also replace the vanilla extract with almond extract and the sugar with honey. For a dairy-free version, use your favorite plant-based milk.

**MAKE-AHEAD TIP:** You can make a single or double batch of baked oatmeal and freeze it for up to 3 months. The night before you plan to serve it, thaw the oatmeal in the refrigerator, then reheat in the microwave for 1 to 2 minutes.

---

Per serving: Calories: 317; Total fat: 8g; Saturated fat: 3g; Protein: 12g; Carbohydrates: 55g; Sugar: 15g; Fiber: 7g; Sodium: 61mg

# Crunchy "Parfait" Toast with Apples, Peanut Butter, and Honey

**DAIRY-FREE, QUICK, VEGETARIAN** .....................................................................

This contemporary take on breakfast was inspired by the "toast mania" on Instagram. It's quick to put together and deliciously wholesome. It's also easy enough for children and teens to make by themselves. Variations are endless and can be customized according to your needs and liking.

.........................................................................................................................

**4 slices multigrain bread**

**4 tablespoons peanut butter, divided**

**2 medium apples, cored and thinly sliced**

**4 tablespoons honey, for topping**

**4 tablespoons granola, for topping**

1. Toast each slice of bread in a toaster or toaster oven. Spread 1 tablespoon of peanut butter on each slice of toast.

2. Evenly divide and layer the apple slices on top of each slice of toast. Then drizzle each toast slice with 1 tablespoon of honey and sprinkle with 1 tablespoon of granola.

**VARIATION TIP:** Use any fruit that pairs well with the nut butter of your choice. Honey can be replaced with maple syrup, and chopped nuts or chocolate can be used in addition to or instead of granola.

**Serves** 4
**Prep time:** 5 minutes
**Cook time:** 5 minutes

Per serving: Calories: 329; Total fat: 10g; Saturated fat: 2g; Protein: 11g; Carbohydrates: 57g; Sugar: 32g; Fiber: 8g; Sodium: 244mg

# Oven–Baked Buttermilk Blueberry Pancakes

NUT-FREE, VEGETARIAN ..........................................................

This recipe is a time-saver since you only have to mix the ingredients and put the batter in the oven. No pancake-flipping! Here I top the finished product with melted chocolate for a fun twist, but you can also use traditional maple syrup. If you use frozen blueberries, just make sure to thaw them before making the batter.

Oil, for greasing the pan

**3 cups buttermilk pancake mix**

1¾ cups water

**2 teaspoons pure vanilla extract**

**1¼ cups blueberries**

**¼ cup bittersweet chocolate chips (optional)**

---

**Makes** 6 square pancakes
**Prep time:** 15 minutes
**Cook time:** 25 minutes

1. Preheat the oven to 425°F. Line a 9-by-13-inch baking pan with aluminum foil. Grease the lined pan well with oil.

2. In a large bowl, whisk together the pancake mix, water, and vanilla. Let the batter rest for 10 minutes.

3. Pour the batter into the prepared pan and spread it to the corners with a rubber spatula. Scatter the blueberries on top. Bake for 15 to 20 minutes, or until set.

4. Remove the pan from the oven and, using potholders, reposition the oven rack so it's about 8 inches away from the broiler. Preheat the broiler.

5. Return the pan to the oven and broil for 1 to 2 minutes, or until browned on top. Remove from the oven and let cool for 2 minutes. Cut into 6 square pancakes.

6. Melt the chocolate chips, if using. Pour them into a microwave-safe bowl and heat in 30-second intervals, stirring in between each interval, until the chocolate has melted. Drizzle the chocolate over the baked pancakes.

**VARIATION TIP:** Blueberries can be replaced by any berry of your choice, or a mixed berry blend.

---

Per serving: Calories: 231; Total fat: 4g; Saturated fat: 1g; Protein: 6g; Carbohydrates: 41g; Sugar: 11g; Fiber: 2g; Sodium: 782mg

# Chai Latte Waffles with Maple Syrup

NUT-FREE, QUICK, VEGETARIAN ..........................................................

Everyone in the family will wake up happy with the warm and cozy aromas of Chai Latte Waffles as their alarm clock. Chai latte powder gives this breakfast treat a comforting flavor that pairs beautifully with the all-natural sweetness of maple syrup. Feel free to use your favorite pancake and waffle mix, though I love using a buttermilk version for these.

**1 cup pancake and waffle mix**

**2 tablespoons chai latte powder**

¾ cup water

3 tablespoons oil, plus more for greasing

**6 tablespoons maple syrup, divided**

---

**Makes** 6 (4-by-4-inch) waffles
**Prep time:** 5 minutes
**Cook time:** 20 minutes, plus 5 minutes to rest

1. Preheat your waffle iron.
2. In a large bowl, whisk together the waffle mix and chai latte powder, then add the water and oil and mix well. Let the batter sit at room temperature for about 5 minutes.
3. Meanwhile, lightly grease the waffle iron with oil. Then pour the batter into the waffle iron and cook according to the manufacturer's instructions until the waffle iron stops steaming and the waffles are crisp and golden on the outside.
4. To serve, drizzle about 1 tablespoon of maple syrup on top of each waffle.

**STORAGE TIP:** Freeze cooled leftover waffles in freezer bags for up to 4 months. Reheat either in a toaster or in the microwave on high for 1 to 2 minutes.

**WASTE-NOT TIP:** You can use leftover chai latte mix to flavor oatmeal, smoothies, and pancake batter. Try adding 1 to 2 tablespoons to the Banana Bread Baked Oatmeal (page 56) or Overnight Chia Pudding with Peanut Butter and Banana (page 54) or substitute it for the espresso powder in the Banana and Mocha Protein Smoothie (page 50). You can also use it to make Chai-Spiced Napoleons (page 244).

Per serving: Calories: 197; Total fat: 9g; Saturated fat: 2g; Protein: 2g; Carbohydrates: 28g; Sugar: 17g; Fiber: <1g; Sodium: 271mg

# Sunny-Side-Up Eggs with Cauliflower Hash Browns and Salsa Verde

**GLUTEN-FREE, NUT-FREE, VEGETARIAN** ...........................................................

This easy, filling, and protein-packed breakfast is low in carbohydrates and perfect for diabetics and those on a keto diet. The salsa verde gives it a punch, but any type of salsa would be great with this dish, so use your favorite or experiment with different brands and styles.

..............................................................................................................

**2 cups shredded cauliflower**

**⅔ cup shredded cheddar cheese**

**5 large eggs, divided**

**¼ teaspoon dried chives, or 1 teaspoon finely chopped fresh chives**

¼ teaspoon salt

Freshly ground black pepper

2 tablespoons olive oil

**½ cup salsa verde**

---

**Serves** 4
**Prep time:** 10 minutes
**Cook time:** 25 minutes, plus 10 minutes to cool

1. Preheat the oven to 400°F. Grease a large baking sheet and set aside.

2. Put the cauliflower in a medium microwave-safe bowl. Cook in the microwave on high for 2 minutes, then let cool for 5 minutes. Wrap the cooked cauliflower in a kitchen towel and wring to squeeze out excess moisture.

3. In a large bowl, combine the cauliflower, cheese, 1 egg, the chives, salt, and pepper to taste. Mix well.

4. Roll the cauliflower mixture into four balls and flatten them with your hands, shaping them into patties. Place the patties on the greased baking sheet and bake for 12 to 15 minutes, or until browned.

5. Turn on the broiler and broil for 2 to 5 minutes, or until crispy. Watch the patties closely, being careful not to burn them. Remove the patties from the oven and allow them to cool for 5 minutes, during which time they will firm up.

6. Meanwhile, in a large nonstick skillet, heat the oil over medium-low heat.

7. Gently crack the remaining 4 eggs into the pan, keeping the yolks intact. Cook until the tops of the whites are set but the yolks are still soft, 2 to 2½ minutes.

8. Remove the pan from the heat and then gently transfer the eggs to a plate using a large metal spatula. Season with additional salt and pepper, if desired. Serve the eggs and hash browns with the salsa verde on the side.

**INGREDIENT TIP:** If you prefer to use frozen cauliflower rice, make sure to thaw it first or cook it to the package instructions and squeeze out any excess water before proceeding with the recipe.

**WASTE-NOT TIP:** Use surplus salsa verde to make Chicken Salsa Verde (page 151).

Per serving: Calories: 243; Total fat: 19g; Saturated fat: 7g; Protein: 13g; Carbohydrates: 5g; Sugar: 2g; Fiber: 2g; Sodium: 448mg

# Mozzarella, Avocado, and Spinach Quesadillas

**NUT-FREE, QUICK, VEGETARIAN** .........................................................

These breakfast quesadillas are crispy on the outside and packed with melted cheese on the inside. They're a great way to incorporate leafy vegetables into breakfast—making the first meal of the day more nutritious—and can be prepared quickly for a breakfast on-the-go.

.............................................................................

Salt

Freshly ground black pepper

**8 (8-inch) flour tortillas**

**2 cups shredded mozzarella cheese, divided**

**1 cup baby spinach, chopped, divided**

**2 avocados, mashed**

---

**Serves** 4
**Prep time:** 5 minutes
**Cook time:** 10 minutes

1. Preheat the oven to 400°F. Line two baking sheets with parchment paper.

2. Place two tortillas on each lined baking sheet. Top each tortilla with ¼ cup of cheese, ½ cup of spinach, and ¼ of mashed avocado.

3. Season each topped tortilla with salt and pepper, sprinkle with another ¼ cup of cheese, and then top with another tortilla, making four complete quesadillas.

4. Bake for 8 to 10 minutes, or until cheese melts. Slice each quesadilla into quarters and serve immediately.

**VARIATION TIP:** I use mozzarella cheese in this recipe, but any melting cheese will work, including cheddar, Monterey Jack, or pepper Jack cheese.

---

Per serving: Calories: 625; Total fat: 30g; Saturated fat: 10g; Protein: 27g; Carbohydrates: 64g; Sugar: <1g; Fiber: 10g; Sodium: 824mg

# Breakfast Tacos with Eggs and Avocado

**DAIRY-FREE, GLUTEN-FREE, NUT-FREE, QUICK, VEGETARIAN** ....................................

I firmly believe tacos are an anytime meal, and I prove it with this quick and comforting breakfast inspired by Tex-Mex cuisine. The pico de gallo brings a subtle spiciness to these tacos, but you can use whatever salsa you prefer. Feel free to add extra toppings such as black beans, sour cream, cooked sausage, or bacon, too.

**4 (6-inch) corn tortillas**
2 tablespoons olive oil
**4 large eggs**
Salt
Freshly ground black pepper
**1 avocado, sliced**
**½ cup pico de gallo**

**Serves** 4
**Prep time:** 5 minutes
**Cook time:** 5 minutes

1. In a large nonstick skillet, heat the tortillas over medium heat for 1 to 2 minutes. Then wrap them tightly in aluminum foil to keep them warm. Set aside.
2. In the same skillet, heat the oil over medium-low heat.
3. In a medium bowl, whisk the eggs and season with salt and pepper. Whisk them until frothy.
4. Pour the eggs into the skillet and leave them undisturbed until edges are about to set, 20 to 30 seconds. Stir until soft curds form, 1 to 2 minutes.
5. Divide the eggs among each warm tortilla and top with the avocado slices and pico de gallo. Serve immediately.

**WASTE-NOT TIP:** Use leftover tortillas to make tacos, quesadillas, or enchiladas, including the Butternut Squash and Roasted Corn Quesadillas (page 142), Sweet Potato and Black Bean Crispy Tacos (page 143), and Refried Beans and Kale Enchiladas with a Kick (page 146). Use leftover pico de gallo to make the Pan-Grilled Pork Chops with Pico de Gallo (page 170).

Per serving: Calories: 268; Total fat: 19g; Saturated fat: 4g; Protein: 9g; Carbohydrates: 18g; Sugar: 1g; Fiber: 5g; Sodium: 164mg

# Cheesy Bacon and Spinach Frittata

**GLUTEN-FREE, NUT-FREE, VEGETARIAN** .............................................................

A frittata is an Italian open-face omelet, usually made with beaten eggs, meats, cheese, and vegetables. This is a simplified version that, unlike the classic, goes directly into the oven to cook. The result is fluffy, savory, and delicious.

.................................................................................................

**6 slices smoked bacon, chopped**

**4 large eggs**

½ teaspoon salt

⅛ teaspoon freshly ground black pepper

**2 cups baby spinach, chopped**

**⅔ cup shredded cheddar cheese, divided**

---

**Serves** 6
**Prep time:** 5 minutes
**Cook time:** 25 minutes, plus 10 minutes to cool

1. Preheat the oven to 400°F.
2. Heat a large ovenproof skillet over medium heat. Put the bacon in the pan and cook for 5 to 7 minutes, or until lightly browned. Using a slotted spoon, transfer the cooked bacon to a plate lined with paper towels and let cool for about 5 minutes.
3. Remove any bits from the bottom of the pan using a spatula and spread the rendered bacon fat all over the inside of the skillet.
4. In a large bowl, vigorously whisk the eggs, salt, and pepper until frothy. Whisk in the spinach, cooled bacon, and ⅓ cup of cheddar cheese until evenly combined.
5. Pour the mixture into the greased skillet and sprinkle the remaining ⅓ cup of cheddar cheese on top.
6. Bake for 15 minutes. Remove from the oven and allow to cool for 5 minutes, then slice and serve.

**STORAGE TIP:** Store any leftovers in an airtight container in the refrigerator for up to 2 days. Reheat in the microwave on high for 30 to 60 seconds.

**WASTE-NOT TIP:** Use leftover spinach as a replacement for mixed greens in the Very Berry Salad with Candied Walnuts (page 112) or in the Pickled Beet and Crumbled Goat Cheese Salad (page 114).

---

Per serving: Calories: 145; Total fat: 11g; Saturated fat: 5g; Protein: 10g; Carbohydrates: 1g; Sugar: <1g; Fiber: <1g; Sodium: 467mg

# Eggs in Chunky Tomato Sauce

**DAIRY-FREE, GLUTEN-FREE, NUT-FREE, QUICK, VEGETARIAN** .......................................

This dish, also known as *shakshuka* or "Eggs in Purgatory," is a Mediterranean dish made by poaching eggs in a spicy and aromatic tomato sauce. This is a shortcut version of the classic—which means it calls for fewer ingredients—and also is less spicy than the traditional recipe. You can add ¼ cup of crumbled feta cheese as a topping, if desired. Serve shakshuka by itself as a low-carb dish, or with pita bread, toast, or a crusty bread to soak up all the sauce.

.......................................

2 tablespoons olive oil

1 white onion, chopped

**2 red bell peppers, seeded and chopped**

4 garlic cloves, minced

**1 (28-ounce) can diced tomatoes**

Salt

Freshly ground black pepper

**½ teaspoon red pepper flakes (optional)**

**4 large eggs**

**2 tablespoons chopped parsley (optional)**

---

**Serves** 4
**Prep time:** 10 minutes
**Cook time:** 20 minutes

1. In a large nonstick skillet, heat the oil over medium heat. Add the onion and bell peppers to the pan and cook, stirring occasionally, for 5 minutes, or until the vegetables have softened. Add the garlic and cook for 1 minute.

2. Pour in the diced tomatoes with their juices. Season with salt and pepper as well as the red pepper flakes, if using. Cook, stirring occasionally, for 5 to 6 minutes, or until the mixture thickens slightly.

3. Using a fork or a potato masher, carefully mash the vegetable mixture so that it doesn't spatter.

4. Make four indentations in the vegetable mixture and gently crack an egg into each one. Reduce the heat to medium-low and cover the pan. Cook for 5 to 8 minutes for soft yolks, or until the eggs are cooked to your liking. Top with parsley, if using, and serve immediately.

**WASTE-NOT TIP:** Use any leftover parsley to make the Chimichurri Sauce (page 208), or to garnish pastas, soups, and stews, such as Mussels in Creamy Wine Sauce (page 190).

---

Per serving: Calories: 207; Total fat: 12g; Saturated fat: 3g; Protein: 9g; Carbohydrates: 15g; Sugar: 8g; Fiber: 3g; Sodium: 459mg

# 4

# Appetizers and Snacks

# Guacamole Dip

It's rare that a bowl of guacamole isn't finished as quickly as you can serve it, which is great since guacamole is best consumed fresh. If, somehow, you do have leftovers, you can store them in the refrigerator for up to one day. To do this, stir in an extra tablespoon of lime juice, place the pit of the avocado in the center of the dip, and tightly cover the container with plastic wrap. Before eating, scrape any lightly browned portions off the surface, and the rest will taste just as fresh as when you made it the day before.

**2 ripe avocados**

¼ yellow or white onion, finely chopped

**¼ cup chopped cilantro**

**1 Roma tomato, finely chopped**

**1 jalapeño, finely chopped (optional)**

2 tablespoons lime juice

Salt

Freshly ground black pepper

**Serves** 4 to 6
**Prep time:** 10 minutes

In a medium bowl, mash the avocado with a fork until relatively smooth (a few small chunks are okay). Stir in the onion, cilantro, tomato, jalapeño (if using), and lime juice. Season with salt and pepper. Taste and adjust the seasoning, if needed.

**WASTE-NOT TIP:** Use any leftover onion to make Slow Cooker Zesty Three Bean and Ham Soup (page 106) or Vegetable Meatballs and Cauliflower Korma (page 128). Use leftover cilantro in Pico de Gallo (page 211), as a garnish for Vegetable Meatballs and Cauliflower Korma (page 128), or add it to Butternut Squash and Roasted Corn Quesadillas (page 142).

Per serving: Calories: 160; Total fat: 14g; Saturated fat: 2g; Protein: 2g; Carbohydrates: 10g; Sugar: 2g; Fiber: 6g; Sodium: 11mg

# Roasted Red Pepper Hummus

**DAIRY-FREE, GLUTEN-FREE, NUT-FREE, QUICK, VEGAN** ................................................

This wonderfully creamy version of the classic Mediterranean dip includes roasted red bell peppers. It's got a bite from the garlic that's tempered by the sweet peppers and pairs well with all kinds of dippers. It makes the perfect no-cook appetizer or a great easy snack.

..........................................................................................................................................

**1 (16-ounce) jar roasted red bell peppers, drained**

**2 (15-ounce) cans chickpeas, rinsed and drained**

**¼ cup tahini paste**

2 tablespoons olive oil

1½ tablespoons lemon juice

4 garlic cloves, crushed

Salt

Freshly ground black pepper

---

**Serves** 4 to 6
**Prep time:** 10 minutes

Put the bell peppers, chickpeas, tahini, oil, lemon juice, garlic, and a pinch each of salt and pepper in a blender and puree until smooth and creamy.

**VARIATION TIP:** For a spicy version, add a pinch of red pepper flakes. To lend a smoky flavor, add a good pinch of smoked paprika.

**WASTE-NOT TIP:** Use leftover tahini as a dip or to make traditional hummus by omitting the roasted red peppers in the recipe above. You can also add 2 to 4 tablespoons of it to the batter of the Almond-Flour Brownies (page 251).

---

Per serving: Calories: 384; Total fat: 17g; Saturated fat: 2g; Protein: 14g; Carbohydrates: 47g; Sugar: 3g; Fiber: 13g; Sodium: 452mg

# Honey and Ricotta Dip with Figs and Granola

QUICK, VEGETARIAN ...................................................................

This sweet and creamy ricotta dip with chunky pieces of dried figs and a crumbly granola topping requires no cooking. It's incredibly delicious and surprisingly healthy, so serve it as a dip or enjoy alone by the spoonful. I like to use dried figs for dipping, but it also tastes great with crackers or multigrain crispbread for added crunch.

....................................................................

**4 ounces cream cheese, softened**

**4 ounces part-skim ricotta cheese, at room temperature**

**2 tablespoons honey, plus extra for drizzling**

**¼ cup finely chopped dried Mission figs, plus 6 figs, halved, for serving**

**2 tablespoons granola**

---

**Serves** 4 to 6
**Prep time:** 10 minutes

1. In a medium bowl, combine the cream cheese, ricotta, and honey. Using an electric mixer, beat until smooth, about 1 minute. Using a wooden spoon, stir in the chopped figs.

2. Transfer the dip to a serving bowl, sprinkle with granola, and drizzle with extra honey. Serve with the halved figs for dipping.

**WASTE-NOT TIP:** Leftover cream cheese can be used to make Portobello Mushrooms Stuffed with Andouille Sausage (page 78). Chop up any leftover dried figs and use them as a topping for the Banana and Mocha Protein Smoothie (page 50).

**MAKE-AHEAD TIP:** To make this dip ahead of time, complete step 1, then put the dip in a covered container in the refrigerator for up to 2 days. When ready to serve, top with granola and a drizzle of honey.

---

Per serving: Calories: 239; Total fat: 12g; Saturated fat: 7g; Protein: 6g; Carbohydrates: 28g; Sugar: 21g; Fiber: 3g; Sodium: 125mg

# Fig, Brie, and Pecan Bites

**QUICK, VEGETARIAN** ...........................................................................................

Your guests will love this sweet and savory appetizer, and you'll love how easy it is to make! To create a mini version of these delicious bites, use a 24-cup mini muffin tin, cut the crescent roll dough and brie into 24 pieces, and use about ½ tablespoon of jam per mini-muffin cup.

..................................................................................................................

Oil, for greasing the tin
Flour, for dusting
**1 (8-ounce) tube refrigerated crescent roll dough**
**1 (8-ounce) wheel Brie**
**¾ cup fig jam**
**¼ cup chopped pecans**
**Fresh rosemary sprigs cut into 1-inch pieces, for garnish**

**Makes** 12 Brie bites
**Prep time:** 10 minutes
**Cook time:** 20 minutes

1. Preheat the oven to 375°F and grease a 12-cup muffin tin with oil. Set aside.
2. Lightly dust a clean work surface with flour. Place the dough on the floured surface and roll it out. Pinch together the seams and cut the dough into 12 squares. Place each square into a muffin cup.
3. Cut the Brie into 12 cubes and place one cube in each muffin cup. Top each with 1 tablespoon of jam and a sprinkling of chopped pecans.
4. Bake for 15 to 20 minutes, or until the pastry is golden. Garnish each of the fig, Brie, and pecan bites with a small rosemary sprig. Serve warm or at room temperature.

**VARIATION TIP:** Try different types of fruit preserves or different kinds of nuts for variation.

**WASTE-NOT TIP:** Use any leftover jam to replace the berries in the Coconut Yogurt Parfait with Mixed Berries and Almond Granola (page 90). Use any leftover rosemary to garnish the Individual Pita Pizzas with Red Onion and Kalamata Olives (page 134) or the Portobello and Caramelized Onion Tart (page 135).

Per serving: Calories: 179; Total fat: 11g; Saturated fat: 5g; Protein: 6g; Carbohydrates: 14g; Sugar: 8g; Fiber: <1g; Sodium: 276mg

# Baked Biscuit Wreath with Garlic Dip

**NUT-FREE, VEGETARIAN** ..................................................................................................

These biscuits are flaky and golden brown, and the dip has a garlicky, cheesy yummi-ness that you won't be able to get enough of. It's a one-pan appetizer dish that's so easy to prepare you'll be coming up with excuses to have friends over so you can share it.

..................................................................................................

**1 (16-ounce) can refrigerated biscuits**

Olive oil, for brushing

**2½ cups shredded mozzarella cheese**

**1 cup ricotta cheese**

**¼ cup mayonnaise**

4 garlic cloves, minced

Salt

Freshly ground black pepper

---

**Serves** 6
**Prep time:** 15 minutes
**Cook time:** 30 minutes

1. Preheat the oven to 350°F.
2. Cut the biscuits in half and flatten them out. Roll each piece of dough into a ball. Arrange each ball of dough, seam-side down, in a large cast-iron skillet, forming a ring around the inside of the skillet. Brush the biscuits with oil and set aside.
3. In a large bowl, mix together the mozzarella, ricotta, mayonnaise, garlic, and a pinch each of salt and pepper. Spoon the dip into the center of the skillet and bake for 25 to 30 minutes, or until the cheese is bubbly and the biscuits are golden.

**WASTE-NOT TIP:** Use any leftover ricotta to make the Honey and Ricotta Dip with Figs and Granola (page 70).

---

Per serving: Calories: 494; Total fat: 30g; Saturated fat: 12g; Protein: 21g; Carbohydrates: 37g; Sugar: 6g; Fiber: 1g; Sodium: 1,171mg

# Baked Brie with Caramelized Walnuts

**GLUTEN-FREE, QUICK, VEGETARIAN** ...................................................................

This is not your average baked brie! It has a caramelized-walnut topping that is to die for and leaves you wondering whether you're eating a scrumptious appetizer or a savory-sweet dessert. Serve this dish with crunchy crackers, flatbread, or crostini.

............................................................................................................................

**1 (8-ounce) wheel brie**

**2 tablespoons
unsalted butter**

¼ cup brown sugar

**3 tablespoons heavy cream**

**¾ cup whole walnuts**

---

**Serves** 6
**Prep time:** 5 minutes
**Cook time:** 25 minutes

1. Preheat the oven to 350°F.
2. Put the brie into a small oven-safe skillet or baking dish.
3. Heat a medium nonstick skillet over low heat, and melt the butter and brown sugar until bubbly, 5 to 10 minutes. Stir in the cream and then the walnuts, making sure that the walnuts are fully coated.
4. Pour the walnuts over the brie and bake for 10 to 15 minutes more, or until the brie has melted.

**VARIATION TIP:** Add ½ teaspoon of ground cinnamon or nutmeg to the sugar and butter in step 2, or try replacing the brie with Camembert cheese.

**WASTE-NOT TIP:** Use leftover heavy cream to make Creamy and Spicy Mushroom Risotto in the Slow Cooker (page 140), Mushroom Fettuccine with Shaved Parmesan (page 139), or the Homemade Frizz Coffee (page 52).

---

Per serving: Calories: 290; Total fat: 25g; Saturated fat: 11g; Protein: 10g; Carbohydrates: 10g; Sugar: 7g; Fiber: 1g; Sodium: 244mg

# Grilled Apricot and Goat Cheese Crostini with Balsamic Reduction and Basil

**NUT-FREE, QUICK, VEGETARIAN** .......................................................

These crostini with grilled fruit and a balsamic reduction are a summer must-try. The grilled bread is crispy; the goat cheese is tart and creamy; the apricot is soft, juicy, and sweet; and the basil adds an herbaceous freshness. This appetizer is sure to be a hit at any party.

.......................................................

¼ **cup balsamic vinegar**

1 tablespoon olive
   oil, divided

6 **(¼-inch-thick) slices**
   **French baguette**

2 **apricots, halved**

3 **tablespoons goat cheese,**
   **softened**

6 **large basil leaves,**
   **thinly sliced**

---

**Makes** 6 crostini
**Prep time:** 5 minutes
**Cook time:** 15 minutes

1. In a small saucepan, bring the vinegar to a boil. Cook for 5 to 8 minutes, or until reduced by half (to about 2 tablespoons). Remove from the heat and set aside.

2. Meanwhile, heat a large grill pan over medium heat. Use half of the oil to brush both sides of the bread. Grill the bread in the pan until golden brown on both sides, 1 to 2 minutes per side. Remove the bread from the pan and set aside.

3. Brush both sides of the halved apricots with the remaining oil. Grill the apricots for 30 to 60 seconds on each side, or until tender and lightly browned. Cool slightly, then cut into thick slices.

4. Spread about ½ tablespoon of goat cheese on each piece of grilled bread, arrange the apricot slices on top, drizzle with the balsamic reduction, and sprinkle with basil.

**WASTE-NOT TIP:** Use leftover bread to make Brazilian Chocolate Bread Pudding Flan (page 238), and use any leftover basil to make Caprese Salad with Peppery Balsamic Reduction (page 110).

---

Per serving: Calories: 86; Total fat: 4g; Saturated fat: 1g; Protein: 2g; Carbohydrates: 11g; Sugar: 2g; Fiber: 1g; Sodium: 115mg

# Bacon-Wrapped Carrot Pops with Honey and Rosemary Glaze

**DAIRY-FREE, GLUTEN-FREE, NUT-FREE** ..........................................................

These bacon-wrapped carrots make a fun appetizer for any occasion, and their smoky-sweet flavor means they'll be a guaranteed hit. For best results, use rosemary sprigs that are about 3 inches long.

..........................................................

**6 medium carrots, peeled**

**6 strips smoked bacon**

**¼ cup honey, divided**

¼ teaspoon freshly ground black pepper

**6 sturdy rosemary sprigs**

---

**Makes** 6 carrot pops
**Prep time:** 10 minutes
**Cook time:** 35 minutes, plus 5 minutes cooling

1. Preheat the oven to 400°F. Line a baking sheet with parchment paper.

2. Fill a large stockpot two-thirds full with water. Bring the water to a boil, then gently slide the carrots into the water and parboil for 5 minutes, or until they start to soften. Using a slotted spoon, remove the carrots from the water. Let cool for 5 minutes, then pat dry.

3. Wrap one strip of bacon around each carrot and arrange the wrapped carrots in a single layer on the prepared baking sheet. Brush bacon with 2 tablespoons of honey and season with pepper.

4. Bake for 10 minutes, then remove the pan from the oven, roll the carrots over, and brush with the remaining 2 tablespoons of honey. Bake for an additional 5 to 10 minutes, or until the carrots are tender and the bacon is crispy.

5. Remove a few rosemary leaves from one of the sprigs and finely chop them. Sprinkle over the bacon-wrapped carrots. Stick the pointy end of one sprig of rosemary into the thicker end of each carrot, using the sprig as a skewer.

**VARIATION TIP:** If you'd like to, use about ¼ teaspoon of dried rosemary and either wood or bamboo skewers to replace the fresh rosemary leaves and sprigs.

---

Per serving: Calories: 114; Total fat: 4g; Saturated fat: 1g; Protein: 3g; Carbohydrates: 18g; Sugar: 15g; Fiber: 2g; Sodium: 178mg

# Tortellini and Caprese Salad Skewers

NUT-FREE, QUICK, VEGETARIAN ...........................................................

These appetizer skewers are inspired by the colors of the Italian flag—green, white, and red. Use small or mini skewers if you are entertaining a larger group of guests or throwing a formal get-together; use long skewers if you are having fewer guests or for picnics and barbecues.

....................................................................................................

**1 (9-ounce) package refrigerated cheese tortellini**

½ cup olive oil

**3 tablespoons balsamic vinegar**

Salt

Freshly ground black pepper

**1 (8-ounce) package fresh mozzarella pearls**

**1 (10-ounce) container grape tomatoes**

**1 bunch fresh basil**

_____

**Makes** about 6 (12-inch) or 12 (6-inch) skewers
**Prep time:** 10 minutes
**Cook time:** 10 minutes, plus 10 minutes to cool

1. Cook the tortellini according to the package instructions. (This should take 8 to 10 minutes.) Drain and let them cool for 10 minutes.

2. Meanwhile, in a large bowl, whisk together the olive oil, balsamic vinegar, and a pinch each of salt and pepper. Add the mozzarella pearls and tomatoes and toss to combine. Once the tortellini are cool, gently toss them into the mixture.

3. Assemble the skewers by alternating layers of mozzarella, tomatoes, basil, and tortellini until all of the ingredients have been used.

**STORAGE TIP:** Store any leftovers, covered, in the refrigerator for up to one day.

**VARIATION TIP:** For a spicy version, add a pinch of red pepper flakes to the oil-and-vinegar mixture.

_____

Per serving out of 6 total: Calories: 358; Total fat: 29g; Saturated fat: 9g; Protein: 11g; Carbohydrates: 13g; Sugar: 4g; Fiber: 1g; Sodium: 275mg

# Portobello Mushrooms Stuffed with Andouille Sausage

NUT-FREE, QUICK ..................................................

These aren't your typical stuffed mushrooms. These little guys are filled with andouille sausage—a spicy smoked pork sausage flavored with garlic, pepper, onions, wine, and seasonings—and melty, gooey mozzarella cheese. It'll be a struggle not to eat them all before your guests arrive!

..................................................

**6 portobello mushrooms, stems and gills removed**

5 tablespoons olive oil, divided

**½ pound andouille sausage, at room temperature**

**6 ounces cream cheese, softened**

**¾ cup shredded mozzarella**

Salt

Freshly ground black pepper

**⅓ cup panko bread crumbs**

---

**Serves** 6
**Prep time:** 10 minutes
**Cook time:** 30 minutes

1. Preheat the oven to 400°F. Grease a large baking sheet. Place the mushrooms stem-side down on the pan and brush with 2 tablespoons of oil. Bake for 10 minutes or until the mushrooms begin to soften. Pat dry any excess water on the pan with a paper towel.

2. Meanwhile, grind the sausage in a blender or food processor. In a large nonstick skillet, heat 1 tablespoon of oil and cook the sausage until lightly browned, 3 to 5 minutes.

3. In a large bowl, combine the cream cheese, sausage, and mozzarella. Season with salt and pepper.

4. In a small bowl, combine the panko bread crumbs, the remaining 2 tablespoons of oil, and a pinch each of salt and pepper.

5. Flip the mushroom caps over and stuff them with the sausage and cheese filling. Top with the panko mixture. Bake for 12 to 15 minutes, or until the cheese has melted and the panko is golden brown.

**WASTE-NOT TIP:** Use leftover mushrooms and mozzarella to make Portobello Mushroom Lasagna Casserole (page 141).

---

Per serving: Calories: 341; Total fat: 27g; Saturated fat: 10g; Protein: 16g; Carbohydrates: 12g; Sugar: 4g; Fiber: 2g; Sodium: 514mg

# Zucchini Roll-Ups

**GLUTEN-FREE, NUT-FREE, QUICK, VEGETARIAN**

I like to think of this as the low-carb version of a vegetarian sushi roll. It's quick, fresh, and flavorful and requires no cooking at all. Enjoy these all by themselves or serve them with Ponzu Sauce (page 215) or Peanut Sauce (page 217).

2 medium zucchini

4 ounces chive and onion cream cheese, softened

½ carrot, peeled and cut into thin matchsticks

½ cucumber, cut into thin matchsticks

1 tablespoon toasted sesame seeds

**Serves** 4 to 6
**Prep time:** 20 minutes

1. Slice each zucchini into thin, flat strips using a vegetable peeler. Lay 2 zucchini slices down lengthwise on top of each other on a cutting board. Spread a thin layer of cream cheese on the top strip.

2. Top either one of the two short sides of the strips with a few carrot and cucumber matchsticks. Starting from the end with the matchsticks, tightly roll up the zucchini.

3. Repeat the same process with the remaining ingredients. Arrange the rolls on a serving platter and sprinkle them with sesame seeds.

**VARIATION TIP:** Add some tofu for protein or switch up the vegetables to whatever you have on hand. If you're not a vegetarian, try adding crabmeat, flaked cooked salmon, or canned tuna.

**WASTE-NOT TIP:** Use any leftover cream cheese to make the Smoked Salmon Wrap with Capers and Cream Cheese (page 120).

Per serving: Calories: 116; Total fat: 8g; Saturated fat: 5g; Protein: 4g; Carbohydrates: 8g; Sugar: 4g; Fiber: 2g; Sodium: 166mg

# No-Knead Brazilian Cheese Rolls

GLUTEN-FREE, NUT-FREE, QUICK, VEGETARIAN ......................................................

These rolls are a family affair. They are very popular in Brazil as well as at Brazilian steakhouses in the United States, where they're called *pão de queijo*. This version is adapted for the blender, which fortunately means no kneading! These rolls are puffy, airy, and addictive. Serve them for breakfast or as a snack or appetizer. They must be consumed right away—otherwise, they become hard and chewy.

Oil, for greasing the tin

**⅔ cup tapioca flour**

**⅓ cup whole milk**

**⅓ cup grated Parmesan cheese**

2½ tablespoons olive oil

**1 small egg, at room temperature**

¼ teaspoon salt

---

**Makes** 12 mini rolls
**Prep time:** 5 minutes
**Cook time:** 20 minutes

1. Preheat the oven to 350°F. Grease a mini muffin tin.
2. Put the flour, milk, cheese, oil, egg, and salt in a blender and blend until smooth, 1 to 2 minutes. You may have to pause the blender to scrape down the sides.
3. Evenly distribute the batter into 12 muffin cups in the mini muffin tin and bake for 14 to 18 minutes, or until puffy and golden brown. Serve warm.

**VARIATION TIP:** For an Italian-style take, stir in ⅛ to ¼ teaspoon of Italian seasoning mix after the batter is blended.

---

Per serving: Calories: 68; Total fat: 4g; Saturated fat: 1g; Protein: 2g; Carbohydrates: 6g; Sugar: <1g; Fiber: 0g; Sodium: 107mg

# Pizza-dilla with Guacamole Salsa

NUT-FREE, QUICK ...................................................................................

These pizza-dillas are quesadillas filled with pizza toppings. They are a yummy fusion of Italian and Mexican cuisine. Pizza-dillas are quick to prepare, crispy on the outside, and melty and gooey on the inside. Kids love them! You can serve them as a casual appetizer, a hearty snack, or even a quick lunch or dinner.

**4 (10-inch) flour tortillas**

**2 cups shredded mozzarella, divided**

**20 pepperoni slices**

**1 cup mild guacamole salsa or guacamole, for dipping**

**Serves** 4 to 6
**Prep time:** 10 minutes
**Cook time:** 10 minutes

1. Place the tortillas on a flat surface. Sprinkle ¼ cup of cheese over one half of each tortilla, arrange five slices of pepperoni over the cheese, then sprinkle another ¼ cup of cheese over the pepperoni. Fold the empty side of the tortilla over the topping.

2. Heat a large nonstick skillet over medium heat and cook two of the pizza-dillas at a time until brown and crispy on the bottom, about 2 minutes. Carefully flip the pizza-dillas and cook until brown and crispy on the second side, about 2 minutes more. Make sure the cheese is melted.

3. Repeat step 2 for the other 2 pizza-dillas. Slice each into thirds and serve with the guacamole salsa for dipping.

**VARIATION TIP:** Replace the guacamole salsa with pizza sauce or Chipotle Sauce (page 213).

Per serving: Calories: 567; Total fat: 30g; Saturated fat: 13g; Protein: 24g; Carbohydrates: 48g; Sugar: 2g; Fiber: 5g; Sodium: 1,348mg

# Fried Garlic and Parmesan Pasta Chips with Marinara Sauce

**NUT-FREE, VEGETARIAN** ....................................................................................

Pasta is truly a versatile ingredient; here it replaces potato or corn chips. The advantage is that these pasta chips are much better for holding the sauce when dipping. This clever and delicious idea is sure to please snack lovers of all ages.

....................................................................................

**1 (12-ounce) package jumbo pasta shells**

**¾ cup grated Parmesan cheese**

**1½ teaspoons garlic powder**

Salt

Freshly ground black pepper

4 cups vegetable oil, for frying

**1½ cups marinara sauce, for dipping**

---

**Serves** 4 to 6
**Prep time:** 5 minutes
**Cook time:** 45 minutes

1. In a large stockpot, cook the pasta according to the package instructions for al dente. Drain the pasta in a colander and reserve.

2. While the pasta is cooking, line a baking sheet with a double layer of paper towels.

3. In a small bowl, mix together the cheese, garlic powder, and a pinch each of salt and pepper.

4. In a large heavy-bottom pot or large cast-iron Dutch oven, heat the oil over medium heat. When the oil is shimmering, add about one-fifth of the pasta, making sure to not overcrowd the pan. Cook until golden and crispy, 3 to 6 minutes. Use a kitchen spider strainer to move the shells around so that they can fry evenly.

5. Scoop the shells out of the oil and set them on the paper-towel-lined baking sheet, with the opening of the pasta shell facing down. Sprinkle about one-fifth of the cheese and garlic seasoning over the shells right away. Repeat from step 4, working in batches, with the remaining pasta and seasoning mixture. Serve with warm marinara sauce.

---

Per serving: Calories: 458; Total fat: 9g; Saturated fat: 3g; Protein: 18g; Carbohydrates: 77g; Sugar: 11g; Fiber: 5g; Sodium: 689mg

# Sweet and Spicy Buffalo Chicken Wings

**DAIRY-FREE, GLUTEN-FREE, NUT-FREE** .........................................

Buffalo wings were created in the 1960s at a bar in Buffalo, New York, and were originally deep-fried. This healthier baked version is sweet, spicy, crispy, and sticky. For a variation, brush the wings with the Five-Spice Barbecue Sauce (page 216). These make one of the best appetizers for a game-day party, but you don't need to wait for a special event to enjoy them!

**1 tablespoon baking powder**

1 teaspoon salt

½ teaspoon freshly ground
  black pepper

**1 teaspoon garlic powder**

**3 pounds chicken wings (if
  frozen, thaw and pat dry)**

**½ cup hot sauce**

2 tablespoons olive oil

**2 tablespoons honey**

**Serves** 6
**Prep time:** 10 minutes
**Cook time:** 45 minutes

1. Preheat the oven to 400°F. Line a baking sheet with foil and then place a nonstick oven-safe rack on top of the sheet pan.
2. In a large bowl, mix together the baking powder, salt, pepper, and garlic powder. Add the chicken wings and toss to evenly coat.
3. Arrange the wings on the rack in a single layer. Bake for 40 to 45 minutes, or until chicken wings are lightly golden brown and crispy.
4. Whisk together the hot sauce, oil, and honey in a small bowl. Brush the wings all over with the sauce mixture.

**STORAGE TIP:** Store leftover chicken in an airtight container in the refrigerator for up to 3 days.

Per serving: Calories: 505; Total fat: 39g; Saturated fat: 11g; Protein: 34g; Carbohydrates: 7g; Sugar: 6g; Fiber: <1g; Sodium: 1,352mg

# Microwave Coconut Curry Popcorn

**GLUTEN-FREE, NUT-FREE, QUICK, VEGETARIAN** ..............................................

If you are a fan of coconut curries, you will fall in love with this snack. It's comforting and buttery with a deep, earthy flavor from the curry. The coconut flakes add a contrasting sweet flavor, making it hard not to come back for seconds . . . or thirds. For a spicy kick, add a pinch of cayenne pepper or a few drops of hot sauce after melting the butter.

2 (2.75-ounce) bags plain
   microwave popcorn
⅔ cup salted butter
1½ tablespoons
   curry powder
1 teaspoon garlic powder
½ cup sweetened
   coconut flakes

**Serves** 4
**Prep time:** 5 minutes
**Cook time:** 10 minutes

1. Cook the popcorn in the microwave according to the package instructions. Be sure to open the popcorn bags carefully to release the steam.

2. In a large microwave-safe bowl, melt the butter in the microwave on high, about 1 minute. Whisk the curry and garlic powder into the butter until combined. Add the popcorn and coconut flakes. Toss to coat and serve immediately.

**WASTE-NOT TIP:** Use any leftover coconut flakes to make the Roasted Pistachio and Coconut Energy Balls (page 89).

Per serving: Calories: 512; Total fat: 42g; Saturated fat: 26g; Protein: 3g; Carbohydrates: 30g; Sugar: 5g; Fiber: 6g; Sodium: 507mg

# Hot Chocolate Popcorn with Marshmallows and Sprinkles

**GLUTEN-FREE, NUT-FREE, QUICK, VEGETARIAN** .....................................

Although corn kernels are an ancient grain, popcorn is a 19th-century invention usually prepared as a savory treat. But I enjoy putting a fun spin on it, making it sweet and adding colorful sprinkles. This not only makes a great afternoon snack or movie treat, but it can also be served at birthday or holiday parties.

.....................................

**4 (2.75-ounce) bags microwave popcorn**

**1 cup bittersweet chocolate chips**

**¾ cup mini marshmallows**

**1 to 2 tablespoons sprinkles**

---

**Serves** 4
**Prep time:** 5 minutes
**Cook time:** 10 minutes, plus 10 minutes to harden

1. Line a baking sheet with parchment paper.
2. Cook popcorn in the microwave according to the package instructions. Be sure to open the popcorn bags carefully to release the steam.
3. In a small microwave-safe bowl, heat the chocolate chips in the microwave in 30-second intervals, stirring well between intervals, until the chocolate is fully melted and smooth, about 2 minutes.
4. Drizzle half of the chocolate onto the prepared baking sheet. Add the popcorn and marshmallows in a single layer and gently press onto the chocolate. Drizzle the remaining chocolate on top and top with the sprinkles. Let the chocolate harden for about 10 minutes. Break into pieces and enjoy!

**WASTE-NOT TIP:** Use leftover chocolate chips to make the No-Bake Dulce de Leche Chocolate Tart (page 248).

---

Per serving: Calories: 585; Total fat: 27g; Saturated fat: 13g; Protein: 7g; Carbohydrates: 81g; Sugar: 31g; Fiber: 10g; Sodium: 512mg

# Pear and Apple "Nachos" with Peanut Butter and Cacao Nibs

**DAIRY-FREE, GLUTEN-FREE, QUICK, VEGAN** ............................................

Do you love nachos? Me, too! But let's face it, nachos are not the healthiest dish. Unlike traditional nachos, these fruit nachos are wholesome, dairy-free, and easy to prepare. They are a great source of vitamins, fiber, and protein, making a satisfying snack. Naturally sweet and nutty with a great crunch, this snack is definitely a fiesta for your mouth!

.............................................................................................

**1 apple, cored and sliced**
**1 pear, cored and sliced**
**⅓ cup creamy peanut butter**
**2 tablespoons cacao nibs**

---

**Serves** 4 to 6
**Prep time:** 10 minutes
**Cook time:** 30 seconds

1. Arrange the apple and pear slices on a serving platter.
2. In a small microwave-safe bowl, melt the peanut butter in the microwave on high for 20 to 30 seconds. Stir, then drizzle over the sliced fruit. Sprinkle cacao nibs over the fruit and serve immediately.

**WASTE-NOT TIP:** Cacao nibs are dairy-free. Though they don't melt like chocolate chips do, they can be used to add flavor and texture to pancakes, waffles, and other baked goods.

**VARIATION TIP:** If you can tolerate dairy, feel free to replace the cacao nibs with chocolate chips.

---

Per serving: Calories: 204; Total fat: 13g; Saturated fat: 3g; Protein: 5g; Carbohydrates: 19g; Sugar: 10g; Fiber: 6g; Sodium: 107mg

# Roasted Cashew Nuts with Honey and Rosemary

**DAIRY-FREE, GLUTEN-FREE, QUICK, VEGETARIAN** .........................................

You'll go nuts for these roasted nuts! They are sweet, crunchy, and smell delicious. They're versatile, too. You can take them as a snack on-the-go, serve them as an appetizer, add them to a cheese board, sprinkle them over salads, or chop them up and use them to garnish your baked goods. What's more, they even make a great edible holiday gift! For a spicy version, stir in a pinch of cayenne before roasting.

..............................................................................................................

1½ tablespoons olive oil

**2½ tablespoons honey**

**3 teaspoons chopped fresh rosemary, divided**

½ teaspoon salt

**2½ cups whole raw cashew nuts**

---

**Serves** 6
**Prep time:** 5 minutes
**Cook time:** 20 minutes, plus 5 minutes to cool

1. Preheat the oven to 350°F. Line a baking sheet with parchment paper.

2. In a large bowl, whisk together the oil, honey, 1½ teaspoons of rosemary, and the salt. Stir in the nuts and mix until they are evenly coated.

3. Pour the nuts onto the lined baking sheet and distribute them in a single layer. Bake for 15 to 20 minutes, stirring every 5 minutes to avoid burning. Remove the baking sheet from the oven and then carefully transfer the parchment paper to a flat surface, trying as much as possible to not disturb the nuts.

4. Let cool for at least 5 minutes, place into a serving bowl, and sprinkle with the remaining 1½ teaspoons of rosemary.

**WASTE-NOT TIP:** Use leftover rosemary to make Bacon-Wrapped Carrot Pops with Honey and Rosemary Glaze (page 75).

Per serving: Calories: 385; Total fat: 30g; Saturated fat: 6g; Protein: 9g; Carbohydrates: 26g; Sugar: 10g; Fiber: 2g; Sodium: 203mg

# Churro Pecans with Chocolate Drizzle

**GLUTEN-FREE, VEGETARIAN** ..............................................................................

Churros are fried pastry treats coated with a mixture of sugar and cinnamon, tradition-ally from Spain and Portugal. These churro-inspired pecans are an adaptation of the recipe in which the pecans replace the pastry and receive a warm, sugary coating. The bittersweet chocolate balances the sweetness of the nuts—just like the chocolate sauce that usually accompanies the pastry in Spain.

½ cup granulated sugar

½ cup brown sugar

**1 tablespoon**
**ground cinnamon**

⅓ cup water

**2 cups raw pecan halves**

**2 to 3 tablespoons**
**bittersweet**
**chocolate chips**

---

**Serves** 4 to 6
**Prep time:** 5 minutes
**Cook time:** 20 minutes,
plus 5 minutes to cool
and 5 minutes to rest

1. In a large nonstick skillet over medium heat, com-bine the granulated sugar, brown sugar, cinnamon, and water. Let the sugars dissolve undisturbed, 5 to 8 minutes. Then add the pecans and stir often, until the pecans are fully coated, the sugar crystallizes, and the mixture becomes dry, 8 to 10 minutes more. Remove the pan from the heat and transfer the pecans to a plate to cool for at least 5 minutes.

2. Meanwhile, in a small microwave-safe bowl, heat the chocolate chips in the microwave in 30-second intervals, stirring well between intervals, until the chocolate is fully melted and smooth, 30 to 90 seconds. Transfer the pecans to a serving bowl, drizzle with the melted chocolate, and let stand for at least 5 minutes, or until the chocolate is set, before serving.

**WASTE-NOT TIP:** Use any leftover pecans and chocolate chips to make the No-Bake Caramel-Pecan Cookie Balls (page 226).

---

Per serving: Calories: 581; Total fat: 41g; Saturated fat: 5g; Protein: 6g; Carbohydrates: 62g; Sugar: 48g; Fiber: 7g; Sodium: 8mg

# Roasted Pistachio and Coconut Energy Balls

**DAIRY-FREE, GLUTEN-FREE, VEGAN** ..........................................................

Roasted pistachios combined with unsweetened coconut and naturally sweet pitted dates create a delicious, nutty snack or a truffle-like dessert. Full of protein, these bite-size balls will keep you full for hours. I suggest doubling the recipe so that you can always have some on hand when a snack attack strikes.

..........................................................................................................................

**1 cup roasted and salted pistachios, shelled**
**½ cup unsweetened coconut flakes, plus extra for topping**
**1 cup pitted Medjool dates**
**1 teaspoon vanilla extract**

---

**Makes** 12 balls
**Prep time:** 10 minutes, plus 30 minutes to chill

1. Line a baking sheet with parchment paper.
2. In a food processor, process the pistachios and coconut flakes until crumbly (not powdered), 10 to 20 seconds. Add the dates and vanilla and process until the mixture pulls together and is sticky when pressed between your fingers, 10 to 20 seconds more. (If needed, add 1 to 2 teaspoons of water to help the mixture come together.)
3. Using a tablespoon, scoop the dough and roll it into balls (about 12). Roll the balls in the extra coconut flakes, pressing a little to make the flakes stick onto the exterior of the balls. Place on the prepared baking sheet and refrigerate for at least 30 minutes before serving, or store in an airtight container in the refrigerator for up to 5 days.

**WASTE-NOT TIP:** Use leftover pistachios, coconut flakes, and chopped dates as a topping for smoothies, such as the Banana and Mocha Protein Smoothie (page 50).

---

Per serving: Calories: 115; Total fat: 6g; Saturated fat: 2g; Protein: 3g; Carbohydrates: 15g; Sugar: 12g; Fiber: 2g; Sodium: 54mg

# Coconut Yogurt Parfait with Mixed Berries and Almond Granola

**DAIRY-FREE, VEGAN** ....................................................................................

This recipe is nutty, sweet, and tangy and goes from creamy to crunchy layer by layer. Whether eaten as breakfast, a snack, or dessert, this parfait is sure to hit all the right notes. I use coconut yogurt here for a vegan option, but if dairy isn't a concern, feel free to replace it with the yogurt of your choice. Try it with fresh berries when they are in season.

**1 pound frozen mixed berries, thawed**

½ cup sugar

2 tablespoons lemon juice

**4 (8-ounce) containers dairy-free coconut milk yogurt**

**1 cup almond granola**

**Serves** 4
**Prep time:** 5 minutes, plus 30 minutes to macerate

1. In a large bowl, mix the berries with the sugar and lemon juice. Let macerate at room temperature for 25 to 30 minutes.

2. Meanwhile, mix the yogurt well and put half of each container into 4 glasses or small bowls. Top each with about 2 tablespoons of granola. Spoon half of the macerated berries into the glasses. Repeat layering in this order: yogurt, granola, berries. Enjoy immediately or cover and refrigerate for up to 1 day.

**WASTE-NOT TIP:** Enjoy leftover granola as a topping for smoothies or smoothie bowls, such as the Protein-Packed Raspberry and Dark Chocolate Smoothie Bowls (page 53).

Per serving: Calories: 432; Total fat: 10g; Saturated fat: 5g; Protein: 5g; Carbohydrates: 84g; Sugar: 58g; Fiber: 8g; Sodium: 63mg

# Grilled Peach Halves with Greek Yogurt and Honey

**GLUTEN-FREE, NUT-FREE, QUICK, VEGETARIAN** .....................................................

These grilled peaches are warm, sweet, juicy, and so luscious—a healthy adaptation of peaches and cream. To create a showstopper at a barbecue or summer get-together, garnish these with fresh mint leaves for a beautiful presentation.

7 tablespoons unsalted butter, melted, divided

3 tablespoons honey, divided, plus extra for drizzling

½ teaspoon ground cinnamon

4 medium peaches, pitted and halved

1 (6-ounce) container vanilla Greek yogurt

**Serves** 4
**Prep time:** 5 minutes, plus 5 minutes to marinate
**Cook time:** 5 minutes

1. In a large mixing bowl, whisk 4 tablespoons of butter, 2 tablespoons of honey, and the cinnamon until just combined. Add the peach halves and toss to coat. Let marinate at room temperature for 5 minutes.

2. Meanwhile, heat a large grill pan over medium heat. Coat the bottom of the pan with the remaining 3 tablespoons of butter. Arrange the peaches in the pan and grill for about 2 minutes on each side, or until grill marks appear.

3. In a small bowl, whisk together the yogurt and remaining 1 tablespoon of honey until just combined and creamy. Dollop the yogurt over the grilled peach halves and drizzle additional honey over all. Serve immediately.

Per serving: Calories: 321; Total fat: 23g; Saturated fat: 14g; Protein: 3g; Carbohydrates: 30g; Sugar: 27g; Fiber: 2g; Sodium: 32mg

# Peaches and Cream Tortilla Rolls

NUT-FREE, VEGETARIAN .......................................................

When your sweet tooth attacks, these tortilla rolls make the perfect 5-ingredient fix. While it may be hard to do, waiting for them to chill ensures that the rolls stay together. Try experimenting with other in-season fruit or fruit combinations—the possibilities are almost endless.

**4 ounces reduced-fat cream cheese, softened**

½ cup powdered sugar, plus extra for sprinkling

**1½ cups whipped cream**

**4 (8-inch) flour tortillas**

**1½ cups chopped fresh peaches**

**Serves** 4 to 6
**Prep time:** 10 minutes, plus 30 minutes to chill

1. In a large bowl, beat the cream cheese and sugar together with an electric mixer until creamy, 1 to 2 minutes. Add the whipped cream and beat just until the mixture comes together, 30 to 60 seconds.

2. Spread about ½ cup of the cream cheese mixture over each tortilla, leaving about 1 inch uncovered around the edges. Divide the chopped peaches evenly among the tortillas and roll them up.

3. Wrap each roll with plastic wrap and refrigerate for at least 30 minutes. Unwrap and sift powdered sugar on top of each roll. Slice and serve.

**WASTE-NOT TIP:** Use any leftover whipped cream to make Strawberry and Cream Panettone (page 252).

Per serving: Calories: 389; Total fat: 14g; Saturated fat: 9g; Protein: 8g; Carbohydrates: 57g; Sugar: 23g; Fiber: 3g; Sodium: 323mg

# Tex–Mex Tortilla Pinwheels with Black Beans and Corn

**NUT-FREE, QUICK, VEGETARIAN** .......................................................................

Delicious and colorful, these pinwheels are a fun take on the humble yet bold flavors of Tex-Mex cuisine. They make a satisfying afternoon snack as well as a quick and affordable school or work lunch.

.......................................................................

1 (8-ounce) container
   jalapeño cream cheese, at
   room temperature
1 cup shredded Monterey
   Jack cheese
4 (8-inch) flour tortillas
1 cup canned black beans,
   drained and rinsed
1 cup canned yellow corn,
   drained and rinsed

**Serves** 4 to 6
**Prep time:** 10 minutes

1. In a medium mixing bowl, mix together the cream cheese and Monterey Jack until well combined. Spread the cheese mixture over the surface of each tortilla, leaving about 1 inch uncovered around the edges. Sprinkle ¼ cup of black beans and ¼ cup of corn on one end of each tortilla.

2. Tightly roll up the tortillas. Slice each tortilla roll crosswise to form pinwheels. Serve immediately or refrigerate in an airtight container for up to one day.

**WASTE-NOT TIP:** Use leftover canned black beans or corn to prepare the Black Beans and Rice Power Bowls with Tofu (page 145) or Butternut Squash and Roasted Corn Quesadillas (page 142).

Per serving: Calories: 531; Total fat: 29g; Saturated fat: 16g; Protein: 18g; Carbohydrates: 51g; Sugar: 6g; Fiber: 6g; Sodium: 678mg

*Very Berry Salad with Candied Walnuts* **112**

# 5

## *Soups, Salads, and Sandwiches*

# Avocado and Kale Gazpacho

**DAIRY-FREE, GLUTEN-FREE, NUT-FREE, QUICK, VEGAN** ..................................................

This healthy soup allows you to spend less time in a hot kitchen and more time enjoying warmer weather with your loved ones. You can serve this as a soup or as a smoothie; either way it's delicious. For an extra-fresh flavor, blend half a cucumber and an extra ¼ cup of water with the other ingredients in step 3 and garnish with leftover fresh mint leaves from the Refreshing Pineapple-Mint Juice (page 43). You can also top the gazpacho with shaved Parmesan cheese for a savory approach.

..................................................

5 tablespoons olive
  oil, divided

**8 cups stemmed and
  chopped kale**

1 garlic clove, minced

**4 small avocados, chopped**

Juice of 2 lemons

3 cups ice water

Salt

Freshly ground black pepper

---

**Serves** 4
**Prep time:** 5 minutes
**Cook time:** 10 minutes,
plus 5 minutes to cool

1. In a large nonstick skillet, heat 2 tablespoons of olive oil over medium heat. Add the kale and sauté, stirring occasionally, for 5 to 8 minutes, or until the kale is soft. Add the garlic and cook for 1 minute more.
2. Remove the pan from the heat, and let the mixture cool for about 5 minutes.
3. Transfer the cooled kale and garlic to a blender. Add the remaining 3 tablespoons of olive oil, avocados, lemon juice, ice water, salt, and pepper. Blend until smooth. Taste and adjust the seasoning, if needed.

**VARIATION TIP:** For a creamier version, add ⅓ cup of plain Greek yogurt in step 3. For a spicy gazpacho, season with red pepper flakes.

---

Per serving: Calories: 430; Total fat: 37g; Saturated fat: 5g; Protein: 8g; Carbohydrates: 27g; Sugar: 4g; Fiber: 13g; Sodium: 68mg

# Miso Soup

This miso soup—made with dashi, a Japanese broth made with kombu (a type of sea-weed) and bonito fish flakes—makes a perfect light appetizer, or it can turn your takeout sushi into a complete meal. While it comes together quickly on the stovetop, you can also make it in a slow cooker (see Appliance Tip). I like to use kitchen shears to cut the seaweed into small pieces. You can store any leftovers in the refrigerator for up to 3 days or freeze them for up to 6 months.

**4 cups dashi**

**½ cup white miso paste**

**½ (14-ounce) block extra-firm tofu, cubed**

**2 dried nori sheets, cut into ¼-inch strips**

½ cup chopped scallions, green parts only

Salt

Freshly ground black pepper

---

**Serves** 4
**Prep time:** 5 minutes
**Cook time:** 20 minutes

1. In a 6-quart nonstick stockpot, combine the dashi, miso, and tofu and bring to a boil over high heat. Once the soup has reached a boil, reduce the heat to medium-low, stir, cover, and cook for 10 to 15 minutes.

2. Stir in the nori and cook for 3 to 5 minutes. Remove from the heat and stir in the scallions. Add salt and pepper to taste.

**WASTE-NOT TIP:** Pan-fry leftover tofu in oil and then mix with sweet chili sauce to make a great plant-based protein dish that can be served over sticky rice with a side of vegetables. Use leftover seaweed in sushi or sushi bowls.

**APPLIANCE TIP:** Place the dashi, miso, and tofu into a 6-quart slow cooker. Stir well and cook on High for 2 to 4 hours or on Low for 6 to 8 hours. When there are 15 to 30 minutes of cooking time remaining, stir in the seaweed and green onions, and cover again for the remaining time. When finished, taste and adjust the seasoning, if needed.

---

Per serving: Calories: 126; Total fat: 2g; Saturated fat: <1g; Protein: 7g; Carbohydrates: 15g; Sugar: <1g; Fiber: 1g; Sodium: 1,113mg

# Pressure Cooker Broccoli and Cheddar Soup

**APPLIANCE, GLUTEN-FREE, NUT-FREE, QUICK, VEGETARIAN** .......................................

Whether you need to warm up or want something that you can put together in no time after a long day of work—or both—this soup has got you covered. Unlike other recipes for this comfort-food staple, this one doesn't use flour as a thickener, so it's gluten-free.

.................................................................................................

1 tablespoon olive oil

6 cloves garlic, minced

**2 pounds frozen broccoli**

**3½ cups low-sodium vegetable broth**

Salt

Freshly ground black pepper

**1 cup heavy cream**

**2 cups shredded cheddar cheese**

---

**Serves** 4
**Prep time:** 5 minutes
**Cook time:** 4 minutes at High Pressure, plus 10 minutes to come to pressure

1. Select the Sauté function to preheat a 6-quart pressure cooker. When hot, pour in the oil, then add the garlic. Sauté for about 1 minute, stirring often.

2. Stir in the broccoli, broth, and a pinch each of salt and pepper. Lock the lid in place. Select High Pressure, close the pressure-release valve, and set the cook time for 4 minutes.

3. When done, turn off the pressure cooker and use the quick pressure release. Once the valve drops, remove the lid. Stir in the cream, then taste and adjust the seasoning, if needed.

4. In small batches, carefully transfer the hot soup to a blender, secure the lid tightly, and blend until mostly smooth.

5. Return the soup to the pressure cooker and add the cheese, stirring until it melts.

**VARIATION TIP:** You can save some calories by substituting half-and-half for heavy cream. Decrease the amount to ¾ cup.

**STORAGE TIP:** Store leftovers in the refrigerator for up to 3 days. Freeze for up to 2 months.

---

Per serving: Calories: 541; Total fat: 44g; Saturated fat: 26g; Protein: 20g; Carbohydrates: 19g; Sugar: 7g; Fiber: 8g; Sodium: 544mg

# Creamy Tomato Bisque

APPLIANCE, GLUTEN-FREE, NUT-FREE, VEGETARIAN .......................................

This creamy, smooth bisque makes for a light and easy weeknight meal. For an extra kick, stir in ¼ teaspoon of red pepper flakes, add leftover harissa from Roasted Cauliflower Steaks with Harissa (page 131), or add leftover chili paste from Garlic Chili Prawns (page 189). To make a vegan version, leave out the heavy cream.

1 tablespoon olive oil, plus more for greasing

2 medium onions, finely chopped

4 cloves garlic, minced

**1 (28-ounce) can whole peeled plum tomatoes**

**3 cups low-sodium vegetable broth**

1 teaspoon salt

**¼ cup heavy cream**

**Serves** 4 to 6
**Prep time:** 15 minutes
**Cook time:** 2 hours on High or 8 hours on Low

1. In a large nonstick skillet, heat the oil over medium-low heat. Add the onions and cook, stirring occasionally, for 10 to 12 minutes, or until the onions have softened. Add the garlic and cook for 1 minute more.

2. Grease a 6-quart slow cooker with some olive oil. Add the cooked onions and garlic as well as the tomatoes, broth, and salt and stir to combine. Cover and cook for 2 to 3 hours on High or 5 to 6 hours on Low.

3. In small batches, carefully transfer the hot soup to a blender, secure the lid tightly, and blend until smooth. Stir in the cream. Taste, and adjust the seasoning, if needed.

**APPLIANCE TIP:** To use a pressure cooker, select the Sauté function to preheat a 6-quart pressure cooker. When hot, pour the oil into the pot and add the onions. Sauté until the onions have softened, 10 to 12 minutes. Add the garlic and cook for 1 minute more. Add the tomatoes, broth, and salt and stir until combined. Lock the lid in place. Select High Pressure and set the cook time for 4 minutes. When done, turn off the pressure cooker and use the quick pressure release. Once the valve drops, remove the lid and continue with step 3.

Per serving: Calories: 170; Total fat: 9g; Saturated fat: 4g; Protein: 3g; Carbohydrates: 17g; Sugar: 9g; Fiber: 3g; Sodium: 1,027mg

# Golden Butternut Squash Bisque

**APPLIANCE, GLUTEN-FREE, NUT-FREE, QUICK, VEGETARIAN** ....................................

This silky soup is comforting but not heavy—perfect for chilly autumn days. You can substitute the same amount of heavy cream or plain Greek yogurt for the sour cream, or skip the dairy altogether to make this soup dairy-free. When leaving out the dairy, I suggest adding a few drops of lemon juice in its place to bring out all the flavors.

2 tablespoons olive oil

½ medium red onion, halved and thinly sliced

**2 pounds frozen butternut squash**

**3 cups low-sodium vegetable broth**

Salt

Freshly ground black pepper

**½ cup sour cream**

**Serves** 4
**Prep time:** 5 minutes
**Cook time:** 25 minutes

1. In a 6-quart nonstick stockpot, heat the oil over medium heat. Add the onion and cook, stirring occasionally, for 5 to 6 minutes, or until the onion has softened.
2. Add the squash, broth, and a pinch of salt and pepper. Stir and bring to a boil over high heat. Once the soup has reached a boil, reduce the heat to medium-low, cover, and cook for 15 to 18 minutes, or until the squash is tender.
3. In small batches, carefully transfer the hot soup to a blender, secure the lid tightly, and blend until smooth.
4. Return the soup to the pot, taste, and adjust the seasoning, if needed. Add the sour cream and stir until just combined.

**STORAGE TIP:** Store any leftovers in the refrigerator for 3 to 4 days. Freeze for up to 2 months. If using dairy in the recipe, thaw frozen soup in the refrigerator and reheat over low heat, stirring often to prevent curdling.

**APPLIANCE TIP:** To make the recipe in a slow cooker, heat the oil in a medium skillet over medium heat and proceed with step 1 as directed. Place the cooked onion, squash, broth, salt, and pepper in a 6-quart slow cooker. Stir, cover, and cook on Low for 6 to 8 hours or on High for 3 to 4 hours, or until the squash is tender. Continue with steps 3 and 4 as directed.

Per serving: Calories: 242; Total fat: 13g; Saturated fat: 6g; Protein: 4g; Carbohydrates: 30g; Sugar: 9g; Fiber: 3g; Sodium: 131mg

# New England Clam Chowder

**APPLIANCE, GLUTEN-FREE, NUT-FREE** ......................................................

This adaptation of classic clam chowder does not use flour to thicken it, which makes it less heavy and also gluten-free. You can substitute half-and-half for heavy cream, just reduce the amount to ¾ cup. For a deeper flavor, replace half of the clam liquid with vegetable broth or seafood stock.

..........................................................................................................

1 tablespoon oil

½ large white onion, finely chopped

4 garlic cloves, minced

**6 large russet potatoes, peeled and cubed**

**1 (51-ounce) can chopped clams, clams and juice separated and refrigerated**

Salt

Freshly ground black pepper

**1 cup heavy cream**

**6 slices cooked bacon, diced, for topping**

---

**Serves** 6
**Prep time:** 5 minutes
**Cook time:** 30 minutes

1. In a 6-quart nonstick stockpot, heat the oil over medium heat. Add the onion and cook, stirring occasionally, for 5 to 6 minutes, or until the onion has softened. Add the garlic and cook for 1 additional minute.

2. Add the potatoes, clam juice, and a pinch each of salt and pepper. Stir and bring to a boil over high heat. Once the soup has reached a boil, reduce the heat to medium-low, cover, and cook for 15 to 18 minutes, or until the potatoes are tender.

3. When the potatoes are tender, mash half of them with a potato masher. Add the clams, stir, and cook for an additional 5 minutes.

4. Turn off the heat and add the cream. (Do not cook any longer, otherwise, the cream will curdle.) Serve immediately, topped with the bacon.

**STORAGE TIP:** Store leftovers in the refrigerator for up to 3 days. Freezing is not recommended.

**APPLIANCE TIP:** To make the soup in a slow cooker, heat the oil in a medium skillet over medium heat. Cook the onions and proceed with step 1 as directed. Transfer the cooked onion and garlic to a 6-quart slow cooker. Add the potatoes, clam juice, salt, and pepper. Stir, cover, and cook on High for 4 to 6 hours or on Low for 8 hours. Continue with steps 3 and 4 as directed.

---

Per serving: Calories: 627; Total fat: 24g; Saturated fat: 11g; Protein: 31g; Carbohydrates: 74g; Sugar: 4g; Fiber: 5g; Sodium: 279mg

# Pressure Cooker Creamy Corn Chowder with Bacon

**APPLIANCE, GLUTEN-FREE, NUT-FREE, QUICK** ........................................................

This effortless soup is ideal for capturing that laid-back summer feeling any time of the year. Packed full of flavor, it all comes together in a snap. I recommend sticking with whole milk for this recipe; otherwise, the soup will be too thin. If you have extra bacon, cook some up for a yummy topping and a bit of crunch.

**6 slices bacon, diced**

6 garlic cloves, minced

**2 (14.75-ounce) cans cream-style sweet corn**

**4 cups whole milk**

**3 cups frozen diced hash brown potatoes**

Salt

Freshly ground black pepper

---

**Serves** 4
**Prep time:** 10 minutes
**Cook time:** 5 minutes at High Pressure, plus 10 minutes to come to pressure

1. Line a plate with a paper towel.

2. Select the Sauté function to preheat a 6-quart pressure cooker. When hot, add the bacon and cook for 5 to 6 minutes, or until brown and crispy. Remove about two-thirds of the bacon and place it on the paper-towel-lined plate.

3. Add the garlic to the pot and cook for 1 minute, stirring often. Stir in the corn, milk, and potatoes. Season with salt and pepper. Lock the lid in place. Select High Pressure, close the pressure-release valve, and set the cook time for 5 minutes.

4. When done, turn off the pressure cooker and use a quick pressure release. Once the valve drops, remove the lid. Taste and adjust the seasoning, if needed. Top the finished soup with the cooked bacon.

**STORAGE TIP:** Store leftovers in the refrigerator for up to 3 days or freeze for up to 2 months. Thaw frozen soup in the refrigerator and reheat over low heat, stirring often to prevent curdling.

---

Per serving: Calories: 512; Total fat: 15g; Saturated fat: 7g; Protein: 19g; Carbohydrates: 81g; Sugar: 18g; Fiber: 5g; Sodium: 1,038mg

# Loaded Potato and Bacon Chowder

**APPLIANCE, GLUTEN-FREE, NUT-FREE** .......................................................

This creamy soup is inspired by the popular recipes for "loaded" potatoes, and it works just as well as a chowder as it does for baked potatoes. If you want a richer, creamier version of this soup, you can add ½ cup of sour cream—a perfect use for leftover sour cream from Charred Corn Salad with Cotija Cheese (page 111)—when blending the soup in step 3.

**6 slices of bacon, diced**

1 yellow onion, chopped

**2 pounds russet potatoes, peeled and chopped**

**3½ cups low-sodium chicken broth**

Salt

Freshly ground black pepper

**1½ cups shredded mild cheddar cheese**

**Serves** 4
**Prep time:** 5 minutes
**Cook time:** 30 minutes

1. Line a plate with a paper towel. Heat a 6-quart nonstick stockpot over medium-high heat. Put the bacon in the pot and cook, stirring occasionally, for 5 to 6 minutes, or until brown and crispy. Transfer the bacon to the paper-towel-lined plate. Put the onion into the pot and cook for about 4 minutes over medium heat, or until soft.

2. Add the potatoes, broth, one-third of the cooked bacon, and a pinch each of salt and pepper to the pot. Stir and bring to a boil over high heat. Once the soup has reached a boil, reduce the heat to medium-low, cover, and cook for 15 to 20 minutes, or until the potatoes are tender.

3. In small batches, carefully transfer the hot soup to a blender, secure the lid tightly, and blend until mostly smooth, but not completely pureed. Return the soup to the pot. Taste and adjust the seasoning, if needed. Add the cheese and stir until it's fully melted. Serve topped with the remaining cooked bacon.

**STORAGE TIP:** Store leftovers in the refrigerator for up to 3 days. Freezing is not recommended.

**APPLIANCE TIP:** To make this using a slow cooker, follow step 1, then heat a large skillet over medium-high heat. Put the bacon in the pan and proceed with step 2 as directed. Place the sautéed onions, potatoes, broth, salt, and pepper into a 6-quart slow cooker. Stir, cover, and cook on Low for 6 to 8 hours or on High for 3 to 4 hours. Continue with steps 4 and 5 as directed.

Per serving: Calories: 410; Total fat: 18g; Saturated fat: 11g; Protein: 20g; Carbohydrates: 41g; Sugar: 3g; Fiber: 6g; Sodium: 612mg

# Southwestern Chicken Soup

APPLIANCE, DAIRY-FREE, GLUTEN-FREE, NUT-FREE, QUICK .........................................

This is a chunky, flavorful soup that can be on the table in 20 minutes, thanks to the time-saving rotisserie chicken. You can also cook it in a slow cooker and have a meal ready and waiting by the time you get home from work. If desired, stir in the juice of a lime right before serving to bring all the flavors together. This recipe is a great way to use up leftover ingredients: toppings such as chopped scallions, shredded cheddar, crushed chips, or a spoonful of sour cream can all kick this soup up a notch.

**4 cups low-sodium chicken broth**

**2 (14.5-ounce) cans diced tomatoes with green chiles**

**1 (1-ounce) package mild taco seasoning**

**1 (14-ounce) package frozen Southwestern blend vegetable mix**

**2 cups shredded rotisserie chicken**

**Serves** 4
**Prep time:** 5 minutes
**Cook time:** 15 minutes

Combine the broth, tomatoes, taco seasoning, vegetable mix, and shredded chicken in a 6-quart nonstick stockpot. Bring to a boil over high heat. Once the soup has reached a boil, reduce the heat to medium-low, cover, and cook for 12 to 15 minutes, or until warmed through.

**STORAGE TIP:** Store leftovers in the refrigerator for up to 3 days or freeze for up to 2 months. Thaw in the refrigerator before reheating.

**WASTE-NOT TIP:** Use leftover rotisserie chicken on nachos, in sandwiches, or to add protein to salads, like the Pad Thai Noodle Salad with Peanut Sauce (page 117).

**APPLIANCE TIP:** To make the recipe in a slow cooker, place the broth, tomatoes, taco seasonings, vegetable mix, and shredded chicken in a 6-quart slow cooker. Cover and cook on High for 4 hours or on Low for 6 to 8 hours.

Per serving: Calories: 251; Total fat: 4g; Saturated fat: 1g; Protein: 26g; Carbohydrates: 22g; Sugar: 9g; Fiber: 4g; Sodium: 796mg

# Slow Cooker Zesty Three Bean and Ham Soup

..................................................

This hearty meal is a savory, all-season dish loaded with protein. It's an effortless soup that is both spicy and tangy. This simple version of the classic requires no soaking since it's made with canned beans. I love to serve it in a warm bowl with a fried egg on top.

....................................................................................

**2 (15-ounce) cans three-bean blend (pinto, kidney, and black beans)**

**1 pound cooked ham, diced**

1 large yellow onion, chopped

**5 cups low-sodium chicken broth**

**1 (1-ounce) package taco seasoning**

Salt

Freshly ground black pepper

Juice of 1 lemon

---

**Serves** 4 to 6
**Prep time:** 5 minutes
**Cook time:** 2 hours on High or 8 hours on Low

1. Combine the beans, ham, onions, broth, taco seasoning, and a pinch each of salt and pepper in a 6-quart slow cooker. Cook on High for 2 to 4 hours or on Low for 6 to 8 hours.

2. Taste and adjust the seasoning, if needed. Then stir in the lemon juice.

**VARIATION TIP:** Feel free to replace the lemon juice with 2 tablespoons of red wine vinegar or lime juice.

**STORAGE TIP:** Store leftovers in the refrigerator for up to 3 days or freeze for up to 2 months. Thaw in the refrigerator before reheating.

---

Per serving: Calories: 474; Total fat: 14g; Saturated fat: 4g; Protein: 47g; Carbohydrates: 35g; Sugar: 7g; Fiber: 9g, Sodium: 893mg

# Slow Cooker Southwestern Meatball Soup

APPLIANCE, DAIRY-FREE, NUT-FREE .........................................................................

This is an adaptation of the Mexican classic *sopa de albóndigas*, or meatball soup. It's a hearty and flavorful soup, perfect for a no-fuss weeknight meal. My version omits the rice that some traditional recipes call for, making this soup lighter. Any combination of canned corn and canned beans may be substituted for the soups mentioned below, so experiment and find your perfect mix. This dish is great topped with shredded cheddar cheese or crushed tortilla chips.

1 (12-ounce) package frozen, fully cooked Italian meatballs

6 cups low-sodium chicken or vegetable broth

1 (14-ounce) can Southwestern vegetable soup, such as Amy's brand or Progresso

2 cups mild tomato salsa

1 (1-ounce) package fajita seasoning mix

Salt

Freshly ground black pepper

Juice of 1 lemon (optional)

**Serves** 4
**Prep time:** 5 minutes
**Cook time:** 4 hours on High or 8 hours on Low

1. Combine the meatballs, broth, vegetable soup, salsa, seasoning mix, and a pinch each of salt and pepper in a 6-quart slow cooker. Cover and cook on High for 3 to 4 hours or on Low for 6 to 8 hours.

2. Taste and adjust the seasoning, if needed. Stir in the lemon juice (if using) to bring out all the flavors.

**APPLIANCE TIP:** You can speed up the cooking time of this recipe by making it in the pressure cooker instead. To do this, combine all the ingredients in the insert of the pressure cooker and mix well. Lock the lid in place. Select High Pressure and set the cook time for 10 minutes. When done, turn off the pressure cooker and use the quick pressure release. Once the valve drops, remove the lid. Taste and adjust the seasoning, if needed.

**STORAGE TIP:** Store any leftovers in the refrigerator for up to 3 days. Freeze for up to 2 months. Thaw in the refrigerator before reheating.

Per serving: Calories: 293; Total fat: 14g; Saturated fat: 5g; Protein: 16g; Carbohydrates: 23g; Sugar: 4g; Fiber: 3g; Sodium: 846mg

# Slow Cooker Beef Chili

**APPLIANCE, DAIRY-FREE, GLUTEN-FREE, NUT-FREE** ...............................................

This adaptation of the Southern Texas chili con carne is unapologetically bold and fla-vorful—and my way of paying homage to my beloved Texas. Since it's made in the slow cooker, you can add all of the ingredients to the pot and go about your day. When you're ready for a warm bowl of chili, all you have to do is season and serve. If you prefer less heat, substitute a mild tomato salsa, or if you'd like to make it leaner, use ground turkey.

½ **pound lean ground beef**

4 garlic cloves, minced

**1 (14.5-ounce) can fire-roasted tomato salsa**

**2½ cups low-sodium chicken broth**

**1 (16-ounce) can kidney beans, undrained**

**1 (1.25-ounce) package chili seasoning mix**

Juice of 1 lemon

Salt

Freshly ground black pepper

----

**Serves** 4
**Prep time:** 5 minutes
**Cook time:** 2 hours on High or 8 hours on Low

1.  Break up the ground beef and put it, along with the garlic, salsa, broth, kidney beans, and seasoning mix, in a 6-quart slow cooker. Stir well and cook on High for 2 to 4 hours or on Low for 6 to 8 hours.

2.  Once cooked, stir in the lemon juice and season with salt and pepper.

**STORAGE TIP:** Store leftovers in the refrigerator for up to 3 days or freeze for up to 2 months. Thaw in the refrigerator before reheating.

----

Per serving: Calories: 256; Total fat: 5g; Saturated fat: 2g; Protein: 21g; Carbohydrates: 33g; Sugar: 9g; Fiber: 10g; Sodium 1,047mg

# Watermelon Salad with Feta, Mint, and Honey–Lime Dressing

**GLUTEN-FREE, NUT-FREE, QUICK, VEGETARIAN** ......................................................

This is truly a refreshing salad. It's perfect for summer snacking or as a surefire winner at picnics, potlucks, and barbecues. Try it for the Fourth of July—just add ½ cup of blueberries to get red, white, and blue!

**8 cups cubed watermelon**

**¼ cup fresh mint leaves**

3 tablespoons olive oil

3 tablespoons fresh
   lime juice

**1½ tablespoons honey**

Salt

Freshly ground black pepper

**¼ cup crumbled feta
   cheese, for topping**

**Serves** 4
**Prep time:** 15 minutes

1. In a large bowl, combine the watermelon and mint leaves.

2. In a small bowl, whisk together the olive oil, lime juice, honey, and a pinch each of salt and pepper.

3. Pour the dressing over the watermelon and mint and toss gently to combine. Top with feta before serving.

**WASTE-NOT TIP:** One of my favorite uses for leftover mint is to make a simple tea. Put mint leaves in a mug and cover them with boiling water. Let steep for 5 to 10 minutes. Then remove and discard the leaves and sweeten as desired. You can also use leftover mint in the Sparkling Strawberry-Mint Juice (page 42), Refreshing Pineapple-Mint Juice (page 43), or as a garnish for Avocado and Kale Gazpacho (page 96).

**VARIATION TIP:** To add a kick, replace the black pepper with red pepper flakes.

Per serving: Calories: 236; Total fat: 13g; Saturated fat: 3g; Protein: 3g; Carbohydrates: 30g; Sugar: 26g; Fiber: 1g; Sodium: 111mg

# Caprese Salad with Peppery Balsamic Reduction

**GLUTEN-FREE, NUT-FREE, QUICK, VEGETARIAN** .................................................................

Caprese salad is a refreshing and satisfying Italian classic that never gets old. It can be served as an appetizer or as a side dish with sandwiches, pastas, and pizzas. My version has a peppery touch and a thick balsamic dressing that takes it to a whole new level. The reduction lends a sweeter note to the salad, making it a restaurant-quality dish that can be prepared right in your kitchen.

.................................................................................................................

¼ cup balsamic vinegar

⅛ teaspoon red pepper flakes

4 tomatoes, cut into ¼-inch-thick slices

16 to 20 fresh basil leaves

1 pound fresh mozzarella cheese, sliced ¼-inch thick

Salt

**Serves** 4
**Prep time:** 10 minutes
**Cook time:** 10 minutes, plus 5 minutes to cool

1. In a small saucepan, heat the balsamic vinegar over medium heat until bubbling, about 2 minutes. Reduce the heat to medium-low and simmer, stirring occasionally, until the liquid is reduced by half and the vinegar has thickened, 4 to 6 minutes.

2. Stir in the red pepper flakes. Let the reduction cool slightly for 2 to 3 minutes.

3. On a large platter, layer the tomato slices, basil leaves, and cheese slices. Season with salt. Drizzle the balsamic reduction over the salad.

**WASTE-NOT TIP:** Use leftover basil to make Grilled Apricot and Goat Cheese Crostini with Balsamic Reduction and Basil (page 74), Spaghetti with Roasted Bell Pepper Sauce and Basil (page 138), or Fire-Roasted Margherita Pizza (page 133). Use leftover balsamic vinegar in the Crispy Caprese Ciabatta Sandwich (page 119).

Per serving: Calories: 318; Total fat: 21g; Saturated fat: 12g; Protein: 21g; Carbohydrates: 12g; Sugar: 3g; Fiber: 1g; Sodium: 361mg

# Charred Corn Salad with Cotija Cheese

**GLUTEN-FREE, NUT-FREE, QUICK, VEGETARIAN** .....................................................

This is one of my favorite summer salads—a twist on Mexican street corn, or *elote*. Cotija is a crumbly, white cheese that can be found in many supermarkets alongside other Mexican cheeses. It can be easily replaced with feta cheese, if needed.

.....................................................................................................

**2 (14.75-ounce) cans fire-roasted corn blend, drained**

**1 cup pico de gallo**

**¼ cup sour cream**

**2 tablespoons chipotle aioli**

Salt

Freshly ground black pepper

**⅓ cup Cotija cheese or feta cheese, finely crumbled, for topping**

**Serves** 4 to 6
**Prep time:** 10 minutes

1. In a large bowl, combine the drained corn and pico de gallo.
2. In a small bowl, whisk together the sour cream, chipotle aioli, and a pinch each of salt and pepper. Taste and adjust the seasoning, if needed.
3. Pour the sauce over the corn mixture and toss to combine. Then, top with the Cotija cheese and serve.

**WASTE-NOT TIP:** Use leftover pico de gallo in tacos and sandwiches, or to top Pan-Grilled Pork Chops with Pico de Gallo (page 170). Chipotle aioli can boost the flavor in any sandwich, including the Fresh Veggie Sandwich with Chipotle Aioli (page 118).

Per serving: Calories: 271; Total fat: 14g; Saturated fat: 6g; Protein: 7g; Carbohydrates: 28g; Sugar: 14g; Fiber: 5g; Sodium: 885mg

# Very Berry Salad with Candied Walnuts

**DAIRY-FREE, GLUTEN-FREE, QUICK, VEGAN** ....................................................

This quick, no-cook salad is jam-packed with antioxidants. It's got everything you want in a salad: sweetness, a tangy zip, and a satisfying crunch. It's one of my favorite things to take to picnics and potlucks. Top the salad with finely crumbled feta or goat cheese if dairy is not a concern.

........................................................................................................

**8 cups mixed greens**
**½ cup fresh blueberries**
**½ cup fresh raspberries**
**2 to 3 tablespoons balsamic vinaigrette**
Freshly ground black pepper
**⅓ cup candied walnuts, for topping**

**Serves** 4 to 6
**Prep time:** 10 minutes

1. Put the greens in a large bowl. Add the blueberries and raspberries, then pour on the vinaigrette.
2. Season with pepper. Toss to combine. Transfer to a platter or salad bowl and top with candied walnuts.

**WASTE-NOT TIP:** Use any leftover berries in smoothies or add them to the Watermelon Salad with Feta, Mint, and Honey-Lime Dressing (page 109). Candied walnuts and balsamic vinaigrette can also be used in the Winter Greens Salad with Pear and Pomegranate (page 113).

**VARIATION TIP:** You can use all blueberries or all raspberries, if you prefer. Or try adding sliced strawberries to the mix. Use any combination of berries you like, just keep the total amount at about 1 cup.

Per serving: Calories: 121; Total fat: 7g; Saturated fat: 1g; Protein: 4g; Carbohydrates: 13g; Sugar: 7g; Fiber: 4g; Sodium: 169mg

# Winter Greens Salad with Pear and Pomegranate

**DAIRY-FREE, GLUTEN-FREE, QUICK, VEGAN** ...............................................

This is a quick seasonal salad chock-full of nutrients. Light yet satisfying, it's the perfect complement to everyday meat dishes. Both the pomegranate and balsamic vinaigrette add a tang, while the walnuts add texture. To lend more festive touches, top the salad with leftover candied walnuts from the Very Berry Salad with Candied Walnuts (page 112) or add crumbled feta cheese (but note that the recipe will no longer be dairy-free).

...............................................

**2 small pears**

**8 cups mixed greens**

**1 cup fresh pomegranate seeds**

**2 to 3 tablespoons balsamic vinaigrette**

Freshly ground black pepper

**¼ cup toasted walnuts, chopped, for topping**

---

**Serves** 4 to 6
**Prep time:** 10 minutes

1. Cut each of the pears into quarters. Remove the core by gently cutting it out of each pear quarter. Cut each quarter of pear into ¼-inch lengthwise slices.

2. In a large bowl, combine the mixed greens with the pear slices and pomegranate seeds.

3. Add the vinaigrette and then season with pepper. Toss gently to combine.

4. Transfer to a platter and top with walnuts before serving.

**WASTE-NOT TIP:** Use leftover pomegranate seeds as a garnish for the Protein-Packed Raspberry and Dark Chocolate Smoothie Bowls (page 53). Use surplus walnuts to make Baked Brie with Caramelized Walnuts (page 73). Refrigerate balsamic dressing after opening and use it on the Very Berry Salad with Candied Walnuts (page 112).

---

Per serving: Calories: 156; Total fat: 7g; Saturated fat: <1g; Protein: 4g; Carbohydrates: 22g; Sugar: 14g; Fiber: 6g; Sodium: 92mg

# Pickled Beet and Crumbled Goat Cheese Salad

GLUTEN-FREE, NUT-FREE, QUICK, VEGETARIAN . . . . . . . . . . . . . . . . . . . . . . . . . . . . . . . . . . . . . . . . . . . . . .

Beets and goat cheese are a match made in heaven. The orange vinaigrette adds a bright note and brings out the wonderful flavor of the beets. If you'd like, add a contrasting texture by sprinkling candied walnuts (a good use for any leftover from the Very Berry Salad with Candied Walnuts on page 112) over the top of the salad right before serving. I like to arrange this salad around cooked hams to instantly transform the meal into a stunner!

. . . . . . . . . . . . . . . . . . . . . . . . . . . . . . . . . . . . . . . . . . . . . . . . . . . . . . . . . . . . . . . . . . . . . . . . . . . . . . . . . . . . . . . .

**8 cups mixed greens**

**1 cup canned or jarred pickled beets, drained**

3 tablespoons olive oil

3 tablespoons fresh orange juice

Salt

Freshly ground black pepper

**⅓ cup crumbled goat cheese**

---

**Serves** 4 to 6
**Prep time:** 10 minutes

1. Put the greens into a large bowl. Add the beets and set aside.

2. In a small bowl, whisk together the oil, orange juice, and a pinch each of salt and pepper. Pour the dressing over the greens and beets and toss to combine.

3. Transfer to a platter to serve, and top with the goat cheese.

**WASTE-NOT TIP:** Use any leftover beets in sandwiches and salads, or as an add-on to the Fresh Veggie Sandwich with Chipotle Aioli (page 118) or the Winter Greens Salad with Pear and Pomegranate (page 113). Use any extra goat cheese in the Grilled Apricot and Goat Cheese Crostini with Balsamic Reduction and Basil (page 74) or simply as a spread on toast—I especially love it topped with honey.

---

Per serving: Calories: 178; Total fat: 13g; Saturated fat: 3g; Protein: 4g; Carbohydrates: 14g; Sugar: 8g; Fiber: 4g; Sodium: 261mg

# Autumn Potato Salad with Apple and Golden Raisins

**DAIRY-FREE, GLUTEN-FREE, NUT-FREE, VEGETARIAN** ..........................................

This autumn potato salad is a popular salad-bar side at many Brazilian steakhouses, as it pairs perfectly with grilled meats. Potatoes and apples might seem to be an odd pairing but this will change your mind! The apples add a crispiness to the soft potatoes. And while it might not seem possible to make this salad even more delicious, try adding about ⅓ cup of cubed pineapple.

**2 pounds Yukon Gold potatoes, peeled and cut into 1-inch cubes**

6 tablespoons lemon juice, divided

**1 cup mayonnaise**

Salt

Freshly ground black pepper

**⅓ cup golden raisins**

**2 tablespoons chopped fresh parsley**

**2 green apples, cored and cubed**

---

**Serves** 4 to 6
**Prep time:** 15 minutes
**Cook time:** 15 minutes, plus 20 minutes to cool

1. Put the potatoes in a large pot and pour in enough water to cover them by 2 inches. Season with salt. Bring the water to a boil over high heat.

2. Once the water has reached a boil, reduce the heat to medium and cook until the potatoes are fork-tender but not crumbly, about 12 minutes. Using a colander, drain the potatoes, then let them cool for about 20 minutes.

3. Meanwhile, in a large bowl, mix 4 tablespoons of lemon juice with the mayonnaise until combined. Stir in a pinch each of salt and pepper. Add the raisins and parsley to the mayonnaise mixture.

4. Put the apples in a medium bowl and coat them with 2 tablespoons of lemon juice to delay oxidation.

5. Add the cooled potatoes and the apples to the bowl with the dressing and gently mix until the potatoes and apples are coated. Serve chilled or at room temperature.

---

Per serving: Calories: 601; Total fat: 40g; Saturated fat: 6g; Protein: 7g; Carbohydrates: 64g; Sugar: 27g; Fiber: 8g; Sodium: 287mg

# Tangy Israeli Couscous Salad

**NUT-FREE, VEGETARIAN** ....................................................................

Israeli couscous, also called pearl couscous, is larger in size than regular couscous and gives this salad a bit more bite. The refreshing, Mediterranean-inspired combination of cucumbers, tomato, mint, and feta makes it a versatile, go-to salad. It's hearty enough to be served as a lunch entrée or light dinner, and it works perfectly as a side dish.

....................................................................

1¼ cups water

**1 cup pearl couscous**

3 tablespoons olive oil

Juice and zest of 1 lemon

1 teaspoon salt

½ teaspoon freshly ground black pepper

**1 medium cucumber, quartered and sliced**

**1 pint cherry or grape tomatoes, halved**

**½ cup crumbled feta cheese**

**¼ cup fresh mint leaves**

---

**Serves** 4
**Prep time:** 15 minutes
**Cook time:** 20 minutes, plus 20 minutes to chill

1. In a medium saucepan over high heat, bring the water to a boil, then add the couscous. Once the couscous starts boiling, reduce the heat to medium-low and cover. Cook for about 20 minutes, or until the water is absorbed. Fluff the couscous with a fork.

2. Meanwhile, in a large bowl, whisk together the olive oil, lemon juice and zest, salt, and pepper until fully combined. Taste and adjust the seasoning, if needed.

3. Add the cooked couscous to the dressing and toss until well coated. Refrigerate for 15 to 20 minutes.

4. Right before serving, add the cucumber, tomatoes, feta, and mint to the couscous and toss until just combined. Serve chilled or at room temperature.

**STORAGE TIP:** Store leftovers in an airtight container in the refrigerator for up to 2 days.

**VARIATION TIP:** To take the salad to a whole new level, add 1 to 2 teaspoons of Dijon mustard to the lemon-oil mixture. If you enjoy spicy foods, try replacing the freshly ground black pepper with red pepper flakes.

---

Per serving: Calories: 299; Total fat: 16g; Saturated fat: 4g; Protein: 9g; Carbohydrates: 34g; Sugar: 6g; Fiber: 3g; Sodium: 801mg

# Pad Thai Noodle Salad with Peanut Sauce

**DAIRY-FREE, QUICK, VEGAN** ........................................................

This simplified twist on pad thai is a quick and tasty way to satisfy a craving for takeout at home. It makes a great vegetarian main dish, and it's the perfect accompaniment for grilled meat skewers, Garlic and Basil Beef (page 180), or Yellow Curry with Beef and Potatoes (page 182). For a spicy version, add 1 teaspoon of sriracha or minced jalapeño. If you can't find Thai basil, regular basil works well in its place.

........................................................

**6 ounces pad Thai rice noodles**

**4 cups broccoli slaw mix**

**2 to 3 tablespoons chopped Thai basil**

**1¼ cups peanut sauce**

Salt

Freshly ground black pepper

**¼ cup roasted peanuts, crushed, for topping**

---

**Serves** 4 to 6
**Prep time:** 15 minutes
**Cook time:** 15 minutes

1.  Cook the noodles according to the instructions on the package, then drain them in a colander and rinse with cold water to chill.

2.  Meanwhile, in a large bowl, combine the broccoli slaw and basil. When the noodles are cool, add them to the bowl and toss to combine.

3.  Add the peanut sauce to the bowl and toss again until the noodles and vegetables are well coated. Season with salt and pepper. Top with the crushed peanuts.

**STORAGE TIP:** Store in an airtight container in the refrigerator for up to 3 days.

**WASTE-NOT TIP:** Use any leftover broccoli slaw in salads or in the Fresh Veggie Sandwich with Chipotle Aioli (page 118). Use leftover peanut sauce with tofu and noodles, such as the Panfried Tofu with Peanut Sauce and Broccoli (page 129).

---

Per serving: Calories: 354; Total fat: 12g; Saturated fat: 3g; Protein: 6g; Carbohydrates: 54g; Sugar: 10g; Fiber: 7g; Sodium: 191mg

# Fresh Veggie Sandwich with Chipotle Aioli

**DAIRY-FREE, NUT-FREE, QUICK, VEGETARIAN** .................................................

This sandwich is perfect packed for a lunch to enjoy at work or school. Serve chilled or at room temperature, and pair it with soup or chips for a meal that will keep you full until dinner. Feel free to use any kind of bread you happen to have on hand. If you are not vegetarian, try adding deli meats or leftover smoked salmon from the Smoked Salmon Wrap with Capers and Cream Cheese (page 120).

**8 slices bread**

**8 tablespoons chipotle aioli**

**3 small cucumbers, thinly sliced**

**2 tomatoes, thinly sliced**

**1⅓ cups broccoli slaw**

Salt

Freshly ground black pepper

**Serves** 4
**Prep time:** 15 minutes

1. Toast the bread in a toaster and let cool to prevent a soggy sandwich.

2. Spread 1 tablespoon of aioli on one side of each slice of bread. Evenly distribute the cucumber, tomato, and broccoli slaw among 4 slices of bread, then season with salt and pepper.

3. Top with another slice of bread with the aioli-covered side facedown. Wrap each sandwich tightly in parchment paper or wax paper to help keep them together, and then slice in half to serve.

**WASTE-NOT TIP:** Use leftover broccoli slaw in Pad Thai Noodle Salad with Peanut Sauce (page 117).

**VARIATION TIP:** To make the sandwich vegan, use your favorite hummus instead of the aioli.

Per serving: Calories: 465; Total fat: 23g; Saturated fat: 2g; Protein: 10g; Carbohydrates: 56g; Sugar: 11g; Fiber: 8g; Sodium: 429mg

# Crispy Caprese Ciabatta Sandwich

APPLIANCE, NUT-FREE, QUICK . . . . . . . . . . . . . . . . . . . . . . . . . . . . . . . . . . . . . . . . . . . . . . . . . . . . . . . . . . . . .

Although these sandwiches look fancy, they are affordable and oh-so-easy to prepare. With the first bite you'll feel like you're eating out at a panino shop, but from the comfort of home. If you don't have ciabatta, use the sliced bread of your choice. You can also replace mozzarella with any other melting cheese. Try it with a small drizzle of balsamic vinegar over the tomatoes.

**4 ciabatta sandwich rolls**

8 tablespoons olive
  oil, divided

**8 slices mozzarella cheese**

**16 basil leaves**

**2 ripe tomatoes, cut in half
  and sliced ¼-inch thick**

---

**Serves** 4
**Prep time:** 10 minutes
**Cook time:** 20 minutes

1. Cut one ciabatta roll in half lengthwise. Brush 1 tablespoon of olive oil on the outside of one half of the roll. Lay the oil-brushed side down, and on the cut side, place one slice of mozzarella, then 4 basil leaves, the slices of one tomato half, and one more slice of cheese.

2. Complete the sandwich by topping the stack with the other half of the roll. Brush the top with more oil. Repeat steps 1 and 2 with the remaining ciabatta rolls.

3. Heat a large grill pan or skillet over medium heat. Place a sandwich into the pan and press down with a spatula—or the bottom of a clean, heavy pan— until the bottom side of the sandwich is golden brown and crisp, 1 to 2 minutes. Flip the sandwich and repeat the process for the other side. Grill the remaining sandwiches and serve while hot.

**WASTE-NOT TIP:** Use leftover basil in recipes like Caprese Salad with Peppery Balsamic Reduction (page 110), One-Pan Gnocchi and Meatballs in Arrabbiata Sauce (page 150), or as a garnish.

**APPLIANCE TIP:** If you are using a grilled cheese machine or a panini press, place a sandwich on the hot press until the outside of the sandwich is crisp and golden brown, about 2 minutes.

---

Per serving: Calories: 574; Total fat: 38g; Saturated fat: 9g; Protein: 17g; Carbohydrates: 45g; Sugar: 3g; Fiber: 3g; Sodium: 716mg

# Smoked Salmon Wrap with Capers and Cream Cheese

NUT-FREE, QUICK ........................................................................

This wrap is perfect for bagel lovers who are watching their carbs or just want a more portable version of a smoked salmon sandwich. If you like a bit of a kick, you can add some red pepper flakes, and a few drops of lemon juice squeezed over the salmon can add a note of brightness. I suggest chive and onion cream cheese here to boost the flavor, but feel free to use plain cream cheese or your favorite savory flavor.

**4 (8- or 10-inch) spinach tortillas**

**½ cup chive and onion cream cheese**

**1⅓ cups mixed greens**

**8 ounces sliced smoked salmon**

**4 tablespoons capers, drained**

**Serves** 4
**Prep time:** 15 minutes

1. Lay one tortilla on a flat surface. Spread 2 tablespoons of cream cheese on the tortilla, being careful to leave some uncovered space around the edge.

2. Place ⅓ cup of mixed greens in the center of the tortilla and top with 2 ounces of smoked salmon and 1 tablespoon of capers.

3. Fold the 2 opposites sides of the tortilla so that the cream cheese slathered along the sides of the tortilla overlaps in the middle to secure the filling, and then roll to secure. Wrap tightly with parchment paper or wax paper.

4. Repeat steps 1 through 3 for each remaining tortilla wrap, and cut each in half to serve.

**WASTE-NOT TIP:** Use leftover cream cheese in the Zucchini Roll-Ups (page 79). Use leftover capers in salads and pastas, or in the Pan-Seared Salmon with Lemon and Garlic Caper Sauce (page 199). Try adding leftover smoked salmon to the Fresh Veggie Sandwich with Chipotle Aioli (page 118).

Per serving: Calories: 302; Total fat: 15g; Saturated fat: 7g; Protein: 17g; Carbohydrates: 27g; Sugar: 2g; Fiber: 2g; Sodium: 1,971mg

# Bacon and Avocado Grilled Cheese Sandwich

**NUT-FREE, QUICK** ....................................................................

These sandwiches are the bomb! Buttery, smoky, peppery, and crispy—they are comfort food at its finest. You can skip the avocados if you don't have any on hand, but you'd be missing out on a fresh and contemporary tweak on a classic. If you wish, choose a different bread or cheese (especially if you're not a fan of spicy foods), but make sure the cheese is a type that melts readily. My kids love these on Texas toast, while for mine I use a multigrain bread. Serve them by themselves, or with a cup of leftover Creamy Tomato Bisque (page 99).

**2 avocados, halved**

**8 slices multigrain bread**

**16 slices pepper Jack cheese**

**12 slices cooked smoked bacon**

**6 tablespoons butter, divided**

**Serves** 4
**Prep time:** 5 minutes
**Cook time:** 10 minutes

1. Scoop out the flesh of the halved avocados and cut it into slices.

2. Next, assemble the sandwich: atop one slice of bread, layer 2 slices of cheese, the slices of half of an avocado, 3 strips of bacon, and 2 more slices of cheese, and then top with another slice of bread. Repeat the same process for each sandwich.

3. In a large nonstick skillet, melt half the butter over medium heat. When the butter starts to foam, place 2 sandwiches into the skillet. Cook until the bottom is golden brown and toasted, 2 to 3 minutes. Flip over and cook for an additional 1 to 2 minutes. Remove the cooked sandwiches and melt the remaining butter. Repeat the same process with the other 2 sandwiches.

Per serving: Calories: 857; Total fat: 59g; Saturated fat: 28g; Protein: 33g; Carbohydrates: 56g; Sugar: 8g; Fiber: 16g; Sodium: 1,360mg

# Pan-Grilled Reuben Sandwich

**NUT-FREE, QUICK** .................................................................

There's nothing quite like a Reuben sandwich, with its toasted rye bread, sauerkraut, and dressing. If you don't have Russian dressing on hand, you can use Thousand Island instead, or try to make your own from ingredients you might already have on hand (see Variation Tip). For a different take, you can make the "Rachel" sandwich by replacing the corned beef with pastrami and the sauerkraut with coleslaw.

.................................................................

2 tablespoons olive oil

**8 slices rye bread**

**½ cup Russian dressing**

**8 slices Swiss cheese**

**8 slices deli sliced corned beef**

**1 cup sauerkraut, drained**

---

**Serves** 4
**Prep time:** 10 minutes
**Cook time:** 20 minutes

1. Lightly brush oil on one side of each slice of bread. Flip and then spread the dressing on the non-oiled sides. Atop the dressing on 4 slices of bread, layer 1 slice of cheese, 2 slices of corned beef, ¼ cup sauerkraut, and a second slice of cheese. Top with remaining slices of bread, keeping the oil-brushed sides faceup.

2. Heat a large grill pan or skillet over medium heat. Grill the sandwiches two at a time until both sides are crisp and golden brown, 4 to 5 minutes per side.

**WASTE-NOT TIP:** Use leftover sauerkraut on sandwiches, hot dogs, and as a side for One-Pan Bratwurst and Vegetables (page 167).

**VARIATION TIP:** To make your own Russian dressing, mix together ½ cup of mayonnaise, 2 to 3 tablespoons of pickle relish, 2 tablespoons of ketchup, and ½ teaspoon of Worcestershire sauce until well combined. Add water to thin (1 to 2 tablespoons) until the dressing reaches your desired consistency.

---

Per serving: Calories: 578; Total fat: 38g; Saturated fat: 10g; Protein: 25g; Carbohydrates: 35g; Sugar: 8g; Fiber: 3g; Sodium: 1,186mg

# Sweet and Spicy BBQ Meatball Sub

NUT-FREE, QUICK ..................................................................

Adding red pepper flakes to your favorite barbecue sauce gives these sandwiches a sweet and spicy zing. In less than 30 minutes, you can whip these up and have a compliment-worthy meal on the table. If you aren't planning to serve the sandwiches right away, you can cook the meatballs in advance, but don't assemble the sandwiches until right before serving; otherwise, the bread will become soggy.

**1 pound fully cooked Italian-style meatballs (about 24 meatballs)**

**2 cups barbecue sauce**

**¼ teaspoon red pepper flakes**

**6 sub rolls, sliced in half lengthwise**

**6 slices provolone cheese**

---

**Serves** 6
**Prep time:** 10 minutes
**Cook time:** 15 minutes

1. Heat the meatballs according to the package instructions. (This should take 6 to 12 minutes.)
2. Meanwhile, in a large microwave-safe bowl, combine the barbecue sauce with the red pepper flakes. Cover and heat in the microwave on high for 2 minutes. Stir, then add the meatballs to the sauce. Toss to combine.
3. Set the oven to broil. Nestle about 4 meatballs into each sub roll and top the meatballs with one slice of cheese per sandwich.
4. Arrange the sandwiches on a baking sheet and broil them just until the cheese is melted and golden brown, 30 to 90 seconds. Keep a close eye on them so that the cheese doesn't burn.

**WASTE-NOT TIP:** Use leftover meatballs and barbecue sauce in Hawaiian-Inspired Turkey Meatballs (page 166). You can also use leftover meatballs in soups and stews such as Slow Cooker Southwestern Meatball Soup (page 107).

---

Per serving: Calories: 438; Total fat: 16g; Saturated fat: 6g; Protein: 20g; Carbohydrates: 54g; Sugar: 33g; Fiber: 3g; Sodium: 1,479mg

*Sweet Potato and Black Bean Crispy Tacos* **143**

# Pressure Cooker Cauliflower Chickpea Vindaloo

**APPLIANCE, GLUTEN-FREE, NUT-FREE, QUICK, VEGETARIAN** ...........................................

Vindaloo is a spicy Indian curry dish from Goa and Kerala, which was originally made with meat and is usually served over white rice or with garlic naan. This vegetarian version is a snap to make in the pressure cooker and only requires one pot. The kick it provides is perfect to combat cold-weather days. If desired, you can replace the Greek yogurt with canned coconut cream, as either one provides a nice balance to the spiciness of the curry.

........................................................................................................................

2 tablespoons olive oil

1 large yellow
  onion, chopped

4 garlic cloves, minced

**2 (12-ounce) packages
  frozen cauliflower**

**1 (15-ounce) can chickpeas,
  rinsed and drained**

**2 (10-ounce) jars
  vindaloo sauce**

½ cup water

Salt

**1 cup plain Greek yogurt**

---

**Serves** 4 to 6
**Prep time:** 10 minutes
**Cook time:** 5 minutes
at High Pressure, plus
10 minutes to come to
pressure

1. Select the Sauté function to preheat a 6-quart pressure cooker. When hot, pour in the olive oil, then add the onion and cook, stirring occasionally, until the onion has softened, about 5 minutes. Add the garlic and cook for 1 minute more.

2. Turn off the sauté function and add the cauliflower, chickpeas, vindaloo sauce, and water. Season with salt and stir. Lock the lid in place. Select High Pressure, close the pressure-release valve, and set the cook time for 4 minutes.

3. When done, turn off the pressure cooker and use a quick pressure release. Once the valve drops, remove the lid and stir in the yogurt. Taste and adjust the seasoning, if needed.

**STORAGE TIP:** Store any leftovers in the refrigerator for up to 3 days. Avoid freezing as the yogurt-based sauce may separate when reheating.

---

Per serving: Calories: 431; Total fat: 21g; Saturated fat: 7g; Protein: 16g; Carbohydrates: 45g; Sugar: 14g; Fiber: 12g; Sodium: 935mg

# Chickpea and Potato Curry

APPLIANCE, DAIRY-FREE, GLUTEN-FREE, NUT-FREE, VEGAN ......................................

This curry is an Indian-inspired stew that's perfect for busy, chilly days. It's creamy, fragrant, and will warm you right up. For a hearty meal, serve it over white rice or with garlic naan. For a creamier stew, you can replace the coconut milk with coconut cream or, for an even thicker dish, you can dissolve ½ tablespoon of cornstarch in 2 tablespoons of water and add it to the fully cooked stew with the heat (or the slow cooker) still turned on, stirring often for 5 to 8 minutes, or until the sauce thickens.

2 tablespoons olive oil

1 medium yellow
   onion, chopped

4 garlic cloves, minced

**1 (13.5-ounce) can
   coconut milk**

**2 tablespoons red
   curry paste**

**1 (16-ounce) package frozen
   sweet potatoes, cubed**

**1 (15-ounce) can chickpeas,
   rinsed and drained**

¼ cup water

Salt

Freshly ground black pepper

---

**Serves** 4 to 6
**Prep time:** 5 minutes
**Cook time:** 30 minutes

1. In a large nonstick stockpot, heat the oil over medium heat. Add the onion and cook, stirring occasionally, for 5 to 6 minutes, or until the onion has softened. Add the garlic and cook for 1 minute more.

2. Add the coconut milk with the red curry paste and whisk until combined. Add the sweet potatoes, chickpeas, and water. Season with salt and pepper. Stir, cover, and cook for 15 to 20 minutes, or until the potatoes are tender. Taste and adjust the seasoning, if needed.

**STORAGE TIP:** Store any leftovers in the refrigerator for up to 3 days. Freeze for up to 2 months. Thaw in the refrigerator. Reheat over low heat, stirring often.

**APPLIANCE TIP:** Follow step 1 as directed. Then, in a 6-quart slow cooker, whisk together the coconut milk with the red curry paste. Add the cooked onion and garlic along with the sweet potatoes, chickpeas, and water. Season with salt and pepper. Stir, cover, and cook for 2 to 4 hours on High, or 6 to 8 hours on Low. Taste and adjust the seasoning, if needed.

Per serving: Calories: 460; Total fat: 28g; Saturated fat: 16g; Protein: 8g; Carbohydrates: 44g; Sugar: 6g; Fiber: 8g; Sodium: 548mg

# Vegetable Meatballs and Cauliflower Korma

**NUT-FREE, QUICK, VEGETARIAN** ......................................................

Inspired by Indian cuisine, this spicy stew is simmered in a creamy curry sauce. For brighter flavors, you can stir in 1 to 2 tablespoons of lemon juice and add 2 tablespoons of chopped cilantro after the stew has fully cooked. Serve over white rice or with garlic naan.

2 tablespoons olive oil

1 large yellow
  onion, chopped

4 garlic cloves, minced

**2 (12-ounce) packages
  frozen vegetable
  meatballs**

**1 (12-ounce) package frozen
  cauliflower**

**1 (15-ounce) jar korma
  curry sauce**

1 cup water

Salt

**Serves** 4 to 6
**Prep time:** 10 minutes
**Cook time:** 30 minutes

1. In a large nonstick saucepan, heat the oil over medium heat. Add the onion and cook, stirring occasionally, for 5 to 6 minutes, or until the onion has softened.

2. Add the garlic and cook for 1 minute. Add the meatballs, cauliflower, korma sauce, and water. Season with salt.

3. Stir, cover, and simmer for 15 to 20 minutes, or until meatballs and cauliflower are fully cooked. Taste and adjust the salt, if needed.

**STORAGE TIP:** Store any leftovers in the refrigerator for up to 3 days. Freeze for up to 2 months.

Per serving: Calories: 654; Total fat: 39g; Saturated fat: 12g; Protein: 36g; Carbohydrates: 41g; Sugar: 17g; Fiber: 13g; Sodium: 1,497mg

# Panfried Tofu with Peanut Sauce and Broccoli

**DAIRY-FREE, GLUTEN-FREE, VEGAN** ..........................................................

Inspired by the cuisines of East and Southeast Asia, this comforting dish is ideal for those on a low-carb diet. For a spicy version, add a pinch of red pepper flakes or a drop of hot sauce. Serve over rice or cauliflower rice. If not served right away, the tofu may lose its crispiness within 15 to 30 minutes.

..........................................................

2 (14-ounce) blocks
  extra-firm tofu

1 (10-ounce) package frozen
  broccoli florets

3 tablespoons cornstarch

3 tablespoons olive oil

2 cups peanut sauce

Salt

---

**Serves** 4
**Prep time:** 10 minutes
**Cook time:** 20 minutes,
plus 30 minutes to drain

1. Place the block of tofu on a large plate. Cover with a paper towel. Then, place the bottom of a cast-iron skillet on top of the towel and let it sit for 15 to 30 minutes. Pat the tofu dry. Discard any liquid on the plate.

2. Cook the broccoli according to the package instructions. Drain, place into a large bowl, cover, and set aside. Cut the pressed tofu into 1-inch cubes. In a large bowl, gently toss the tofu with the cornstarch until coated. (The cubes will be sticky.)

3. In a large nonstick skillet, heat the oil over medium heat for 2 to 3 minutes. Add one cube of tofu to make sure the oil is hot enough to make it sizzle. If so, add half of the tofu in a single layer and cook until browned, 2 to 3 minutes. Use a spatula to flip the cubes and cook for 2 to 3 additional minutes, or until crispy. Add the cooked tofu to the bowl of broccoli. Repeat the process with the other half of the tofu.

4. Once finished, add the peanut sauce and a pinch of salt to the bowl and toss until the tofu and broccoli are well coated. Taste and adjust the salt, if needed.

Per serving: Calories: 520; Total fat: 32g; Saturated fat: 7g; Protein: 23g; Carbohydrates: 36g; Sugar: 13g; Fiber: 9g; Sodium: 310mg

# Roasted Cauliflower Steaks with Harissa

**DAIRY-FREE, GLUTEN-FREE, VEGETARIAN** .................................................

These cauliflower steaks are a Moroccan-inspired plant-based meal. The combination of the fiery harissa and the sesame seeds elevates the humble cauliflower to diva status. If desired, garnish the dish with 2 tablespoons of chopped cilantro or parsley. Serve the steaks over semolina couscous or white rice.

.................................................................................................

**2 heads cauliflower, outer leaves removed and stems trimmed**

⅓ cup olive oil

1½ teaspoons salt

**½ cup harissa paste (see tip)**

**2 tablespoons honey**

2 tablespoons freshly squeezed lemon juice

¼ teaspoon freshly ground black pepper

**1 tablespoon toasted white sesame seeds**

---

**Serves** 4 to 6
**Prep time:** 15 minutes
**Cook time:** 50 minutes

1. Preheat the oven to 425°F. Line a baking sheet with foil.

2. Place one head of cauliflower on a cutting board. Using a large, sharp knife, cut the cauliflower in half lengthwise through the center. Then cut each half into 1½-inch-thick steaks. Repeat the process with the second head of cauliflower. Place the cauliflower steaks onto the prepared baking sheet.

3. In a small bowl, whisk together the oil, salt, and harissa paste. Spread the mixture over both sides of each cauliflower steak. Bake for 40 to 50 minutes or until tender, turning once halfway through.

4. Transfer steaks to a serving platter. In a separate small bowl, whisk the honey, lemon juice, and pepper until combined. Drizzle the sauce over the steaks and sprinkle with sesame seeds before serving.

**WASTE-NOT TIP:** Harissa is a thick and spicy chili paste made by blending the peppers with garlic, olive oil, and spices. You can use it as a replacement for the Thai chili paste in the Garlic Chili Prawns recipe (page 189) or use it to make a spicy version of the Creamy Tomato Bisque (page 99).

---

Per serving: Calories: 315; Total fat: 21g; Saturated fat: 3g; Protein: 7g; Carbohydrates: 29g; Sugar: 17g; Fiber: 10g; Sodium: 961mg

# Baked Rice with Cheddar and Broccoli

NUT-FREE, VEGETARIAN ..................................................................

Say cheese—literally! This creamy rice casserole is loaded with cheese. It's a real family favorite and is perfect for taking care of rice leftovers. You can easily make it gluten-free by using a gluten-free flour blend. Note that low-fat milk unfortunately won't work as a replacement for heavy cream, and the rice must be cool, or at room temperature, when mixing with the other ingredients; otherwise, the egg yolks could curdle, and the sauce might separate.

..................................................................

1 tablespoon olive oil

2 to 3 tablespoons all-purpose flour

**3 large egg yolks**

3½ cups heavy cream

½ small white onion, diced

**1 (16-ounce) package frozen chopped broccoli, thawed and drained**

1 teaspoon salt

½ teaspoon freshly ground black pepper

**1 (16-ounce) package shredded cheddar cheese**

**2 cups cooked long-grain white rice, chilled or at room temperature**

---

**Serves** 4 to 6
**Prep time:** 10 minutes
**Cook time:** 35 minutes

1. Place an oven rack in the lowest position. Preheat the oven to 350°F. Grease a 9-by-13-inch baking pan with the olive oil. Then flour the pan, tapping away any excess.

2. In a large bowl, whisk together the egg yolks and heavy cream. Add the onion, broccoli, salt, pepper, cheddar cheese, and rice. Stir until combined.

3. Place the rice mixture into the prepared baking dish. Bake, uncovered, on the low oven rack for 25 to 35 minutes, or until the casserole is bubbly and the cheese is fully melted.

**STORAGE TIP:** Leftovers should be covered and refrigerated for up to 2 days. Freezing is not recommended.

**WASTE-NOT TIP:** Use the egg whites to make the Mini Lemon Pavlovas with Lemon Curd (page 228).

---

Per serving: Calories: 1,381; Total fat: 121g; Saturated fat: 74g; Protein: 36g; Carbohydrates: 40g; Sugar: 8g; Fiber: 4g; Sodium: 1,407mg

# Fire-Roasted Margherita Pizza

**NUT-FREE, QUICK, VEGETARIAN** .........................................................................

Making pizza at home couldn't be any easier than this. With a few affordable ingredients, you can quickly put together an Italian classic by yourself for a fraction of the price you would pay at a pizzeria. You can make variations by adding red pepper flakes (for a spicy version) or adding toppings such as arugula, avocado, Parmesan shavings, etc. Using the same method, you can come up with different pizzas. The sky is the limit!

.........................................................................

**1 package refrigerated pizza dough**

1 tablespoon olive oil, plus extra for drizzling

**½ cup canned fire-roasted crushed tomatoes, drained**

**8 ounces fresh mozzarella cheese pearls, drained and patted dry**

**½ cup fresh basil leaves**

**Serves** 4 to 8
**Prep time:** 10 minutes
**Cook time:** 20 minutes

1. Place an oven rack in the lowest position. Preheat the oven to 400°F. Line a baking sheet with parchment paper.
2. Unroll the pizza dough onto the baking sheet. Brush the dough with olive oil. Top with tomatoes and the mozzarella pearls. Make sure to leave an inch around the perimeter uncovered for the crust.
3. Bake for 17 to 22 minutes, or until the bottom of crust is golden brown and the cheese has melted. Top with the basil and a drizzle of olive oil before serving.

**WASTE-NOT TIP:** Use leftover tomatoes in stews and to make tomato sauce or salsa from scratch, or to make Individual Pita Pizzas with Red Onion and Kalamata Olives (page 134).

Per serving: Calories: 421; Total fat: 17g; Saturated fat: 7g; Protein: 18g; Carbohydrates: 49g; Sugar: 8g; Fiber: 2g; Sodium: 875mg

# Individual Pita Pizzas with Red Onion and Kalamata Olives

**NUT-FREE, QUICK, VEGETARIAN** ........................................................

These personal pizzas use pita bread as crust and kalamata olives for a delicious twist on a classic. To further channel the flavors of the Greek islands, right before serving, top these pizzas with any combination of crumbled feta cheese, chopped cucumber, fresh basil leaves, or dried oregano.

........................................................

**4 pita breads**

2 tablespoons olive oil, plus extra for drizzling

**½ cup canned fire-roasted crushed tomatoes, drained**

**1 (8-ounce) package shredded mozzarella cheese**

½ cup diced red onion

**12 pitted kalamata olives, sliced**

---

**Serves** 4
**Prep time:** 10 minutes
**Cook time:** 10 minutes

1. Place an oven rack in the lowest position. Preheat the oven to 400°F. Line a baking sheet with parchment paper.

2. Place the pita breads onto the baking sheet. Lightly brush each one with olive oil and top each evenly with 2 tablespoons of tomatoes and about ¼ cup of cheese.

3. Evenly distribute the red onion and the olives among the four pizzas. Bake for 5 to 7 minutes, or until the cheese has melted. Drizzle with olive oil before serving.

**WASTE-NOT TIP:** Use leftover tomatoes in stews and to make tomato sauce or salsa from scratch, or to make Fire-Roasted Margherita Pizza (page 133).

---

Per serving: Calories: 440; Total fat: 22g; Saturated fat: 8g; Protein: 20g; Carbohydrates: 40g; Sugar: 3g; Fiber: 2g; Sodium: 1,022mg

# Portobello and Caramelized Onion Tart

**NUT-FREE, VEGETARIAN** ..................................................

This gourmet tart draws inspiration from French cuisine and is great for entertaining. It sounds fancy but it's easier to make than you might think. The preparation time is cut down by using store-bought puff pastry and jarred caramelized onions. The result is a buttery, sweet, and earthy tart that will impress your family and friends. Serve it with a side of fresh salad or steamed asparagus and a glass of pinot noir.

..................................................

**1 pound portobello
   mushrooms**
2 tablespoons olive oil, plus
   extra for brushing
Salt
Freshly ground black pepper
**⅓ cup jarred caramelized
   onion spread, such as
   Gracious Gourmet brand**
**1 sheet puff pastry, thawed
   to package instructions**
**½ cup shredded
   Swiss cheese**

---

**Serves** 4
**Prep time:** 15 minutes
**Cook time:** 30 minutes

1. Preheat the oven to 400°F. Separate the mushroom stems from the caps; discard the stems. Slice the caps into ¼-inch slices.

2. In a large nonstick skillet, heat the olive oil over medium heat. Add the mushrooms and cook for 5 to 7 minutes, or until they are tender and release their juices. Season with salt and pepper. Stir in the caramelized onion spread.

3. Roll the puff pastry out into a 10-by-16-inch rectangle. Score the dough to create a 1-inch border around the edges. Sprinkle the cheese over the puff pastry, minding the 1-inch border. Distribute the mushroom-and-onion topping over the cheese in an even layer.

4. Brush the border with olive oil. Bake for 15 to 25 minutes, or until the pastry is golden brown and the cheese has melted.

**WASTE-NOT TIP:** Use any leftover onion spread in sandwiches, pizzas, salads, and over grilled meats.

---

Per serving: Calories: 513; Total fat: 37g; Saturated fat: 7g; Protein: 12g; Carbohydrates: 36g; Sugar: 4g; Fiber: 3g; Sodium: 229mg

# Buttery Sweet Potato Noodles with Garlic and Parmesan

**GLUTEN-FREE, NUT-FREE, QUICK** ...........................................................................

This contemporary dish is perfect for pasta lovers who have a gluten allergy, or anyone looking try something new. It's buttery and garlicky with a lemon-and-pepper punch. You can use store-bought frozen butternut squash or carrot spiral noodles as a replacement for sweet potato noodles, but the cooking time should be adjusted according to the package instructions.

......................................................................................................

**4 medium sweet potatoes**

**4 tablespoons unsalted butter**

4 garlic cloves, minced

**¼ teaspoon red pepper flakes**

Salt

4 to 6 tablespoons water

1 tablespoon lemon juice

**½ cup grated Parmesan cheese**

---

**Serves** 4
**Prep time:** 15 minutes
**Cook time:** 15 minutes

1. Peel the sweet potatoes, slice off the two pointy end tips, and cut the potatoes in half. Place in the spiralizer and spiralize into noodles. If you don't have a spiralizer, grate the sweet potatoes on the coarse side of the grater.

2. In a large nonstick skillet, melt the butter over medium heat. Add the garlic and cook for about 1 minute, stirring occasionally. Add the red pepper flakes and season with salt. Stir in the sweet potato noodles. Toss to coat and cook for 2 to 3 minutes, gently tossing occasionally.

3. Add the water to the pan and toss again. Make sure the noodles are not sticking to the bottom of the pan. Cover and cook for 5 to 7 minutes, or until the noodles are al dente. (They'll break apart if they start to overcook, so check them often.)

4. Add the lemon juice and toss. Taste and adjust the salt, if needed. Transfer to bowls and sprinkle with Parmesan cheese before serving.

---

Per serving: Calories: 301; Total fat: 16g; Saturated fat: 10g; Protein: 8g; Carbohydrates: 33g; Sugar: 6g; Fiber: 4g; Sodium: 253mg

# Zucchini Noodles with Pesto Sauce and Shaved Parmesan

..............................................................

This is a contemporary low-carb dish, perfect for pasta lovers who are on a keto diet or are diabetic. The red pepper flakes and pesto sauce give the mild zucchini noodles, or "zoodles," a punch of rich flavor, taking the dish to a whole new level. If desired, pair with panfried tofu or fried eggs and avocado slices.

**4 (12-ounce) packages zucchini noodles**

2 tablespoons olive oil

1 large yellow onion, thinly sliced

**1½ cups pesto sauce**

**¼ teaspoon red pepper flakes**

**½ cup shaved Parmesan cheese**

---

**Serves** 4
**Prep time:** 10 minutes
**Cook time:** 15 minutes

1. Cook the zucchini noodles according to the package instructions. Drain and set aside.

2. In a large nonstick skillet, heat the oil over medium heat. Add the onion and cook until softened, 5 to 6 minutes.

3. Add the zoodles, pesto, and red pepper flakes. Toss until combined and let cook for an additional 30 to 60 seconds, or until warm. Serve with Parmesan shavings on top.

**WASTE-NOT TIP:** Use any surplus pesto in pastas, sandwiches, and on pizzas. You can also add it to the Buttery Sweet Potato Noodles with Garlic and Parmesan (page 136).

---

Per serving: Calories: 653; Total fat: 58g; Saturated fat: 10g; Protein: 19g; Carbohydrates: 14g; Sugar: 7g; Fiber: 6g; Sodium: 996mg

# Spaghetti with Roasted Bell Pepper Sauce and Basil

NUT-FREE, QUICK, VEGETARIAN ...........................................

Bell peppers are one of the most popular ingredients in Spanish and Southern Italian cuisine. This dish brings both of those influences together by blending the smoky sweet flavor of roasted red pepper with garlic and a hint of spice. Feel free to replace the red pepper flakes with freshly ground black pepper for a milder version of this dish.

..................................................................................................

**1 pound dry spaghetti pasta**

4 tablespoons olive oil, divided

4 garlic cloves, minced

**½ cup heavy cream**

**1 (16-ounce) jar roasted red bell peppers, drained**

Salt

**½ teaspoon red pepper flakes**

**¼ cup lightly packed fresh basil leaves, chopped, for garnish**

---

**Serves** 4
**Prep time:** 10 minutes
**Cook time:** 15 minutes

1. In a large stockpot, cook the pasta according to package instructions for al dente. (This should take 8 to 10 minutes.) Drain and return to the pot.

2. Meanwhile, in a medium nonstick skillet, heat 1 tablespoon of oil over medium heat. Add the garlic and cook for 1 minute. Add the cream and let simmer for 2 to 3 minutes, or until just warm.

3. Transfer the garlic and cream to a blender or food processor. Add the remaining 3 tablespoons of oil, red peppers, and a pinch of salt and puree until smooth.

4. Pour the sauce over the pasta, add the red pepper flakes, and toss to combine. Serve immediately with the basil leaves on top.

**VARIATION TIP:** You can replace the heavy cream with sour cream or plain Greek yogurt, adding 2 to 3 tablespoons of full-fat milk to loosen the sauce.

---

Per serving: Calories: 676; Total fat: 27g; Saturated fat: 9g; Protein: 16g; Carbohydrates: 92g; Sugar: 7g; Fiber: 4g; Sodium: 270mg

# Mushroom Fettuccine with Shaved Parmesan

**NUT-FREE, QUICK**......................................................................

I truly feel that pasta is one of the most comforting dishes ever created. Don't you agree? It never gets old or outdated. Although I am a fan of cremini mushrooms for their stronger flavor, you can replace them with oyster or shiitake mushrooms. Stick with heavy cream for a creamy texture. If desired, garnish with 2 tablespoons of chopped parsley. Serve the pasta immediately for the best results.

......................................................................

**1 pound dry fettuccine**

4 tablespoons olive oil, divided

**1 pound cremini mushrooms, chopped**

Salt

Freshly ground black pepper

4 garlic cloves, minced

**¾ cup heavy cream**

Zest and juice of ½ lemon

**¾ cup shaved Parmesan cheese, plus more for garnishing**

---

**Serves** 4
**Prep time:** 10 minutes
**Cook time:** 20 minutes

1. Cook the pasta according to the package instructions for al dente. (This should take 8 to 10 minutes.)
2. Meanwhile, in a large nonstick skillet, heat 2 tablespoons of oil over medium heat. Cook half of the mushrooms, stirring occasionally, for 5 to 6 minutes, or until browned.
3. Transfer the mushrooms to a bowl and season with salt and pepper. Repeat step 2 with the remaining 2 tablespoons of oil and the remaining mushrooms. Add the garlic to the mushrooms and cook for 1 minute. Transfer to the bowl and season again.
4. Making sure that you have set aside ½ cup of the pasta water, drain the pasta. Transfer the mushrooms and garlic to the pot used to cook the pasta. Add the cream and stir in the reserved pasta water. Bring to a simmer over medium heat, and cook for 3 to 4 minutes.
5. Add the pasta and toss. Add the lemon zest and juice and the Parmesan. Toss to coat. Taste and adjust the seasoning, if needed. Transfer to serving bowls and top with Parmesan shavings.

Per serving: Calories: 663; Total fat: 23g; Saturated fat: 6g; Protein: 27g; Carbohydrates: 90g; Sugar: 5g; Fiber: 4g; Sodium: 314mg

# Creamy and Spicy Mushroom Risotto in the Slow Cooker

**APPLIANCE, GLUTEN-FREE, NUT-FREE, VEGETARIAN** .................................

This is an umami-rich risotto with a kick. If you are not a fan of spicy foods, replace the pepper Jack cheese with mozzarella, or any melting cheese of your choice. Cremini mushrooms have a stronger flavor than white button mushrooms and work best in this dish, but you can replace them with any mushroom available at your grocery store.

.................................

3 tablespoons olive oil

**1 (8-ounce) package sliced fresh cremini mushrooms**

½ medium white onion, chopped

4 garlic cloves, minced

**1½ cups uncooked Arborio rice**

**4¾ cups chicken broth**

Salt

**1 cup heavy cream**

**⅓ cup shredded pepper Jack cheese**

---

**Serves** 4
**Prep time:** 5 minutes
**Cook time:** 10 minutes on the stovetop, plus 1 hour 30 minutes on High in a slow cooker

1. In a large nonstick skillet, heat the oil over medium heat. Add the mushrooms, onion, and garlic and cook, stirring occasionally, for 5 to 7 minutes, or until the mushrooms are lightly browned and the onion has softened. Add the rice and cook 1 minute more, stirring often.

2. Transfer the rice and vegetables to a 6-quart slow cooker. Add the broth and season with salt. Cover and cook on High for 30 minutes.

3. Remove the cover and stir, then cover and cook for an additional 40 to 60 minutes, or until the rice is just tender and the liquid is mostly absorbed.

4. In a small saucepan, heat the heavy cream over medium heat until just warm, 2 to 3 minutes. Stir the warm cream and the cheese into the rice mixture. Taste and adjust the salt, if needed.

---

Per serving: Calories: 606; Total fat: 36g; Saturated fat: 17g; Protein: 11g; Carbohydrates: 61g; Sugar: 5g; Fiber: 2g; Sodium: 759mg

# Portobello Mushroom Lasagna Casserole

. . . . . . . . . . . . . . . . . . . . . . . . . . . . . . . . . . . . . . . . . . . . . . . . . . . . . . . . . . . . . . . . . . . . . . . . . . . . . . . . . . . . . . . . . . .

This mushroom-loaded vegetarian lasagna is a delicious casserole, perfect for when you need a helping of comfort food. I like to make it for a weekend meal, and then have leftovers throughout the week. When cooking tomato sauce–based dishes, avoid using aluminum pans because the combination can cause a reaction that results in a metallic taste and could ruin aluminum cookware.

. . . . . . . . . . . . . . . . . . . . . . . . . . . . . . . . . . . . . . . . . . . . . . . . . . . . . . . . . . . . . . . . . . . . . . . . . . . . . . . . . . . . . . . . . . . . . . . . . . . . . . . . .

6 tablespoons olive oil, plus
   more for greasing
**3 pounds portobello
   mushrooms, stems
   removed, cut
   into ¼-inch-thick
   slices, divided**
Salt
Freshly ground black pepper
**5 cups marinara
   sauce, divided**
**1 (12-ounce) package
   no-boil lasagna sheets**
**10 cups shredded
   mozzarella cheese**

---

**Serves** 4 to 6
**Prep time:** 20 minutes
**Cook time:** 75 minutes,
plus 15 minutes to rest

1. In a large nonstick skillet, heat 2 tablespoons of oil over medium heat. Add one-third of the mushrooms and cook for about 5 minutes, or until they are tender and release their juices. Season with salt and pepper. Transfer the mushrooms to a large bowl and set aside. Repeat the same process with the remaining two batches of mushrooms.

2. Preheat the oven to 375°F. Spread 1 cup of marinara sauce in the bottom of an 8-by-12-inch baking dish.

3. Arrange one-quarter of the lasagna sheets on top, slightly overlapping the edges. Spread another 1 cup of sauce on top of the lasagna sheets. Then top with 1 cup of mozzarella cheese and one-third of the mushrooms. Top with an additional 1 cup of cheese. Repeat this process until all ingredients are used.

4. Grease one side of a foil sheet with olive oil and cover the pan tightly with the oiled-side down to prevent sticking.

5. Bake the casserole for 50 to 60 minutes, or until the sauce is bubbly and the cheese is melted. Let rest at room temperature for 15 minutes before serving.

**STORAGE TIP:** Store any leftovers in the refrigerator for up to 3 days or in the freezer for up to 2 months.

---

Per serving: Calories: 1,562; Total fat: 80g; Saturated fat: 40g; Protein: 94g; Carbohydrates: 124g; Sugar: 27g; Fiber: 13g; Sodium: 3,208mg

# Butternut Squash and Roasted Corn Quesadillas

**NUT-FREE, QUICK, VEGETARIAN** ......................................................

These sweet and spicy vegetarian quesadillas can be served by themselves or with a simple chopped salad. Feel free to use gluten-free, whole-wheat, or spinach tortillas instead—depending upon your needs and preferences. However, I advise against corn tortillas because they can break apart. If you have leftover cilantro from the Guacamole Dip (page 68) or Pico de Gallo (page 211), try chopping up a couple of tablespoons and sprinkling it inside each quesadilla before folding.

1 (10-ounce) package frozen butternut squash

Salt

Freshly ground black pepper

**4 (8-inch) flour tortillas**

**¾ cup canned fire-roasted corn blend, drained and rinsed**

**1 cup shredded pepper Jack cheese**

1 to 2 tablespoons olive oil

**¾ cup mild salsa**

**Serves** 4
**Prep time:** 10 minutes
**Cook time:** 10 minutes

1. Cook the squash according to the package instructions. Drain excess water.

2. In a medium bowl, mash the cooked squash well while it's still hot and mix in a pinch each of salt and pepper. Taste and adjust seasoning if needed.

3. Spread the squash onto half of each tortilla and then top each evenly with the corn and the cheese. Fold the other half of each tortilla over the filling and lightly brush olive oil on both sides of each folded quesadilla.

4. Heat a large nonstick skillet over medium heat. Cook the quesadillas for 1 to 2 minutes per side, or until they are lightly golden brown and the cheese is melted. Serve with salsa.

**VARIATION TIP:** To use fresh butternut squash: Pierce a small butternut squash all over with a fork. Put the squash on a microwave-safe plate, microwave on high for 4 to 5 minutes, then test it with a fork for doneness. Cook in 1- to 2-minute intervals until fully cooked and soft. When cool enough to handle, cut it in half, remove the seeds, and scoop the flesh. Proceed with step 2.

Per serving: Calories: 399; Total fat: 20g; Saturated fat: 8g; Protein: 12g; Carbohydrates: 45g; Sugar: 5g; Fiber: 6g; Sodium: 798mg

# Sweet Potato and Black Bean Crispy Tacos

NUT-FREE, QUICK, VEGETARIAN ..............................................................

Inspired by the flavors of Mexican cuisine, these tacos make a wonderful quick meal. For a more robust meal, serve them with a side of Charred Corn Salad with Cotija Cheese (page 111) or a simple fresh salad. Chopped cilantro and sour cream can be added as toppings, if you have either of them on hand. If you are not familiar with queso fresco, or "fresh cheese," it's a crumbly and mild Mexican cheese available at most supermarkets alongside other Mexican cheeses. Feta cheese makes a suitable substitute.

**1 (10-ounce) package frozen roasted sweet potatoes**

Salt

Freshly ground black pepper

**4 (8-inch) flour tortillas**

1 to 2 tablespoons olive oil

**1 cup canned vegetarian refried black beans**

**½ cup guacamole**

**1 cup queso fresco or feta cheese, crumbled, for topping**

---

**Serves** 4
**Prep time:** 5 minutes
**Cook time:** 15 minutes

1. Cook the sweet potatoes according to the package instructions. Drain excess water. Season with salt and pepper. Set aside.

2. Heat a large nonstick skillet over medium heat. Lightly brush both sides of each tortilla with oil. Add them to the skillet in batches and cook for 1 to 2 minutes per side, or until lightly brown and crispy. Remove from the pan and place on a flat surface.

3. Spread the refried beans in the center of each tortilla, then top each with a quarter of the sweet potatoes, guacamole, and cheese.

**VARIATION TIP:** You may replace flour tortillas with gluten-free, whole-wheat, or spinach tortillas according to your preference and needs—or even use crunchy taco shells. But avoid using corn tortillas because they can break apart easily.

**WASTE-NOT TIP:** Use leftover refried beans to make Refried Beans and Kale Enchiladas with a Kick (page 146).

---

Per serving: Calories: 467; Total fat: 23g; Saturated fat: 6g; Protein: 16g; Carbohydrates: 52g; Sugar: 2g; Fiber: 8g; Sodium: 807mg

# Black Bean Fiesta Quinoa Bowls

. . . . . . . . . . . . . . . . . . . . . . . . . . . . . . . . . . . . . . . . . . . . .

When you're busy and in need of a complete, simple, and nutritious meal, this delicious quinoa bowl inspired by Mexican cuisine is the solution. It can be served warm, at room temperature, or chilled. For extra zing, try mixing in 2 to 3 tablespoons of chopped cilantro or a dash of red pepper flakes.

**1⅓ cups uncooked quinoa**

2½ tablespoons olive oil

Juice of 3 lemons

Salt

Freshly ground black pepper

**1 (15-ounce) can black beans and corn mix, rinsed and drained**

**¾ cup halved grape tomatoes**

**2 avocados, cubed**

**Serves** 4
**Prep time:** 10 minutes
**Cook time:** 25 minutes, plus 10 minutes to cool

1. Cook the quinoa according to the package instructions. (This should take 20 to 25 minutes.) When the quinoa is done cooking, drain any excess liquid, fluff with a fork, and let cool for about 10 minutes.

2. While the quinoa is cooling, in a small bowl, whisk together the olive oil, lemon juice, and a pinch each of salt and pepper.

3. Add the bean and corn mix, tomatoes, and avocado to the quinoa. Pour the lemon dressing over the quinoa and vegetables, then toss gently to combine. Taste and adjust the seasoning, if needed.

4. Divide evenly among four serving bowls.

Per serving: Calories: 559; Total fat: 27g; Saturated fat: 3g; Protein: 16g; Carbohydrates: 70g; Sugar: 6g; Fiber: 16g; Sodium: 117mg

# Black Beans and Rice Power Bowls with Tofu

**DAIRY-FREE, GLUTEN-FREE, NUT-FREE, QUICK, VEGAN** .....................................

This quick, healthy bowl is inspired by the bold, spicy flavors of Mexican cuisine. I use parboiled rice, which takes less time to cook than regular rice and makes this recipe quicker to prepare. But feel free to use your favorite rice and adjust your cooking time accordingly.

1 cup parboiled white rice, sorted and rinsed

1 (15-ounce) can black beans, rinsed and drained

2 cups red enchilada sauce, divided

Salt

Freshly ground black pepper

1 (14-ounce) block extra-firm tofu, pressed to remove excess liquid (see step 1 on page 129)

2 tablespoons cornstarch

2 tablespoons olive oil

**Serves** 4 to 6
**Prep time:** 10 minutes
**Cook time:** 20 minutes

1. In a large pot, cook the rice according to the package instructions. (This should take 12 to 15 minutes.) Add the beans and 1½ cups of enchilada sauce. Season with salt and pepper and stir. Cover to keep warm and set aside.

2. Cut the pressed tofu into 1-inch cubes. In a large bowl, gently toss the tofu with the cornstarch until coated. (The cubes will be sticky.)

3. In a large nonstick skillet, heat the oil over medium heat for 2 to 3 minutes. Add one cube of tofu to make sure the oil is hot enough to make the tofu sizzle. In batches, if necessary, cook the tofu in a single layer, until browned, 2 to 3 minutes. Use a spatula to flip cubes and cook for 2 to 3 additional minutes, or until crispy. Add all of the tofu back to the pan.

4. Add the remaining enchilada sauce and toss to combine. Distribute the rice and bean mixture evenly among four serving bowls. Place one-quarter of the tofu and sauce into each bowl and serve immediately, as the tofu may lose its crispiness within 15 to 30 minutes.

Per serving: Calories: 483; Total fat: 16g; Saturated fat: 2g; Protein: 20g; Carbohydrates: 67g; Sugar: 2g; Fiber: 10g; Sodium: 658mg

# Refried Beans and Kale Enchiladas with a Kick

**GLUTEN-FREE, NUT-FREE, VEGETARIAN** .......................................................

Enchiladas might seem complicated, but they are actually easy to put together. They make a great weeknight dinner that can be assembled a day ahead and baked before serving. These are soaked in a delicious medium-spicy tomatillo sauce and loaded with melted cheese. This dish is easily customizable: Replace green salsa with your favorite enchilada sauce, use any other melting cheese, or swap refried pinto beans for refried black beans. Chopped cilantro, avocado slices, and sour cream all make great toppings for these enchiladas.

**1 (16-ounce) jar medium salsa verde, divided**

2 tablespoons olive oil

**1 (16-ounce) bag fresh chopped kale**

4 garlic cloves, minced

**1 (16-ounce) can refried beans**

Salt

Freshly ground black pepper

**10 corn tortillas**

**1 (16-ounce) package shredded cheddar cheese**

---

**Serves** 5 to 6
**Prep time:** 15 minutes
**Cook time:** 25 minutes

1. Preheat the oven to 400°F. Coat the bottom of a 9-by-13-inch baking dish with 1 cup of salsa.

2. In a large nonstick skillet, heat the oil over medium heat. Add the kale and cook for 5 to 6 minutes, or until the kale has wilted. Stir occasionally. Slide all the kale to one side of the pan. Put the garlic in the free side of the pan and cook for 1 minute, stirring occasionally.

3. Add the beans to the pan and mix them together with the kale and garlic. Cook for about 1 minute. Season with salt and pepper.

4. Wrap the corn tortillas in plastic wrap and microwave them for 30 seconds. This will steam them enough to roll without cracking.

5. Fill each tortilla with a few tablespoons of the kale and bean filling and top with 2 tablespoons of cheese. Make sure they are not too full; otherwise, you won't be able to roll them up.

6. Roll up the enchiladas and place them, seam-side down, into the prepared baking dish. Arrange the enchiladas into 2 rows with the rolls oriented lengthwise, parallel to the long side of the pan. They should snuggle close to one another and all fit into the pan.

7. Pour the remaining 1 cup of salsa over the enchiladas. Sprinkle with the remaining cheese. Bake for 15 minutes or until the enchiladas are bubbly and the cheese is melted.

**STORAGE TIP:** Store leftovers covered in the refrigerator for up to 3 days. Freeze for up to 2 months.

**PREP TIP:** Don't use an aluminum pan to make these enchiladas, as the aluminum will react with the salsa.

Per serving: Calories: 657; Total fat: 37g; Saturated fat: 21g; Protein: 29g; Carbohydrates: 51g; Sugar: 5g; Fiber: 13g; Sodium: 1,460mg

Pan-Grilled Pork Chops
with Pico de Gallo **170**

# 7

## *Meat and Poultry*

# One-Pan Gnocchi and Meatballs in Arrabbiata Sauce

**NUT-FREE, QUICK** .................................................................

What's not to love about a quick and mess-free meal, especially after a long day of work? This gnocchi and meatballs dish is comforting, spicy, and hearty—not to mention easy to make and clean up. Feel free to use the meatballs of your choice—vegetarian, turkey, beef—or mix it up! For a mild version, use marinara sauce.

.................................................................

1 (16-ounce) package
   potato gnocchi

1 (12 to 16-ounce) package
   frozen cooked meatballs

4 cups arrabbiata sauce

1 cup shredded
   mozzarella cheese

2 tablespoons chopped
   basil, for topping

**Serves** 4 to 6
**Prep time:** 5 minutes
**Cook time:** 25 minutes

1. Preheat the oven to 375° F.

2. In a large oven-safe skillet or a 4-quart or larger Dutch oven, toss the gnocchi and meatballs with the sauce until evenly coated. Top with mozzarella and bake for 20 to 25 minutes, or until all is bubbly and the cheese melts. Sprinkle basil over the top and serve hot.

**WASTE-NOT TIP:** Use any leftover arrabbiata sauce as a replacement for marinara sauce in Fried Garlic and Parmesan Pasta Chips with Marinara Sauce (page 82). Use leftover mozzarella as a replacement for pepper Jack for a milder version of Creamy and Spicy Mushroom Risotto in the Slow Cooker (page 140). Leftover basil can be chopped and sprinkled on the Individual Pita Pizzas with Red Onion and Kalamata Olives (page 134) or Buttery Sweet Potato Noodles with Garlic and Parmesan (page 136).

Per serving: Calories: 718; Total fat: 39g; Saturated fat: 12g; Protein: 27g; Carbohydrates: 69g; Sugar: 9g; Fiber: 7g; Sodium: 2,770mg

# Chicken Salsa Verde

**APPLIANCE, DAIRY-FREE, GLUTEN-FREE, NUT-FREE** ......................................

Salsa verde is a spicy Mexican sauce made from tomatillos and green chiles. It's versatile and can be used in a variety of dishes such as tacos, quesadillas, enchiladas, and stews. It's one of the stars of this recipe, adding acidity and bold flavors to the dish.

**2 pounds bone-in, skin-on chicken thighs, at room temperature**

Salt

Freshly ground black pepper

2 tablespoons olive oil

8 garlic cloves, minced

**1 (16-ounce) bottle medium salsa verde**

**1 cup chicken broth**

Juice of 2 limes

---

**Serves** 4
**Prep time:** 5 minutes
**Cook time:** 55 minutes

1. Pat the chicken thighs dry and season them with salt and pepper.

2. Heat a medium nonstick stockpot or Dutch oven over medium-high heat. Pour in the oil and swirl it around the pot to evenly coat the bottom. Place the chicken thighs skin-side down and sear for 2 to 4 minutes, or until the skin is golden brown. Flip the chicken and sear it for 2 to 4 minutes on the second side. Transfer the chicken thighs to a plate.

3. Reduce the heat to medium, add the garlic to the pot and cook, stirring occasionally, for about 1 minute, or until fragrant.

4. Place the chicken thighs back into the pot and pour the salsa verde and broth over the top. Stir, cover tightly, and reduce the heat to medium-low, then cook for 45 to 55 minutes, or until the thighs are cooked through. Make sure to stir and to turn the chicken over occasionally while cooking.

5. Stir in the lime juice. Taste and adjust the seasoning, if needed.

**APPLIANCE TIP:** To use a slow cooker, follow steps 1 and 2. Transfer the chicken thighs to the slow cooker, and stir in the salsa verde and broth. Cover and cook on High for 2 to 4 hours or on Low for 6 to 8 hours. Stir in the lime juice. Taste and adjust the seasoning, if needed.

Per serving: Calories: 614; Total fat: 45g; Saturated fat: 11g; Protein: 39g; Carbohydrates: 10g; Sugar: 5g; Fiber: 2g; Sodium: 819mg

# One–Pan Chipotle Chicken Thighs with Guacamole Salsa

**DAIRY-FREE, GLUTEN-FREE, NUT-FREE, QUICK** ....................................................

This is a quick, mess-free, one-pan meal that's ideal for busy weekdays. The chicken comes out spicy and juicy inside, with a crispy, golden-brown skin. Drawing on the bold flavors of Mexico, the recipe uses guacamole salsa to complement the chipotle flavor while adding creaminess. But you can try this dish with store-bought versions of different sauces, or make your own Chimichurri Sauce (page 208), Spicy Cilantro Sauce (page 209), Pico de Gallo (page 211), or Spinach Pesto Sauce (page 207).

**2 teaspoons chipotle powder**
**1 teaspoon garlic powder**
Salt
Freshly ground black pepper
**4 bone-in, skin-on chicken thighs, at room temperature**
3 tablespoons olive oil
**½ cup mild guacamole salsa**

**Serves** 4
**Prep time:** 5 minutes
**Cook time:** 25 minutes

1. Place a rack in the middle of the oven, then preheat the oven to 425°F.

2. In a small bowl, mix the chipotle powder, garlic powder, and a pinch each of salt and pepper. Pat dry the chicken thighs with a paper towel. Season the chicken on both sides with the spices.

3. Heat a large, oven-safe skillet over medium-high heat. Pour in the oil and swirl it around the skillet to evenly coat the bottom of the skillet. Place the chicken thighs skin-side down in the skillet and sear for 4 to 6 minutes, or until the skin is crisp and golden brown. Flip the chicken and remove the pan from the heat.

4. Transfer the pan to the middle rack of the oven and bake for about 15 minutes, or until chicken has cooked through. Pour about 2 tablespoons of guacamole salsa over each thigh and serve.

**STORAGE TIP:** Store leftover chicken in an airtight container in the refrigerator for up to 3 days. Freeze for up to 3 months without the salsa.

Per serving: Calories: 402; Total fat: 35g; Saturated fat: 8g; Protein: 20g; Carbohydrates: 3g; Sugar: 1g; Fiber: 1g; Sodium: 230mg

# Chicken Fajitas

**APPLIANCE, DAIRY-FREE, GLUTEN-FREE, NUT-FREE** .............................................

Fajitas are a Tex-Mex dish of meat strips cooked with onions and peppers. They're usually served with tortillas and condiments such as sour cream, guacamole, and pico de gallo. The fajitas presented here are made from chicken strips flavored with taco seasoning and pan-seared. This dish makes a flavorful, easy dinner or a delicious lunch on the go.

5 tablespoons olive oil, divided

Juice of 2 limes

**1 (1-ounce) package taco seasoning mix**

Salt

Freshly ground black pepper

**2 pounds boneless, skinless chicken breasts, cut into thin strips, at room temperature**

1 large yellow onion, cut in half and then cut into half-moons

**2 red bell peppers, seeded and cut into strips**

**Serves** 4 to 6
**Prep time:** 5 minutes
**Cook time:** 20 minutes, plus 15 minutes to marinate

1. In a large bowl, whisk together 2 tablespoons of oil, lime juice, taco seasoning, and a pinch each of salt and pepper. Add the chicken strips and toss to coat. Cover and let marinate at room temperature for at least 15 minutes.

2. Heat a large cast-iron skillet over medium heat. Pour in 1 tablespoon of oil. Add the onions and peppers and cook until softened, 6 to 8 minutes. Using a slotted spoon, transfer the onions and peppers to a plate.

3. Drain the chicken from the marinade and discard the marinade. Heat the same skillet over medium-high heat, pour in the remaining 2 tablespoons of oil and swirl it around the skillet to evenly coat the bottom. Place the chicken in the skillet and sauté until cooked through, 5 to 7 minutes. Return the vegetables to the pan and cook for 2 minutes more.

**APPLIANCE TIP:** To make this dish using a slow cooker, place half of a 16-ounce jar of tomato salsa into the slow cooker and spread to cover the bottom. In a large bowl, whisk 2 tablespoons of oil, the lime juice, taco seasoning, salt, and pepper. Add the chicken strips and toss to coat. Place the strips into the slow cooker and cover with the onion and peppers. Pour the remaining salsa on top, cover, and cook on Low for 3 to 4 hours or until the chicken and vegetables are cooked through.

Per serving: Calories: 428; Total fat: 23g; Saturated fat: 4g; Protein: 47g; Carbohydrates: 13g; Sugar: 4g; Fiber: 2g; Sodium: 1,203mg

# Chicken Thighs in Garlic and Balsamic Sauce

APPLIANCE, DAIRY-FREE, GLUTEN-FREE, NUT-FREE ...........................................

Balsamic vinegar, an Italian dark and concentrated grape-based vinegar, can not only dress salads, it can also be a condiment and tenderizer for meats. This mess-free, easy one-pot dish is the perfect dinner for a busy night. Store leftovers in an airtight container in the refrigerator for up to 3 days, or make the dish ahead of time and freeze for up to 3 months.

**2½ pounds boneless, skinless chicken thighs, at room temperature**

Salt

Freshly ground black pepper

2 tablespoons olive oil

8 garlic cloves, minced

**½ cup balsamic vinegar**

**2 tablespoons tomato puree**

**1 cup chicken broth**

**Serves** 4 to 6
**Prep time:** 5 minutes
**Cook time:** 30 minutes

1. Pat the chicken thighs dry and season them with salt and pepper.

2. Heat a large stockpot or Dutch oven over medium-high heat. Pour in the oil and swirl it around the pot to evenly coat the bottom. Place the chicken thighs skin-side down and sear for 2 to 4 minutes or until the skin is golden-brown. Flip and sear for 2 to 4 minutes on the second side. Transfer the chicken thighs to a plate. Reduce the heat to medium, add the garlic, and cook, stirring occasionally, for about 1 minute, or until fragrant.

3. Put the chicken thighs back into the pan and stir in the vinegar, tomato puree, and broth. Cover, reduce the heat to medium-low, and cook for about 25 minutes, or until thighs are cooked through. Make sure to stir and turn the chicken over occasionally while cooking.

4. Taste and adjust the seasoning, if needed.

**APPLIANCE TIP:** To make this dish using a slow cooker, follow steps 1 and 2. Transfer the chicken thighs to the slow cooker and stir in the cooked garlic, vinegar, tomato puree, and broth. Cover and cook on High for 2 to 4 hours or on Low for 6 to 8 hours. Taste and adjust the seasoning, if needed.

Per serving: Calories: 285; Total fat: 18g; Saturated fat: 4g; Protein: 25g; Carbohydrates: 7g; Sugar: 1g; Fiber: <1g; Sodium: 425mg

# One-Pan Roasted Chicken Thighs with Pesto and Cherry Tomatoes

**APPLIANCE, DAIRY-FREE, GLUTEN-FREE** ....................................................

This recipe finds inspiration in the flavors of Italy. Roasting brings out the tangy-sweetness of vine-ripened tomatoes, which pair perfectly with the succulent chicken. It's an easy meal that the whole family will enjoy.

**2 pounds bone-in, skin-on chicken thighs, at room temperature**

1½ teaspoons salt, plus extra

4 tablespoons olive oil, divided

**½ cup pesto sauce**

**12 ounces cherry tomatoes on the vine or regular cherry tomatoes**

---

**Serves** 4
**Prep time:** 5 minutes
**Cook time:** 35 minutes

1. Preheat the oven to 400°F. Line a baking sheet with aluminum foil. Pat the chicken thighs dry with a paper towel. Sprinkle 1½ teaspoons of salt over the chicken, making sure to season both sides.

2. In a medium bowl, combine 3 tablespoons oil and the pesto. Add the chicken and toss to coat. Transfer the chicken thighs to the baking sheet, skin-side up. Place the tomatoes onto the sheet pan. Drizzle the remaining 1 tablespoon of oil over the tomatoes and season them with salt.

3. Bake for 35 minutes, or until the chicken is cooked through. Scoop up any pesto sauce that has collected on the baking sheet and spoon it over the chicken thighs. For crispy skin, broil for an additional 5 to 8 minutes.

**VARIATION TIP:** Swap ¼ cup of red curry paste for the pesto, and add 1 to 2 extra tablespoons of oil to the curry paste mixture.

**APPLIANCE TIP:** To use a slow cooker, begin with: Follow step 1. Then, place the thighs in a slow cooker in a single layer. Add the pesto, tomatoes, ½ cup of chicken broth, and ½ teaspoon of red pepper flakes, if desired. Stir to combine. Cover and cook on High for 3 to 4 hours or on Low for 6 to 8 hours.

---

Per serving: Calories: 785; Total fat: 68g; Saturated fat: 14g; Protein: 41g; Carbohydrates: 3g; Sugar: 2g; Fiber: 1g; Sodium: 1,140mg

# Chicken Puttanesca with Orzo

APPLIANCE, DAIRY-FREE, NUT-FREE, QUICK ..........................................................

This dish is inspired by a Neapolitan classic, spaghetti alla puttanesca. The delicious sauce consists of tomatoes, garlic, oil, anchovies, capers, and olives, which are mixed with cooked chicken and served over orzo instead of spaghetti.

..........................................................................................

1½ cups dried orzo pasta

3 cups low-sodium chicken broth

2 pounds boneless, skinless chicken thighs, at room temperature

Salt

Freshly ground black pepper

2½ tablespoons olive oil, divided

6 garlic cloves, minced

1 (24-ounce) jar puttanesca sauce

Serves 4
**Prep time:** 5 minutes
**Cook time:** 15 minutes

1. In a medium nonstick stockpot, cook the orzo in the chicken broth until the liquid is absorbed and the pasta is tender, about 15 minutes.

2. Meanwhile, season the chicken with salt and pepper on both sides. Then, heat a nonstick skillet over medium-high heat. Pour in 2 tablespoons of oil and cook the chicken, undisturbed, for 3 minutes. Flip and cook for another 3 minutes, or until lightly golden brown.

3. Remove the chicken from the pan, add the remaining ½ tablespoon of oil, and cook the garlic until fragrant, stirring often, about 1 minute. Place the chicken back into the pan, add the sauce, and cook for about 5 minutes, or until heated.

4. Serve over a bed of the cooked orzo or mixed with the orzo.

**APPLIANCE TIP:** To use a slow cooker: Season the chicken with salt and pepper, then place it in the slow cooker with the sauce and the garlic. Cover and cook on Low for 4 hours. Remove the chicken to a plate. Add the orzo and the broth. Stir and add the chicken thighs. Cook for another 30 to 45 minutes on Low, or until the orzo is tender. If needed, add more liquid to cook the orzo completely.

Per serving: Calories: 655; Total fat: 27g; Saturated fat: 5g; Protein: 44g; Carbohydrates: 58g; Sugar: 8g; Fiber: 4g; Sodium: 1,101mg

# Herby Roast Chicken with Potatoes

**DAIRY-FREE, GLUTEN-FREE, NUT-FREE** ...........................................................

This roast chicken is seasoned with an Italian herb blend and prepared with potatoes. The result is a dinner the whole family will enjoy.

..................................................................................................................

**1 (4-pound) whole chicken, at room temperature**

5½ tablespoons olive oil, divided

**2 teaspoons Italian seasoning**

Salt

Freshly ground black pepper

**1 pound small red potatoes, quartered**

---

**Serves** 6
**Prep time:** 5 minutes
**Cook time:** 60 minutes

1. Position a rack in the upper third of the oven. Preheat the oven to 425°F. Remove the giblets and neck from the chicken cavity and discard them.

2. In a small bowl, mix 3 tablespoons of olive oil, the Italian seasoning, and a generous amount of salt and pepper.

3. Pat the chicken dry with a paper towel. Using your fingertips, gently separate the skin from the meat of the chicken breast. Rub about 1 tablespoon of the seasoned olive oil on the meat beneath the skin. Then, tie the legs together with kitchen string. Rub the chicken all over with the remaining 2 tablespoons of the seasoned oil.

4. In a large bowl, toss the potatoes with 1½ tablespoons of oil and a good pinch of salt and pepper until coated. Pour the remaining 1 tablespoon of oil into a large cast-iron skillet and swirl it around to evenly coat the bottom. Place the chicken, breast-side up, in the center and arrange the potatoes around it.

5. Roast for 55 to 60 minutes, or until the juices run clear when the thickest part of the thigh is pierced with a knife, or a thermometer inserted reaches 155°F. The potatoes should be fork-tender and crisp. Let the chicken rest for 10 to 15 minutes (it will reach 165°F), before carving.

---

Per serving: Calories: 733; Total fat: 52g; Saturated fat: 14g; Protein: 58g; Carbohydrates: 16g; Sugar: 4g; Fiber: 2g; Sodium: 1,754mg

# Ginger and Soy Chicken Thighs

APPLIANCE, DAIRY-FREE, NUT-FREE ...................................................

This dish was inspired by Mongolian beef and borrows the sweet and savory sauce, inflected with ginger and garlic, as a braising liquid for chicken thighs. To make this dish gluten-free, use tamari or gluten-free soy sauce. To speed up the cooking time considerably, make this in the pressure cooker (see Appliance Tip).

**2 pounds bone-in, skin-on chicken thighs, at room temperature**

Salt

Freshly ground black pepper

**1 teaspoon ground ginger**

2 to 3 tablespoons olive oil

6 garlic cloves, minced

**½ cup low-sodium soy sauce**

**2 cups low-sodium chicken broth**

½ cup dark brown sugar

---

**Serves** 4
**Prep time:** 5 minutes
**Cook time:** 55 minutes

1. Pat the chicken thighs dry and season them with salt, pepper, and ground ginger.

2. Heat a medium nonstick stockpot or Dutch oven over medium-high heat. Pour in the oil and swirl it around the pot to evenly coat the bottom. Place the chicken thighs in the pot skin-side down and sear for 2 to 4 minutes, or until the skin is golden-brown. Flip and sear for 2 to 4 minutes on the other side.

3. Transfer the chicken thighs to a plate. Reduce the heat to medium. Add the garlic to the pot and cook, stirring occasionally, for about 1 minute.

4. Place the chicken thighs back into the pot and pour in the soy sauce, broth, and brown sugar. Stir, then cover tightly, reduce the heat to medium-low, and cook for 45 to 55 minutes, or until the thighs are cooked through. Stir occasionally while the chicken is cooking.

**APPLIANCE TIP:** Select the Sauté function to preheat a 6-quart pressure cooker. Follow step 1. When the pressure cooker is hot, pour in the oil and sear the chicken as directed in step 2, then move to steps 3 and 4. When all ingredients are in the pot, lock the lid in place. Select High pressure and cook for 10 minutes. When done, use quick pressure release.

Per serving: Calories: 658; Total fat: 45g; Saturated fat: 11g; Protein: 41g; Carbohydrates: 29g; Sugar: 18g; Fiber <1g; Sodium: 1,193mg

# Orange Chicken

Orange Chicken is a Chinese American dish that consists of battered, fried chicken pieces coated in a thick, sweet, orange-flavored sauce. This is a quick, leaner version of the classic. It can be prepared either on the stovetop or with the convenience of the slow cooker. It makes a fuss-free dinner ideal for busy weekdays. For a spicy version, add a pinch of red pepper flakes to the sauce. Try garnishing it with chopped scallions and toasted sesame seeds.

**2 pounds boneless, skinless chicken thighs, cut into 1½-inch chunks, at room temperature**

Salt

Freshly ground black pepper

**¼ cup cornstarch**

2 to 3 tablespoons olive oil

**1 cup barbecue sauce**

**¾ cup orange marmalade**

**½ cup low-sodium soy sauce**

**Serves** 4 to 6
**Prep time:** 5 minutes
**Cook time:** 20 minutes

1. Pat the chicken pieces dry. Put them into a large sealable plastic bag, season generously with salt and pepper, and sprinkle the cornstarch into the bag. Seal the bag and shake well to fully coat the chicken with cornstarch.

2. Heat a medium nonstick stockpot or Dutch oven over medium-high heat. Pour in the oil and swirl the pot to evenly coat the bottom. Add the chicken and cook, undisturbed, until the chunks are browned, 2 to 3 minutes per side.

3. Add the barbecue sauce, marmalade, and soy sauce. Stir, and then reduce heat to medium-low, cover, and cook for 10 minutes, or until the chicken is cooked through.

**APPLIANCE TIP:** To make this dish using a slow cooker, follow steps 1 and 2 as directed. Then place the chicken, barbecue sauce, marmalade, and soy sauce into the slow cooker. Stir, cover, and cook on Low for 2 to 3 hours, or until the chicken is cooked through.

**WASTE-NOT TIP:** Use leftover marmalade, barbecue sauce, and soy sauce to make the Slow Cooker Falling-Off-the-Bone Five-Spice Barbecue Pork Ribs (page 169).

Per serving: Calories: 565; Total fat: 20g; Saturated fat: 4g; Protein: 47g; Carbohydrates: 57g; Sugar: 57g; Fiber: 1g; Sodium: 1,883mg

# Butter Chicken

APPLIANCE, GLUTEN-FREE, NUT-FREE .................................................

Butter chicken is an Indian dish originally made by stewing leftover chicken in a tomato gravy flavored with spices, butter, and cream. This is an abbreviated version of the classic. To make it dairy-free, replace the Greek yogurt with a plant-based yogurt.

**2 pounds boneless, skinless chicken thighs, cut into 1½-inch chunks, at room temperature**

Salt

Freshly ground black pepper

**5 tablespoons unsalted butter, divided**

1 large yellow onion, thinly sliced

**1 (15-ounce) jar butter chicken sauce**

**1 cup plain Greek yogurt, at room temperature**

---

**Serves** 4
**Prep time:** 5 minutes
**Cook time:** 30 minutes

1. Pat the chicken pieces dry and season them with salt and pepper.

2. Meanwhile, heat a medium nonstick stockpot or Dutch oven over medium-high heat. Drop in 3 tablespoons of butter. Once melted, add the chicken and cook, undisturbed, until lightly browned, 5 to 7 minutes. Using a slotted spoon, transfer the chicken to a bowl. Reduce the heat to medium and put the remaining 2 tablespoons of butter into the pan. Once melted, add the onion and cook until softened, about 5 minutes.

3. Increase the heat to medium-high, add the chicken back to pan, stir in the sauce, and let it come to a boil. Reduce the heat to medium-low, stir, and cover, letting simmer for 15 minutes, or until the chicken is cooked through. Stir in the yogurt. Taste and adjust the seasoning, if needed.

**APPLIANCE TIP:** To use a slow cooker: Follow steps 1 and 2. Transfer the browned chicken and cooked onions to the slow cooker, stir in the sauce, cover, and cook on High for 2 to 4 hours or on Low for 6 to 8 hours. Stir in the yogurt.

**STORAGE TIP:** Store leftovers in an airtight container in the refrigerator for up to 3 days.

---

Per serving: Calories: 569; Total fat: 40g; Saturated fat: 19g; Protein: 36g; Carbohydrates: 18g; Sugar: 13g; Fiber: 1g; Sodium: 751mg

# Creamy Chicken Tikka Masala

**GLUTEN-FREE, NUT-FREE, QUICK** ......................................................

Chicken Tikka Masala consists of marinated pieces of chicken cooked in a savory, creamy curry sauce with a hint of spice. This shortcut version uses a store-bought sauce, which lets you enjoy the finished product in only 30 minutes.

......................................................

**2 pounds boneless, skinless chicken thighs, cut into 1½-inch chunks, at room temperature**

Salt

Freshly ground black pepper

4 tablespoons olive oil, divided

6 garlic cloves, minced

**1 (15-ounce) jar tikka masala sauce**

**1 cup plain Greek yogurt, at room temperature**

---

**Serves** 4 to 6
**Prep time:** 5 minutes
**Cook time:** 25 minutes

1. Pat the chicken pieces dry and season them with salt and pepper.

2. Heat a medium nonstick stockpot or Dutch oven over medium-high heat. Pour in 3 tablespoons of oil and swirl it around the pot to evenly coat the bottom. Add the chicken and cook, undisturbed, until the pieces are lightly browned, 5 to 7 minutes. Using a slotted spoon, transfer the chicken to a bowl.

3. Reduce the heat to medium. Pour the remaining 1 tablespoon of oil into the pan and cook the garlic until fragrant, about 1 minute. Increase the heat to medium-high, add the chicken back to the pan, stir in the tikka masala sauce, and let it come to a boil. Then, reduce the heat to medium-low, stir, and cover the pan.

4. Let simmer for 15 minutes, or until the chicken is cooked through. Stir in the yogurt. Taste and adjust the seasoning, if needed.

**STORAGE TIP:** Store leftovers in an airtight container in the refrigerator for up to 3 days. Freezing is not recommended because sauce may separate.

---

Per serving: Calories: 502; Total fat: 34g; Saturated fat: 8g; Protein: 36g; Carbohydrates: 11g; Sugar: 8g; Fiber: 2g; Sodium: 658mg

# Shortcut Chicken Curry

**APPLIANCE, DAIRY-FREE, GLUTEN-FREE, NUT-FREE, QUICK** .........................................

Curry is an Indian stew made from a complex combination of spices, chiles, and herbs, in addition to other ingredients. This time-saving version is a very loose adaptation. If desired, replace the flavorful curry paste with curry powder and add about 1 tablespoon each of garlic powder and onion powder to the stew along with the tomato puree. Store any leftovers in an airtight container in the refrigerator for up to 3 days.

**2 pounds boneless, skinless chicken breasts, cut into 1½-inch chunks, at room temperature**

Salt

Freshly ground black pepper

2 tablespoons olive oil

**2 tablespoons green curry paste**

**1½ cups tomato puree**

**1 (14-ounce) can coconut milk, divided**

---

**Serves** 4
**Prep time:** 5 minutes
**Cook time:** 25 minutes

1. Pat the chicken chunks dry and season them with salt and pepper.
2. Meanwhile, heat a medium nonstick stockpot or Dutch oven over medium-high heat. Pour in the oil and swirl it around the pot to evenly coat the bottom. Add the chicken and cook, undisturbed, until the chunks are lightly browned, about for 5 to 7 minutes.
3. Add the curry paste, tomato puree, and half of the coconut milk and stir until the ingredients are well combined. Reduce the heat to medium-low, cover, and let simmer for 10 to 15 minutes. Stir in the remaining coconut milk. Taste and adjust the seasoning, if needed.

**APPLIANCE TIP:** To use a slow cooker: Follow steps 1 and 2. Then transfer the chicken to the slow cooker, and stir in the curry paste and tomato puree until well combined. Cover and cook on High for 4 hours or on Low for 6 to 8 hours. Stir in the coconut milk for 10 to 15 minutes before the cooking time ends. Taste and adjust the seasoning, if needed.

**WASTE-NOT TIP:** Use leftover curry paste in the Chickpea and Potato Curry (page 127).

Per serving: Calories: 522; Total fat: 32g; Saturated fat: 18g; Protein: 49g; Carbohydrates: 12g; Sugar: 6g; Fiber: 2g; Sodium: 1,149mg

# Bacon–Wrapped Turkey Breast

**APPLIANCE, DAIRY-FREE, GLUTEN-FREE, NUT-FREE** .......................................................

The Cajun seasoning blend gives this slightly smoky Bacon-Wrapped Turkey Breast a real burst of flavor. You can prepare this either in the oven or in the slow cooker (see Appliance tip). It's the perfect dish to provide delicious leftovers for a couple or to feed your family. If you are preparing this in the oven, make sure to brine the turkey to make it moist. Skip the brining if you are preparing it in the slow cooker.

4 quarts cold water

⅔ cup salt

¼ cup sugar

**1 (4-pound) boneless, skinless turkey breast**

1 to 2 tablespoons olive oil, plus more for greasing

**2 tablespoons Cajun seasoning**

**14 to 16 slices thick-cut smoked bacon**

**1 to 2 tablespoons honey**

---

**Serves** 4 to 6
**Prep time:** 10 minutes
**Cook time:** 1 hour 40 minutes, plus 8 hours to brine

1. In a large bowl or medium stockpot, combine the water, salt, and sugar, mixing until the salt and sugar dissolve. Place the turkey breast into the brine. Cover and transfer to the refrigerator for least 8 hours to brine.

2. Preheat the oven to 325°F. Grease both a metal cooking rack and a baking sheet with oil and position the rack on top the baking sheet.

3. Remove the turkey breast from the brine and pat very dry with a paper towel.

4. In a small bowl, mix the Cajun seasoning with the oil until it becomes a thick, spreadable paste. Spread the seasoning evenly all over the breast and place the breast on the greased rack.

5. On a sheet of parchment paper, arrange the bacon slices in a weave pattern, or any other pattern of your liking. Place the bacon weave over the turkey breast and tuck the edges underneath very well.

6. Roast the turkey for 1 hour and 40 minutes (or 25 minutes per pound), or until the bacon is crispy and the internal temperature of the turkey is 160°F. About 15 minutes before the roasting time comes to an end, brush the bacon with honey and return to the oven.

7. If the turkey breast is still not fully cooked, rotate the turkey and bake for 15 to 30 minutes more, or it until reaches the requisite internal temperature. For extra browning of the bacon, broil for 2 to 3 minutes or until crispy. (Watch carefully in order for it not to burn.) Let the turkey breast rest for 10 to 15 minutes before slicing.

APPLIANCE TIP: To use a slow cooker: In a small bowl, mix the Cajun seasoning with the 1 to 2 tablespoons of oil until it becomes a thick, spreadable paste. Evenly spread the paste all over the turkey breast. On a sheet of parchment paper, arrange the bacon slices in a weave pattern, or to your liking. Place the bacon over the turkey, then gently transfer the bacon-wrapped breast to the slow cooker, tucking the edges underneath securely. Cover and cook on Low for 5 to 6 hours. Do not cook the breast on High. During hour 5, use a meat thermometer to see if the internal temperature reaches 160°F; if not, cook for another hour. When the breast is fully cooked, remove it from the slow cooker and place it on a baking sheet lined with parchment paper. Brush the honey over the bacon and broil for 2 to 5 minutes or until the bacon is crispy and golden brown.

Per serving: Calories: 779; Total fat: 33g; Saturated fat: 11g; Protein: 110g; Carbohydrates: 20g; Sugar: 17g; Fiber: 0g; Sodium: 1,918mg

# Hawaiian–Inspired Turkey Meatballs

**APPLIANCE, DAIRY-FREE, NUT-FREE, QUICK**............................................................

Get the tropical vibes of Hawaii without ever having to jump on a plane. These turkey meatballs are cooked in a robust, sweet barbecue sauce, making a comforting and flavorful weeknight meal in half an hour. This is a loose adaptation of Hawaiian hulihuli chicken, which is barbecued and basted in a sweet sauce made of barbecue sauce, pineapple, bell peppers, and other delights.

........................................................................................................

1 (20- to 24-ounce) bag
frozen cooked turkey
meatballs

1 (8-ounce) can
pineapple chunks

2 red bell peppers, seeded
and chopped

1 (28-ounce) bottle
barbecue sauce

¼ cup chopped scallions,
white and green parts, for
topping (optional)

**Serves** 4 to 6
**Prep time:** 5 minutes
**Cook time:** 25 minutes

1. Heat a large nonstick stockpot or Dutch oven over medium heat. Put the meatballs, pineapple chunks with their juices, bell peppers, and barbecue sauce into the pot. Stir gently, but thoroughly, in order to coat all of the solid ingredients with the barbecue sauce.

2. Cover and cook for 20 to 25 minutes, stirring occasionally, until the sauce is bubbly and the meatballs are fully heated.

3. If you prefer a saucier dish, stir in ¼ to ⅓ cup of water 5 to 10 minutes before the cooking time ends. Sprinkle the scallions over the top (if using) and serve hot.

**APPLIANCE TIP:** To make this dish using a slow cooker: Combine all of the ingredients in the slow cooker. Stir, cover, and cook on High for 2 to 4 hours.

Per serving: Calories: 415; Total fat: 14g; Saturated fat: 1g; Protein: 30g; Carbohydrates: 40g; Sugar: 82g; Fiber: 4g; Sodium: 2,684mg

# One–Pan Bratwurst and Vegetables

**DAIRY-FREE, GLUTEN-FREE, NUT-FREE** ...........................................................

Bratwurst is a German fresh link sausage made from veal, beef, or pork that's great for roasting. In this recipe, the sausages are roasted along with potatoes and red peppers on a baking sheet, making a comforting dish that's both colorful and super easy to clean up!

**1 pound bratwurst sausages**

¼ cup olive oil, plus extra for drizzling

**1 (1-ounce) package onion soup mix**

**1 pound small yellow potatoes, quartered**

**1 red bell pepper, seeded and sliced**

**Serves** 4 to 6
**Prep time:** 5 minutes
**Cook time:** 40 minutes

1. Preheat the oven to 400°F. Line a baking sheet with aluminum foil. Place the sausages onto the lined baking sheet and drizzle oil over them.

2. Mix ¼ cup of oil with the onion soup mix in a large bowl until combined. Put the potatoes and bell pepper into the bowl and toss to coat. Arrange the vegetables in a single layer around the sausages.

3. Bake for 30 to 40 minutes, or until the sausages are cooked through, making sure to flip the sausages halfway through the cooking time. The potatoes should be fork-tender.

Per serving: Calories: 600; Total fat: 47g; Saturated fat: 13g; Protein: 18g; Carbohydrates: 27g; Sugar: 2g; Fiber: 4g; Sodium: 1,588mg

# Pressure Cooker Pulled Pork

APPLIANCE, DAIRY-FREE, NUT-FREE

This pulled pork makes some of the best pulled-pork sandwiches. The meat comes out tender and juicy, infused with a smoky flavor. Since this version is cooked in the pressure cooker, the prep time is cut down considerably. For a gluten-free version, use a gluten-free soy sauce or tamari.

3 tablespoons olive
   oil, divided
**2 pounds boneless pork
   shoulder, cut into two
   equal pieces**
1½ cups barbecue
   sauce, divided
¼ **cup low-sodium soy sauce**
¼ **cup low-sodium
   chicken broth**

**Serves** 4 to 6
**Prep time:** 5 minutes
**Cook time:** 1 hour
40 minutes, plus 10 minutes to come to pressure and 20 minutes to release pressure

1. Select the Sauté function to preheat a 6-quart pressure cooker. When hot, pour in 1½ tablespoons of oil and brown half of the pork on both sides, about 3 minutes per side. Repeat the process with the other half of the oil and pork. Transfer the pork to a platter.

2. Add ¾ cup of barbecue sauce, the soy sauce, and broth to the bowl of the pressure cooker and stir to combine. Add the browned pork and any pork juices. Lock the lid in place. Select High Pressure, close the pressure-release valve, and set the cook time for 75 minutes.

3. Allow the pressure to release naturally, which will take about 20 minutes. Remove the lid, transfer the pork to a large bowl or platter, and shred it using two forks. Discard any excess fat. Strain the cooking liquid, reserving ½ cup.

4. Put the shredded pork back in the pressure cooker with the remaining ¾ cup of barbecue sauce and the reserved ½ cup of cooking liquid. Stir, then select the Sauté function and bring to a simmer for about 5 minutes, stirring often.

**STORAGE TIP:** Store leftover pulled pork in an airtight container in the refrigerator for up to 3 days, or freeze for up to 3 months.

Per serving: Calories: 709; Total fat: 54g; Saturated fat: 16g; Protein: 41g; Carbohydrates: 13g; Sugar: 31g; Fiber: 1g; Sodium: 1,473mg

# Slow Cooker Falling-Off-the-Bone Five-Spice Barbecue Pork Ribs

**APPLIANCE, DAIRY-FREE, NUT-FREE** .................................................................

These ribs are cooked in the slow cooker, resulting in a tender, falling-off-the-bone, sticky-sweet delight. You can store leftover ribs in an airtight container in the refrigerator for up to 4 days or freeze them in small portions in freezer-safe bags for up to 4 months.

½ cup low-sodium soy sauce

⅔ cup orange marmalade

½ cup barbecue sauce

1 teaspoon
   five-spice powder

4 garlic cloves, minced

1 (3-pound) rack baby back
   ribs, membrane removed

---

**Serves** 4
**Prep time:** 5 minutes
**Cook time:** 4 hours on
High, or 6 to 8 hours
on Low

1. In a small bowl, mix together the soy sauce, marmalade, barbecue sauce, five-spice powder, and garlic. Spread three-quarters of the sauce on both sides of the ribs. Reserve the remaining sauce.

2. Transfer the ribs to a 6-quart slow cooker. You may have to curl the rack of ribs along the inner wall of the pot to fit it. Cover and cook on High for 4 hours or on Low for 6 to 8 hours, or until tender.

3. About 5 minutes before the cooking time ends, place the remaining sauce mixture in a small nonstick saucepan or skillet and heat over medium heat until thickened, 3 to 5 minutes. Brush the ribs on both sides with sauce and serve. If desired, transfer the ribs to a parchment-paper-lined baking sheet and broil for 5 to 8 minutes.

**PREP TIP:** To remove the membrane, place the pork ribs on a large cutting board and slip a dull knife under the membrane (starting from the narrower end). Using a paper or kitchen towel, grasp the membrane and pull it away from the bones.

**WASTE-NOT TIP:** Use leftover marmalade to replace the fig jam in the Fig, Brie, and Pecan Bites (page 71).

---

Per serving: Calories: 1,135; Total fat: 82g; Saturated fat: 30g; Protein: 57g; Carbohydrates: 43g; Sugar: 42g; Fiber: 1g; Sodium: 1,684mg

# Pan-Grilled Pork Chops with Pico de Gallo

**DAIRY-FREE, GLUTEN-FREE, NUT-FREE** .................................................

Grilling is a healthy cooking method that you can perform both indoors and outdoors. If you miss grilled meats during the wintertime, don't worry! Just grab your grill pan or skillet and prepare these pan-grilled pork chops. Alternatively, follow the variation tip below to cook these on an outdoor grill. For a twist, you can replace the pico de gallo with a store-bought pesto, or with the Spinach Pesto Sauce (page 207), Chipotle Sauce (page 213), Chimichurri Sauce (page 208), or Spicy Cilantro Sauce (page 209).

.................................................

3 tablespoons olive oil, divided

**1 tablespoon Dijon mustard**

Juice of 2 lemons, divided

1 tablespoon salt

1 tablespoon ground black pepper

**3 pounds bone-in, thick center-cut pork chops (4 to 6 chops)**

**1 cup pico de gallo, for topping**

---

**Serves** 4 to 6
**Prep time:** 5 minutes
**Cook time:** 25 minutes, plus 30 minutes to marinate

1. In a large bowl, whisk together 1½ tablespoons of oil, the mustard, half of the lemon juice, and the salt and pepper, until just combined. Brush the mixture over both sides of the chops and let them marinate in the bowl, refrigerated, for 30 minutes.

2. Heat a large grill pan, or a large skillet, over high heat until sizzling hot, about 5 minutes. Brush the pan well with the remaining oil. Place the pork chops into the pan in a single layer. Cook for about 3 minutes on one side, or until grill marks appear. Flip and cook for 3 minutes on the other side, or until grill marks form.

3. Flip the chops again and position them so that the current grill lines will cross the first to form a checkerboard pattern. Reduce heat to medium and let cook for 5 minutes.

4. Using tongs, hold each chop up vertically, with the closest end to the bone resting against the pan, for 30 to 60 seconds (to prevent that part from being undercooked).

5. Transfer the pork chops to a plate, drizzle with the remaining lemon juice, and let them rest for 3 to 5 minutes. Top with pico de gallo and serve.

**STORAGE TIP:** Store leftover pork chops (without the pico de gallo) in an airtight container in the refrigerator for 3 to 4 days. Freeze for up to 2 months.

**VARIATION TIP:** To make these pork chops on an outdoor grill, follow step 1 as directed. Then preheat the grill to medium-high heat and oil the grate. Grill the chops until they are no longer pink in the center, for 5 to 6 minutes per side. Proceed with step 4 as directed.

Per serving: Calories: 699; Total fat: 50g; Saturated fat: 17g; Protein: 61g; Carbohydrates: 7g; Sugar: 2g; Fiber: 2g; Sodium: 2,999mg

# Slow Cooker Ham with Orange and Brown Sugar Sauce

**APPLIANCE, DAIRY-FREE, GLUTEN-FREE, NUT-FREE** ....................................................

This ham is one of the easiest dishes to prepare for a holiday—or any day. It's flavored with a sweet orange sauce and only needs to be heated up in the slow cooker. You don't need to worry about basting the ham like you would if it were baked in the oven. This gives you time to make other dishes for your get-together while your beautiful golden-brown and flavorful main dish practically cooks itself.

....................................................

**1 (6- to 7-pound) spiral-cut ham, bone-in and fully cooked**

1 cup brown sugar

**1 cup honey**

1 cup freshly squeezed orange juice

---

**Serves** 4 to 6
**Prep time:** 10 minutes
**Cook time:** 3 to 4 hours on Low

1. Grease a 6-quart slow cooker.
2. Place the ham, cut-side down, in the slow cooker. Rub brown sugar all over the ham and pour the honey and the orange juice over the top.
3. Cover and heat on Low for 3 to 4 hours, or until the sugar has dissolved and the ham is fully heated.
4. Carefully transfer the ham to a serving platter.
5. Transfer the liquid to a medium saucepan. Heat it over medium-high heat until thickened, 5 to 8 minutes.
6. Pour the sauce over the ham.

**STORAGE TIP:** Store leftover ham in an airtight container in the refrigerator for up to 3 days. Freeze for up to 3 months.

**PREP TIP:** Any bone-in ham that weights more than 7 pounds will probably require a slow cooker larger than 6 quarts.

---

Per serving: Calories: 1,462; Total fat: 56g; Saturated fat: 20g; Protein: 113g; Carbohydrates: 173g; Sugar: 150g; Fiber: <1g; Sodium: 6,499mg

# Pan–Seared Pork Chops with Sweet Teriyaki Sauce

**DAIRY-FREE, NUT-FREE, QUICK** .....................................................

This is one of the most visually appetizing dishes you'll ever lay eyes on, and although I like to gaze at it, I love eating it even more. The teriyaki—a sweet, sour, and salty Japanese sauce—gives the glaze a beautiful brown color, while imparting extra flavor and making the chops oh so succulent.

**4 center-cut boneless pork chops, at room temperature**
Salt
Freshly ground black pepper
3 tablespoons olive oil, divided
6 cloves garlic, minced
**¼ cup honey**
**¼ cup teriyaki sauce**
2 tablespoons freshly squeezed lemon juice

**Serves** 4
**Prep time:** 5 minutes
**Cook time:** 25 minutes

1. Preheat the broiler. Season the chops with salt and pepper.
2. Heat a large cast-iron skillet over medium-high heat until very hot, about 5 minutes. Pour in 2 tablespoons of oil, then sear the pork chops for 4 to 5 minutes per side, or until cooked through and golden. Transfer to a plate.
3. Reduce the heat to medium. Pour in the remaining 1 tablespoon of oil and scrape up the browned bits from the bottom of the pan. Add the garlic and cook for about 30 seconds. Add the honey, teriyaki sauce, and lemon juice.
4. Increase the heat to medium-high. Let the sauce cook for 3 to 4 minutes, stirring occasionally, until it thickens slightly. Add the pork chops back into the pan and baste them with the sauce.
5. Transfer the skillet to the oven and broil until the edges of the pork are slightly charred, 1 to 2 minutes.

Per serving: Calories: 318; Total fat: 16g; Saturated fat: 4g; Protein: 22g; Carbohydrates: 21g; Sugar: 20g; Fiber: <1g; Sodium: 1,213mg

# Sweet and Sour Pork Chops

....................................................

This version of the Cantonese dish uses barbecue sauce as the sweet and sour component. The chops are beautifully seared and tender, cooked in a delicious sauce with vegetables and sweet pineapple. You can store leftovers in an airtight container in the refrigerator for up to 3 days or freeze for up to 3 months.

**1 (20-ounce) can
   pineapple chunks**
**1½ cups barbecue sauce**
**4 center-cut boneless pork
   chops, 1-inch thick, at
   room temperature**
Salt
Freshly ground black pepper
2 tablespoons vegetable oil
**2 medium carrots, peeled
   and cut into ¼-inch rounds**
**1 red bell pepper, seeded
   and chopped**

---

**Serves** 4
**Prep time:** 5 minutes
**Cook time:** 45 minutes

1. Preheat the oven to 350°F.
2. Into a medium bowl, strain the juice from the canned pineapple and reserve the pineapple. Add the barbecue sauce to the pineapple juice and mix well.
3. Pat the chops dry and season them on both sides with salt and pepper. Heat a large skillet over medium-high heat. Pour in the oil and evenly coat the bottom. Add the chops and sear, undisturbed, for 2 to 4 minutes per side, or until golden brown.
4. Transfer the chops to a 9-by-13-inch baking dish. Arrange the pineapple chunks, carrots, and bell pepper in the baking dish (both on top of the chops and surrounding them). Pour the pineapple barbecue sauce on top, cover tightly with foil, and bake for 25 to 35 minutes, or until everything is tender and cooked through.

**APPLIANCE TIP:** To use a slow cooker: Follow step 3. Then, arrange the seared pork chops, the pineapple chunks and their juices, the carrots, bell pepper, and barbecue sauce in the slow cooker. Stir, cover, and cook on High for about 2 hours or on Low for about 6 hours.

---

Per serving: Calories: 370; Total fat: 14g; Saturated fat: 3g; Protein: 24g; Carbohydrates: 35g; Sugar: 50g; Fiber: 4g; Sodium: 1,386mg

# Creamy Green Curry with Pork

APPLIANCE, DAIRY-FREE, GLUTEN-FREE, NUT-FREE ........................................

This is a dish inspired by the many curries of Thailand. It's made with green chili curry paste, which makes the dish mildly spicy. The coconut cream adds creaminess to the dish while tamping down the heat from the curry paste. You may replace the green curry paste with any other curry paste of your liking, including red curry paste for a spicier version.

**2 pounds boneless pork shoulder, cut into ¾-inch cubes, at room temperature**

Salt

Freshly ground black pepper

2 tablespoons olive oil

**¼ cup green curry paste**

**2 cups low-sodium chicken broth**

**1 (12-ounce) bag frozen broccoli florets**

**1 (13.5-ounce) can coconut cream**

---

**Serves** 4 to 6
**Prep time:** 5 minutes
**Cook time:** 50 minutes

1. Pat the pork dry and season with salt and pepper. Heat a large Dutch oven over medium-high heat. Pour in the oil and swirl it around the pot to evenly coat the bottom. Add the pork pieces and cook, stirring occasionally, for 6 to 8 minutes, or until lightly browned.

2. Stir in the green curry paste and broth, then add the broccoli. Bring to a boil. Reduce the heat to medium-low, cover, and cook, stirring occasionally, for 30 to 40 minutes, or until the pork is tender.

3. Stir in the coconut cream. Taste and adjust the seasoning, if needed. Serve.

**APPLIANCE TIP:** To make this dish using a slow cooker, follow step 1 as directed. Then, transfer the pork to the slow cooker, and stir in the green curry paste, broth, and broccoli. Cover and cook on High for 2 to 3 hours, or on Low for 6 to 8 hours. Stir in the coconut cream, adjust the seasoning if necessary, and serve.

**WASTE-NOT TIP:** Use leftover green curry paste to replace the curry paste in the Shortcut Chicken Curry (page 163).

---

Per serving: Calories: 851; Total fat: 50g; Saturated fat: 15g; Protein: 62g; Carbohydrates: 38g; Sugar: 28g; Fiber: 3g; Sodium: 750mg

# Pork Adobo

.....................................................

Adobo is the unofficial national dish of the Philippines. It's a stew that consists of meat marinated in a tangy sauce, then browned in oil and simmered. This recipe takes a shortcut by using an adobo sauce mix to coat the meat. You can cut the cooking time significantly by using a pressure cooker (see the Appliance tip below).

**2 pounds boneless pork shoulder, cut into ½-inch cubes, at room temperature**

Salt

Freshly ground black pepper

**2 (1.76-ounce) packages adobo sauce mix, such as Mama Sita's brand, divided**

2 tablespoons olive oil

2 cups water

**Serves** 4 to 6
**Prep time:** 5 minutes
**Cook time:** 45 minutes

1. Pat the pork pieces dry and season with salt and pepper. Put the pork in a large bowl and then stir in one package of the adobo mix until the pork is fully coated with the spices.

2. Heat a large Dutch oven over medium-high heat. Pour in the oil and swirl it around the pot to evenly coat the bottom. Add the pork pieces and cook, stirring occasionally, for 4 to 7 minutes, or until browned.

3. Stir in the remaining package of adobo mix and then stir in the water. Bring to a boil. Reduce the heat to medium-low, cover, and cook, stirring occasionally, for 25 to 35 minutes, or until the pork is tender. Taste and adjust the seasoning, if needed. Serve.

**APPLIANCE TIP:** To use a pressure cooker: Select the Sauté function to preheat a 6-quart pressure cooker. Follow step 1. When the pressure cooker is hot, pour in the oil and brown the pork for 4 to 7 minutes, stirring occasionally. Stir in the remaining package of adobo mix and the water. Lock the lid, select High Pressure, and set the cook time for 15 minutes. Let the pressure naturally release for about 10 minutes once the cooking time is done, then quick-release any remaining pressure.

**STORAGE TIP:** Leftovers can be frozen for up to 3 months.

Per serving: Calories: 680; Total fat: 49g; Saturated fat: 15g; Protein: 42g; Carbohydrates: 16g; Sugar: 12g; Fiber: 0g; Sodium: 2,050mg

# Cuban-Style Beef Picadillo

**APPLIANCE, DAIRY-FREE, GLUTEN-FREE, NUT-FREE, QUICK**..........................................

Picadillo (from the Spanish verb *picar*, meaning "to mince") is a traditional Cuban dish. It's made from ground beef, tomatoes or tomato sauce, olives, and raisins, which give it a touch of sweetness. It's usually served with white rice or used as a filling for tacos, croquettes, and empanadas.

**2 pounds lean ground beef**

1 medium yellow
    onion, chopped

Salt

Freshly ground black pepper

**2 (8-ounce) cans
    tomato sauce**

**1 (10-ounce) jar green
    olives, drained**

**¼ cup raisins**

Juice of 1 lemon

**Serves** 4 to 6
**Prep time:** 5 minutes
**Cook time:** 15 minutes

1. Heat a large nonstick skillet over medium-high heat. Put the ground beef in the skillet and cook, stirring and breaking up the meat, for about 5 minutes, or until lightly browned. Drain off most of the fat. Reduce the heat to medium, add the onion, and cook, stirring occasionally, for about 5 minutes, or until softened. Season with salt and pepper.

2. Stir in the tomato sauce, olives, and raisins. Increase the heat to medium-high and bring to a boil. Reduce the heat to medium-low and let simmer, uncovered, for about 5 minutes, or until the raisins are softened. Stir in the lemon juice.

**APPLIANCE TIP:** To use a slow cooker: Follow step 1. Then, transfer the beef and onion to the slow cooker and stir in the tomato sauce. Cover and cook on High for 2 hours or on Low for 6 to 8 hours. One hour before the cooking time ends, stir in the olives and raisins, cover, and complete the remaining cooking time. Finally, stir in the lemon juice.

**STORAGE TIP:** Store any leftover picadillo in an airtight container in the refrigerator for up to 3 days. Freeze for up to 3 months.

Per serving: Calories: 479; Total fat: 24g; Saturated fat: 6g; Protein: 46g; Carbohydrates: 23g; Sugar: 11g; Fiber: 3g; Sodium: 1,293mg

# Spaghetti Bolognese

APPLIANCE, DAIRY-FREE, NUT-FREE, QUICK ..................................................

This recipe is a loose interpretation of an Italian classic, typical of the city of Bologna. It consists of a meat-based sauce, *ragù alla Bolognese*, served with pasta. It's homey, comforting, and robust, a dish adored by adults and children of all ages around the world.

**1 pound dry spaghetti**

2 tablespoons olive oil

1 yellow onion, chopped

**2 pounds lean ground beef**

**1 cup red wine or broth**

**1 (8-ounce) can
    tomato sauce**

---

**Serves** 4 to 6
**Prep time:** 5 minutes
**Cook time:** 25 minutes

1. Cook the pasta in a large pot of boiling salted water according to package instructions for al dente. (This should take 8 to 12 minutes.) Before draining the pasta, remove ½ cup of the water from the pot and reserve, then drain the pasta.

2. In a large nonstick skillet, heat the oil over medium heat. Add the onion and cook, stirring occasionally, for 5 to 6 minutes, or until the onion has softened. Using a slotted spoon, transfer the cooked onion to a bowl.

3. Increase the heat to medium-high, put the ground beef into the skillet, and cook, stirring and breaking up the meat, for about 5 minutes, or until lightly brown. Place onion back into the skillet. Add the wine and let cook for about 2 minutes, or until reduced by half.

4. Reduce the heat to medium-low and stir in the tomato sauce. Cook for about 5 minutes, or until heated through.

5. Put the pasta back into the pot, and then pour on the Bolognese sauce and the ½ cup of reserved pasta water. Toss gently over medium heat for about 2 minutes, or until the sauce has thickened and coats the pasta.

**APPLIANCE TIP:** To make this dish using a slow cooker, heat a large nonstick skillet over medium heat, add the oil, and cook the onion, stirring occasionally, until softened, 5 to 7 minutes. Transfer the onion to the slow cooker. Increase the heat to medium-high, put the ground beef into the skillet, and cook, stirring and breaking up the meat, for about 5 minutes, or until lightly browned. Transfer the beef to the slow cooker. Stir in the wine and tomato sauce. Cover and cook on High for 2 hours, or on Low for 6 to 8 hours. About 15 minutes before the cooking time ends, cook the pasta as directed in step 1.

**WASTE-NOT TIP:** Use any leftover red wine as an add-on to beef stews such as the Cuban-Style Beef Picadillo (page 177), giving the dish added depth of flavor.

Per serving: Calories: 883; Total fat: 25g; Saturated fat: 7g; Protein: 60g; Carbohydrates: 94g; Sugar: 7g; Fiber: 4g; Sodium: 502mg

# Garlic and Basil Beef

**APPLIANCE, DAIRY-FREE, NUT-FREE, QUICK** ............................................................

Garlic and Basil Beef is a loose adaptation of the popular Thai dish pad kra pao ("stir-fried holy basil"). It's quick and easy to make, as well as fragrant, garlicky, and spicy, with a savory-sweet flavor. It makes the perfect weeknight meal for busy days. For a mild version, skip the chiles. For a gluten-free dish, use tamari or a gluten-free soy sauce.

............................................................

**2 pounds ground beef**

8 garlic cloves, minced

**2 bird's-eye chiles, thinly sliced**

2 tablespoons brown sugar

**¼ cup low-sodium soy sauce**

Juice of 2 limes

**1 cup Thai basil**

---

**Serves** 4 to 6
**Prep time:** 5 minutes
**Cook time:** 10 minutes

1. Heat a large nonstick skillet over medium-high heat. Put the ground beef in the skillet and cook, stirring and breaking up the meat, for about 5 minutes, or until lightly browned. Drain any excess fat.
2. Add the garlic and chiles and cook, stirring occasionally, until fragrant, 1 to 2 minutes.
3. Add the sugar, soy sauce, lime juice, and basil. Cook until the basil just starts to wilt, about 1 minute.

**VARIATION TIP:** Replace the bird's-eye chiles with either serrano peppers or with 1 teaspoon of ground cayenne pepper. You may also substitute regular basil for Thai basil.

**APPLIANCE TIP:** To make this dish using a slow cooker, place the ground beef, garlic, chiles, sugar, and soy sauce in the slow cooker. Add 1 cup of water. Stir until combined, cover, and cook on High for 2 hours, or on Low for 6 to 8 hours. About 20 minutes before the cooking time ends, stir in the lime juice and the basil. Cover and let cook for the remaining 20 minutes.

---

Per serving: Calories: 365; Total fat: 16g; Saturated fat: 6g; Protein: 46g; Carbohydrates: 10g; Sugar: 5g; Fiber: 1g; Sodium: 745mg

# Creamy Red Curry with Beef

**APPLIANCE, DAIRY-FREE, GLUTEN-FREE, NUT-FREE**..............................................

This is another Thai-inspired curry. Unlike the green curry, it's much spicier because the base is made from red chiles. Its spiciness is calmed a bit by the coconut cream, which also adds a velvety texture. For a milder version, you can replace the red curry paste with green curry paste.

**2 pounds lean stew beef, at room temperature**

Salt

Freshly ground black pepper

2 tablespoons olive oil

**2 tablespoons red curry paste**

**2 cups beef broth**

**1 (6- to 10-ounce) bag fresh baby spinach**

**1 (13.5-ounce) can coconut cream**

**Serves** 4 to 6
**Prep time:** 5 minutes
**Cook time:** 75 minutes

1. Pat the beef pieces dry and season with salt and pepper.
2. Heat a large Dutch oven over medium-high heat. Pour in the oil and swirl it around the pot to evenly coat the bottom. Add the beef and cook, stirring occasionally, for 5 to 7 minutes, or until browned.
3. Stir in the red curry paste and then stir in the broth. Bring to a boil. Reduce the heat to medium-low, cover, and cook, stirring occasionally, for 55 to 60 minutes, or until beef is fork-tender. Add the spinach and the coconut cream, and let the dish cook, uncovered, for about 5 minutes. Taste and adjust seasoning, if needed.

**APPLIANCE TIP:** To make this dish using a slow cooker, follow steps 1 and 2 as directed. Then, transfer the beef to the slow cooker and stir in the red curry paste and broth. Cover and cook on High for 2 to 4 hours, or on Low for 6 to 8 hours. About 10 minutes before the cooking time ends, stir in the spinach and the coconut cream. Cover and let the dish cook for the remaining 10 minutes. Taste and adjust the seasoning, if needed.

**WASTE-NOT TIP:** You can use the red curry paste to make a spicier spin on Creamy Green Curry with Pork (page 175).

Per serving: Calories: 596; Total fat: 43g; Saturated fat: 23g; Protein: 46g; Carbohydrates: 3g; Sugar: 1g; Fiber: 1g; Sodium: 292mg

# Yellow Curry with Beef and Potatoes

DAIRY-FREE, GLUTEN-FREE, NUT-FREE .................................................

This curry is a Thai-inspired dish with the addition of creamy Yukon Gold potatoes. The yellow curry makes the dish medium-spicy. To help remember how spicy different curry pastes are, use a traffic light analogy: red (stop) = spicy, yellow (caution) = medium-spicy, and green (go) = mild. Easy, right?

**2 pounds lean stew beef, at room temperature**

Salt

Freshly ground black pepper

2 tablespoons olive oil

6 garlic cloves, minced

**¼ cup yellow curry paste**

**3 cups beef broth**

**12 ounces Yukon Gold potatoes, cut into chunks**

**1 (13.5-ounce) can coconut cream**

---

**Serves** 4 to 6
**Prep time:** 5 minutes
**Cook time:** 1 hour
15 minutes

1. Pat the beef pieces dry and season them with salt and pepper.
2. Heat a large Dutch oven over medium-high heat. Pour in the oil and swirl it around the pot to evenly coat the bottom. Add the beef and cook, stirring occasionally, for 5 to 7 minutes, or until browned. Add the garlic and cook, stirring occasionally, for 1 to 2 minutes or until fragrant.
3. Stir in the yellow curry paste and then stir in the broth and the potatoes. Bring to a boil. Reduce the heat to medium-low, cover, and cook, stirring occasionally, for 55 to 60 minutes, or until the beef and potatoes are both tender. Add the coconut cream and let the dish cook, uncovered, for about 5 minutes. Taste and adjust the seasoning, if needed. Serve.

**STORAGE TIP:** Store any leftovers in an airtight container in the refrigerator for up to 3 days. Freezing is not recommended as the sauce may separate.

**WASTE-NOT TIP:** Use the broth and yellow curry paste to make the Creamy Green Curry with Pork (page 175) and the Creamy Red Curry with Beef (page 181). The yellow curry paste can replace the green and red curry pastes in those recipes.

---

Per serving: Calories: 673; Total fat: 43g; Saturated fat: 23g; Protein: 51g; Carbohydrates: 20g; Sugar: 3g; Fiber: 2g; Sodium: 823mg

# Spicy Lamb Madras

**APPLIANCE, DAIRY-FREE** ...........................................................

Madras curry sauce, usually made with lamb, is rich in red chiles, which makes it spicy. The preparation in this recipe has been shortened significantly by using a store-bought sauce. To calm the fiery taste, you can serve the dish with yogurt or stir one cup of yogurt into the stew once it's fully cooked.

**2 pounds lamb shoulder, cut into 1½-inch chunks, at room temperature**

Salt

Freshly ground black pepper

⅓ cup all-purpose flour

4 tablespoons olive oil, divided

6 garlic cloves, minced

**2 cups beef broth, divided**

**1 (10- to 12-ounce) jar Madras curry sauce**

---

**Serves** 4 to 6
**Prep time:** 5 minutes
**Cook time:** 40 minutes

1. Pat the lamb pieces dry. Place them into a large resealable plastic bag, generously season with salt and pepper, and add the flour. Seal and shake well to fully coat the lamb.

2. Heat a medium nonstick stockpot or Dutch oven over medium-high heat. Add 3 tablespoons of oil and evenly coat the bottom. Add the lamb and cook, undisturbed, until the lamb is lightly browned, 3 to 4 minutes. Using a slotted spoon, transfer the lamb to a bowl.

3. Reduce the heat to medium, add the remaining 1 tablespoon of oil, and cook the garlic until fragrant, about 1 minute. Pour in a little bit of the broth and scrape the browned bits from the bottom.

4. Add the lamb back to the pan, increase the heat to medium-high, stir in the remaining broth and the Madras sauce, and bring all to a boil. Reduce the heat to medium-low, stir, and cover the pan. Let simmer for 30 to 35 minutes, or until the lamb is cooked through. Taste and adjust the seasoning, if needed.

**APPLIANCE TIP:** To use a slow cooker: Follow steps 1 and 2. Then put the lamb, garlic, only 1 cup of broth, and the Madras sauce into the slow cooker. Stir, cover, and cook on High for 3 to 4 hours or on Low for 6 to 8 hours.

---

Per serving: Calories: 667; Total fat: 43g; Saturated fat: 13g; Protein: 48g; Carbohydrates: 22g; Sugar: 8g; Fiber: 2g; Sodium: 933mg

*Mussels in Creamy Wine Sauce* **190**

# 8

## *Fish and Seafood*

# Shrimp a la Diabla

DAIRY-FREE, GLUTEN-FREE, NUT-FREE, QUICK..................................................

This dish was inspired by the Mexican dish *camarones a la diabla*, which translates to "deviled shrimp," and has some spice to it, as the name suggests. For a milder version, substitute ½ teaspoon of red pepper flakes for the chipotle pepper. Serve over white rice or pasta, or with crusty bread to soak up the sauce.

**2 pounds raw large shrimp, peeled, deveined, and tails off, at room temperature (see Prep Tip)**

Salt

Freshly ground black pepper

3 tablespoons olive oil, divided

7 garlic cloves, minced

**2 (29-ounce) cans tomato puree**

¼ cup water

**2 chipotle chiles, in adobo sauce**

**Serves** 4
**Prep time:** 10 minutes
**Cook time:** 20 minutes

1. Pat the shrimp dry with paper towels and season them with salt and pepper.
2. Heat a large nonstick saucepan over medium heat. Pour in 1 tablespoon of oil, then add the garlic and cook for 1 minute, stirring occasionally.
3. Transfer the garlic to a blender with the tomato puree, water, chipotle peppers, and a pinch each of salt and pepper. Blend until smooth. Pour the sauce into the saucepan, cover, and cook over medium-low heat for 15 minutes, or until the sauce thickens slightly.
4. Heat a large nonstick skillet over medium heat, add the remaining 2 tablespoons of oil, and cook the shrimp until they turn pink, 3 to 4 minutes. Add the shrimp to the sauce and toss to combine. Taste and adjust the seasoning, if needed.

**PREP TIP:** Thaw frozen shrimp in the refrigerator and let drain in a colander to remove excess water. Pat the shrimp dry before seasoning. Make sure to use raw shrimp—not cooked and then frozen shrimp.

**WASTE-NOT TIP:** Use leftover chipotle peppers to make Chipotle Sauce (page 213) or to add punch to soups and stews.

Per serving: Calories: 515; Total fat: 16g; Saturated fat: 2g; Protein: 54g; Carbohydrates: 43g; Sugar: 22; Fiber: 9g; Sodium: 2,188mg

# Shrimp Scampi with Orzo

NUT-FREE, QUICK ...........................................................................................

Comforting, creamy, and satisfying—this dish is an Italian American meal at its best! It's also easy to customize to your needs: for a spicier version of the dish, add ½ teaspoon of red pepper flakes along with the wine and cream. You can replace the orzo with spaghetti or any other pasta, and you can substitute chicken or vegetable broth for the wine. To add an extra touch of freshness, try sprinkling 1 to 2 tablespoons of chopped parsley over the top.

.............................................................................................................

**1¼ pounds large raw shrimp, peeled, deveined, and tails-off, thawed to room temperature**

Salt

Freshly ground black pepper

**8 ounces dried orzo**

2 tablespoons olive oil

6 cloves garlic, minced

**½ cup white wine or broth**

**½ cup heavy cream**

Juice of 1 lemon

**½ cup shredded Parmesan cheese (optional)**

---

**Serves** 4
**Prep time:** 5 minutes
**Cook time:** 25 minutes

1. Pat the shrimp dry and season it with salt and pepper.
2. In a large nonstick pot, prepare the orzo according to the package instructions, cooking it for about 15 minutes or until the liquid is absorbed and the orzo is tender (or the time indicated on the package instructions). Transfer the cooked orzo to a large bowl.
3. Heat the same pot over medium heat. Pour in the oil, then add the garlic and cook for 1 minute, stirring occasionally. Add the shrimp and cook until they almost turn pink, about 3 minutes.
4. Add the wine and reduce for 1 minute. Stir in the heavy cream and cook for 1 to 2 minutes more.
5. Stir in the lemon juice. Taste and adjust the seasoning, if needed. Add the cooked orzo and toss until well combined. Serve with Parmesan on top, if desired.

**WASTE-NOT TIP:** Use leftover heavy cream in the Creamy Tomato Bisque (page 99), Mushroom Fettuccine with Shaved Parmesan (page 139), or Spaghetti with Roasted Bell Pepper Sauce and Basil (page 138).

---

Per serving: Calories: 543; Total fat: 22g; Saturated fat: 8g; Protein: 37g; Carbohydrates: 46g; Sugar: 3g; Fiber: 2g; Sodium: 227mg

# Quick Paella with Broiled Shrimp

**DAIRY-FREE, GLUTEN-FREE, NUT-FREE, QUICK** ............................................................

This one-pot dish is a quick and easy version of the iconic Spanish paella. The colorful presentation is just beautiful, and because it's a cinch to make, it works well as both a family weeknight dinner and a show-stopping centerpiece for a dinner party. Either sauvignon blanc or chardonnay would make a great pairing, along with good company.

..............................................................................................................

3 tablespoons olive
   oil, divided

6 cloves garlic, minced

**1½ cups long-grain
   parboiled rice**

**1 (14.5-ounce) can diced
   tomatoes, drained**

**3 cups chicken broth**

Salt

Freshly ground black pepper

**1 pound large raw shrimp,
   peeled, deveined, and
   tails-off, thawed to
   room temperature and
   patted dry**

Juice of 1 lemon

**½ cup fresh basil leaves**

**Serves** 4
**Prep time:** 5 minutes
**Cook time:** 25 minutes

1. In a 5- to 6-quart oven-safe skillet, heat 2 tablespoons of oil over medium heat. Add the garlic and cook for 1 minute, stirring occasionally. Add the rice and cook for 1 minute more, stirring occasionally. Stir in the tomatoes, the broth, and a pinch each of salt and pepper. Increase the heat to high and bring to a boil.

2. Reduce the heat to medium-low, stir, and cover. Simmer for 15 to 20 minutes, or until the rice is soft but still holds a firm shape. Remove from the heat and lightly fluff the rice with a fork.

3. While the rice is cooking, place an oven rack in the top position. Preheat the broiler.

4. In a large bowl, toss the shrimp with the remaining 1 tablespoon of oil and season with salt and pepper.

5. Once the rice is cooked, arrange the shrimp on top of the rice and broil until the shrimp turns pink, 3 to 4 minutes. Squeeze the lemon juice on top of the shrimp and garnish with the basil.

**VARIATION TIP**: For a spicy version, stir in ½ to 1 teaspoon of red pepper flakes when adding the broth. Replace the white rice with any other rice, adjusting the cooking time and amount of broth according to the package instructions.

Per serving: Calories: 504; Total fat: 13g; Saturated fat: 2g; Protein: 30g; Carbohydrates: 63g; Sugar: 4g; Fiber: 2g; Sodium: 795mg

# Garlic Chili Prawns

**DAIRY-FREE, GLUTEN-FREE, NUT-FREE, QUICK** .....................................................

These chili prawns are simple, spicy, and garlicky, with a fresh touch of basil. They may be served as an appetizer or over rice or noodles to make a complete meal. If you can't find Thai basil, Italian basil is a great substitute. For a mild version, substitute tomato puree for chili paste.

**16 to 20 raw prawns or extra-large or jumbo shrimp, peeled, deveined, and tails-off, at room temperature**

Salt

Freshly ground black pepper

2 tablespoons olive oil

6 garlic cloves, minced

**2 teaspoons chili paste**

Juice of 1 lemon

**2 tablespoons chopped Thai basil**

---

**Serves** 4
**Prep time:** 5 minutes
**Cook time:** 10 minutes, plus 10 to 15 minutes to come to room temperature

1. Pat the prawns dry with paper towels and season them with salt and pepper.
2. Heat a large nonstick skillet over medium heat. Pour in the oil, and then add the garlic and cook for 1 minute, stirring occasionally. Stir in the chili paste.
3. Add the prawns and cook for 4 to 5 minutes or until they turn pink. Squeeze the lemon juice over the prawns and add the basil, either stirred in or as a garnish for the top of the dish.

**PREP TIP:** If using frozen prawns or shrimp, make sure to thaw them in the refrigerator and let them drain in a colander to remove excess water. Pat the prawns dry before seasoning.

**WASTE-NOT TIP:** Use surplus chili paste in soups and stews, to make the spicy version of our Creamy Tomato Bisque (page 99), to replace harissa in Roasted Cauliflower Steak with Harissa (page 131), or to replace chipotle peppers in Shrimp a la Diabla (page 186).

---

Per serving: Calories: 123; Total fat: 8g; Saturated fat: 1g; Protein: 10g; Carbohydrates: 4g; Sugar: 1g; Fiber: <1g; Sodium: 142mg

# Mussels in Creamy Wine Sauce

**GLUTEN-FREE, NUT-FREE, QUICK** ...........................................................

This is an adaptation of the classic French dish *moules marinières*, or "mussels in white wine." It's a quick, one-pot meal that is best served with crusty bread for soaking up the garlicky broth. You can also serve this with French fries, a common accompaniment for mussels. A glass of pinot grigio, sauvignon blanc, or chardonnay is the perfect pairing for the grown-ups at the table.

...........................................................

3 tablespoons
   unsalted butter

8 garlic cloves, minced

1½ cups dry white wine
   or broth

2 pounds fresh, uncooked
   mussels (see tip)

⅓ cup heavy cream

Salt

Freshly ground black pepper

2 tablespoons
   chopped parsley

---

**Serves** 4
**Prep time:** 15 minutes
**Cook time:** 15 minutes

1. Heat a large Dutch oven over medium heat. Drop in the butter and let it melt, and then add the garlic and cook it for about 2 minutes, stirring occasionally, until softened and fragrant. Stir in the wine, increase the heat to high, and bring the wine to a boil. Then reduce the heat to medium-low and let simmer until the wine is reduced by half, 5 to 6 minutes.

2. Stir in the mussels, cover, and let them cook for about 4 minutes. Stir in the cream and simmer for 2 to 3 minutes more, or until the mussels open. Discard any shells that have not opened.

3. Season with salt and pepper and top with parsley.

**PREP TIP:** Buy tightly closed mussels (a sign of freshness). Store them in the refrigerator and cook them on the day of purchase. Before cooking, place the mussels in a colander under cold running water. Discard any that are open. Scrub each to get rid of grime and barnacles, and pull off the hairy "beard" that sticks out of the shell. Do not submerge them under water as this will kill them.

**VARIATION TIP:** For a spicy version, stir in ½ teaspoon of red pepper flakes when adding the wine. You can also swap a light ale-style beer for the wine.

---

Per serving: Calories: 604; Total fat: 26g; Saturated fat: 12g; Protein: 55g; Carbohydrates: 20g; Sugar: 2g; Fiber: <1g; Sodium: 852mg

# Seared Scallops with Honey–Soy Glaze

**DAIRY-FREE, NUT-FREE, QUICK** ................................................................

These scallops are sweet and tangy with an appealing golden-brown sear. It's easy to adapt this recipe to your preferences. You can substitute pineapple juice for the lemon juice for a tropical twist or replace the soy sauce with teriyaki. If you're allergic to gluten, use tamari or another gluten-free soy sauce. Serve the scallops by themselves as an appetizer or over sticky rice as a main dish.

..............................................................................................

**1 cup honey**

**½ cup low-sodium soy sauce**

6 garlic cloves, minced

Juice of 2 lemons

**2 pounds raw large sea scallops, thawed and patted dry**

2 tablespoons olive oil

Salt

Freshly ground black pepper

**2 teaspoons toasted sesame seeds (optional)**

---

**Serves** 4

**Prep time:** 5 minutes

**Cook time:** 10 minutes, plus 30 minutes to marinate

1. In a large bowl, whisk together the honey, soy sauce, garlic, and lemon juice. Transfer half of the mixture to a small bowl and set aside.

2. Place the scallops in the large bowl containing half of the marinade and toss to coat. Marinate for 30 minutes in the refrigerator. After the scallops have marinated, drain them and discard the marinade.

3. Heat a large nonstick pan over high heat. Pour in the oil, then add the scallops to the pan. Season with salt and pepper.

4. Cook the scallops for 3 to 3½ minutes on each side, or until they have a golden-brown sear. Transfer the scallops to a plate.

5. Pour the marinade reserved in the small bowl into the pan and cook until the sauce starts to thicken, about 2 minutes. Add the scallops back into the pan and coat with the sauce. If using, sprinkle with sesame seeds before serving.

**VARIATION TIP**: For a spicy version, add a few drops of hot sauce or ¼ teaspoon red pepper flakes to the sauce.

---

Per serving: Calories: 547; Total fat: 9g; Saturated fat: 1g; Protein: 41g; Carbohydrates: 81g; Sugar: 70g; Fiber: 1g; Sodium: 1,512mg

# Baked Cajun Tilapia with White Wine

..............................................

This dish uses the French technique *en papillote*, which retains moisture by steaming the fish in packets made of parchment paper (or, in this case, aluminum foil). It's an easy, mess-free preparation that doesn't require any special cooking skills. All you have to do is assemble the packets with a few ingredients and bake. Feel free to use a mix of the frozen vegetables you like best and replace the white wine with chicken broth, if desired. If using frozen tilapia fillets, make sure to thaw them in the refrigerator, press to remove excess water, and pat dry before cooking.

..............................................

**4 (4- to 6-ounce) tilapia fillets, patted dry**

Salt

Freshly ground black pepper

**4 teaspoons Cajun seasoning**

**1 pound frozen bell pepper and onion blend**

4 tablespoons olive oil

**4 tablespoons white wine**

---

**Serves** 4
**Prep time:** 5 minutes
**Cook time:** 15 minutes, plus 15 minutes to rest

1. Preheat the oven to 400°F. Season the fillets on both sides with salt, pepper, and Cajun seasoning.

2. Tear off four (15-inch-long) sheets of heavy-duty aluminum foil. Place ½ cup of the frozen vegetables in the center of each foil sheet and top with one tilapia fillet. Drizzle each fillet with 1 tablespoon of olive oil and 1 tablespoon of wine.

3. Fold the aluminum foil over the center contents, crimp edges to seal, and place the packets in a single layer on a baking sheet.

4. Bake the packets for about 15 minutes. The fish will be done when it's opaque and flakes easily when tested with a fork.

**STORAGE TIP:** Store the cooked fish and vegetables in an airtight container in the refrigerator for 2 to 3 days. Freeze for up to one month. Thaw in the refrigerator and reheat in the microwave for 1 to 2 minutes, or until heated through.

**WASTE-NOT TIP:** Use leftover frozen vegetables to make Hawaiian-Inspired Turkey Meatballs (page 166) or Chicken Fajitas (page 153).

---

Per serving: Calories: 271; Total fat: 16g; Saturated fat: 3g; Protein: 23g; Carbohydrates: 8g; Sugar: 4g; Fiber: 1g; Sodium: 265mg

# Panfried Brown Sugar and Bourbon—Blackened Tilapia

**DAIRY-FREE, GLUTEN-FREE, NUT-FREE, QUICK** ....................................................

This dish channels New Orleans with its bold Cajun spices. If you're adventurous, add ¼ to ½ teaspoon of red pepper flakes to the brown sugar and bourbon seasoning, or serve the fillets with a few drops of hot sauce on top.

**4 (4- to 6-ounce) tilapia fillets, at room temperature**

Salt

Freshly ground black pepper

**2 tablespoons brown sugar bourbon seasoning, such as McCormick brand**

2 tablespoons olive oil

**1 tablespoon unsalted butter**

2 lemons

**1 tablespoon chopped chives (optional)**

---

**Serves** 4
**Prep time:** 5 minutes
**Cook time:** 10 minutes, plus 15 minutes to rest

1. Pat the tilapia fillets dry with paper towels and season them on both sides with salt, pepper, and the brown sugar bourbon seasoning.

2. Heat a large nonstick skillet over medium-high heat. Pour in the oil. Place the fillets in the pan and cook for 2 to 3 minutes. Flip them, add the butter to the pan, and cook the fillets for an additional 2 to 3 minutes, or until browned.

3. Squeeze the juice of 1 lemon over the fillets and sprinkle with the chives, if using. Serve the fish immediately with wedges of the remaining 1 lemon on the side.

**INGREDIENT TIP**: I've had good lucking finding the brown sugar bourbon seasoning at stores like Walmart and Target, but if you can't find it near you, or if it's too sweet, use a combination of 1 tablespoon of brown sugar and 1 teaspoon each of salt, garlic powder, and onion powder. Feel free to experiment with these proportions to make your own signature blend.

**VARIATION TIP**: If using frozen tilapia, make sure to thaw the fillets in the refrigerator, press them well to remove excess water, and pat dry; otherwise, they won't turn out crisp.

---

Per serving: Calories: 221; Total fat: 12g; Saturated fat: 4g; Protein: 24g; Carbohydrates: 9g; Sugar: 2g; Fiber: 3g; Sodium: 662mg

# Baked Cod with Tomatoes, Artichokes, and Bell Peppers

**DAIRY-FREE, GLUTEN-FREE, NUT-FREE** .....................................................

In this Mediterranean-inspired dish, the wine and vegetables add zing while still allowing the cod to shine. If you want to use frozen cod, just thaw it in the refrigerator and press to remove excess water before baking. Serve with crusty bread, or over pasta or rice.

2 tablespoons olive oil, plus more for greasing

**4 (4- to 6-ounce) fresh cod fillets, at room temperature**

Salt

Freshly ground black pepper

Juice of 1 lemon

**1 pound frozen bell pepper and onion blend, thawed and excess water removed**

**1 (14.5-ounce) can diced tomatoes, half drained**

**1 (14-ounce) can quartered artichoke hearts, drained**

**½ cup white wine or broth**

**Serves** 4
**Prep time:** 5 minutes
**Cook time:** 25 minutes

1. Position a rack in the center of the oven and preheat the oven to 375°F. Lightly grease a 9-by-13-inch baking dish with oil.

2. Pat the cod fillets dry with paper towels and season with salt and pepper on both sides. Arrange the fillets in the prepared dish and drizzle lemon juice over the top.

3. Heat a large nonstick skillet over medium heat. Pour in the 2 tablespoons of oil and cook the bell pepper and onion blend, stirring occasionally, for 6 to 8 minutes, or until tender.

4. Add the diced tomatoes with half of their juices, along with the artichokes, wine, and a pinch each of salt and pepper. Stir and let cook for 1 to 2 minutes to blend the flavors together.

5. Pour the vegetable mixture over and around the cod in the baking dish. Cover with foil and bake for 10 to 12 minutes, or until the cod is opaque and flakes easily when tested with a fork.

Per serving: Calories: 285; Total fat: 8g; Saturated fat: 1g; Protein: 28g; Carbohydrates: 17g; Sugar: 8g; Fiber: 4g; Sodium: 550mg

# Portuguese–Style Cod with Potatoes and Olives

**DAIRY-FREE, GLUTEN-FREE, NUT-FREE** ...............................................................

This is a complete, one-pan dish inspired by the cuisine of my Portuguese ancestors. To use frozen fish, make sure to thaw it in the refrigerator and press it to remove excess water.

.........................................................................................................................

4 (4- to 6-ounce) fresh cod fillets, at room temperature

2 pounds baby potatoes, patted dry and quartered

2 tablespoons olive oil, divided, plus more for drizzling

Salt

Freshly ground black pepper

1 teaspoon garlic powder

1 (14.5-ounce) can diced tomatoes, drained

½ cup pitted green or kalamata olives, drained

Juice of 1 lemon

---

**Serves** 4
**Prep time:** 10 minutes
**Cook time:** 40 minutes

1. Pat the cod fillets dry with paper towels. Preheat the oven to 450°F.

2. Toss the potatoes with 1 tablespoon of oil on a large baking sheet. Season them well with salt and pepper. Arrange the potatoes in a single layer, cut-side down, and bake for 20 to 25 minutes, or until they begin to brown. Make sure to toss potatoes once halfway through the baking time.

3. Five minutes before the baking time ends, brush the cod fillets on both sides with the remaining 1 tablespoon of oil and season with salt and pepper on both sides. Sprinkle the garlic powder on the tops of the fillets only.

4. Remove the pan from the oven, add the tomatoes and olives to the potatoes, and stir. Slide all of the vegetables to one side of the pan and place the fillets in a single layer next to the vegetables. Bake for 8 to 12 minutes, or until the cod is tender and flaky and the potatoes are browned and cooked through.

5. Drizzle lemon juice over the fish and the vegetables. Pour just a drizzle of olive oil on top of the fillets.

---

Per serving: Calories: 405; Total fat: 12g; Saturated fat: 1g; Protein: 30g; Carbohydrates: 43g; Sugar: 5g; Fiber: 6g; Sodium: 573mg

# Panfried Crispy Catfish

DAIRY-FREE, NUT-FREE, QUICK ...................................................

These catfish fillets are incredibly easy to make and can be served on a bed of cooked vegetables or topped with a remoulade sauce (see page 214 to make your own), garlic mayonnaise, or tartar sauce. They are crispy, with a mouthwatering golden-brown crust. I like to use Cajun or Creole seasoning for this dish, but you can use the seasoning blend of your choice, such as taco seasoning, to create your own variation.

......................................................................................

**4 (4- to 5-ounce) catfish fillets, thawed and patted dry, at room temperature**
Salt
Freshly ground black pepper
1 cup all-purpose flour
**1 tablespoon Cajun seasoning**
4 tablespoons olive oil
Juice of 1 lemon

**Serves** 4
**Prep time:** 10 minutes
**Cook time:** 10 minutes, plus 10 minutes to rest

1. Season the catfish fillets with salt and pepper on both sides.
2. In a large bowl, mix together the flour and the Cajun seasoning.
3. Coat the fillets with the flour mixture, pressing down firmly so the mixture adheres. Shake off any excess seasoning.
4. Heat a large nonstick skillet over medium-high heat. Pour in the oil and heat it until it shimmers. Swirl the oil around the skillet to evenly coat the bottom.
5. Place the fillets in the skillet and cook for 2 to 3 minutes per side, or until golden brown and crispy. Squeeze the lemon juice on top and serve immediately—otherwise, they will lose crispness.

Per serving: Calories: 333; Total fat: 20g; Saturated fat: 3g; Protein: 17g; Carbohydrates: 23g; Sugar: <1g; Fiber: 1g; Sodium: 625mg

# Pan-Grilled Salmon with Garlic-Maple Sauce

**DAIRY-FREE, GLUTEN-FREE, NUT-FREE, QUICK** ......................................................

Pan-grilling is a clever way to enjoy grilled seafood and meats all year round. Serve this dish with cooked vegetables and rice for a complete meal. For a high-quality and safe product, give preference to farmed Norwegian salmon, which is available in many supermarkets.

**4 (4-ounce) fresh salmon fillets, skin off, at room temperature**

Salt

Freshly ground black pepper

2 tablespoons olive oil

4 garlic cloves, minced

**4 tablespoons maple syrup**

1 tablespoon water

**2 teaspoons low-sodium soy sauce**

**1 tablespoon lemon juice, plus extra to drizzle**

---

**Serves** 4
**Prep time:** 5 minutes
**Cook time:** 10 minutes, plus 15 minutes to rest

1. Pat the salmon fillets dry with paper towels, and season them with salt and pepper on both sides.
2. Heat a large grill pan over medium-high heat. Pour in the oil. Add the garlic and cook for 30 seconds, stirring constantly. Add the maple syrup, water, and soy sauce and stir. Let the mixture heat for 40 to 60 seconds, and then stir in the lemon juice.
3. Add the salmon fillets to the pan and cook them for 3 to 4 minutes, or until they are golden and grill marks appear. Make sure to baste the tops with the pan juices.
4. Flip the fillets with a spatula and cook for an additional 3 to 4 minutes, or until cooked through. Baste the fillets again.
5. Serve the salmon drizzled with the pan juices and extra lemon juice.

**STORAGE TIP:** Store cooked fish in an airtight container in the refrigerator for 2 to 3 days. Freeze for up to 1 month. To reheat, thaw in the refrigerator and heat in the microwave for 1 to 2 minutes, or until heated through.

---

Per serving: Calories: 259; Total fat: 12g; Saturated fat: 2g; Protein: 23g; Carbohydrates: 15g; Sugar: 12g; Fiber: <1g; Sodium: 95mg

# Pan-Seared Salmon with Lemon and Garlic Caper Sauce

**DAIRY-FREE, GLUTEN-FREE, NUT-FREE, QUICK** .........................................

This simple yet flavorful dish is perfect for serving with cooked vegetables or over pasta. You can top it with chopped fresh parsley or dill, or serve it with lemon wedges, if desired. For a spicy version, add a pinch of red pepper flakes along with the butter.

**4 (4-ounce) fresh salmon fillets, skin off, at room temperature**
Salt
Freshly ground black pepper
1 tablespoon olive oil
**3 tablespoons unsalted butter**
6 garlic cloves, minced
**1 tablespoon capers, drained**
Juice of 2 lemons

**Serves** 4
**Prep time:** 5 minutes
**Cook time:** 10 minutes, plus 15 minutes to rest

1. Pat the salmon fillets dry with paper towels and season them with salt and pepper on both sides.

2. Heat a large nonstick skillet over medium-high heat, and then pour in the oil. Place the fillets into the pan and sear them for 3 to 4 minutes, or until crispy. Flip them and sear for an additional 2 to 3 minutes.

3. Add the butter and let it melt. Stir in the garlic and cook for 30 seconds. Stir in the capers and lemon juice and let cook for 30 to 60 seconds. Baste the salmon with the sauce and serve immediately.

**WASTE-NOT TIP:** Use surplus capers in the Smoked Salmon Wrap with Capers and Cream Cheese (page 120) or Olive Tapenade (page 206). They would make a nice addition to the Tangy Israeli Couscous Salad (page 116), Spaghetti with Roasted Bell Pepper Sauce and Basil (page 138), or the Individual Pita Pizzas with Red Onion and Kalamata Olives (page 134).

Per serving: Calories: 260; Total fat: 17g; Saturated fat: 7g; Protein: 24g; Carbohydrates: 4g; Sugar: 1g; Fiber: <1g; Sodium: 66mg

# Pan–Seared Ahi Tuna Bowls

**DAIRY-FREE, GLUTEN-FREE, NUT-FREE, QUICK** ......................................................

This is a dish with roots in Hawaiian cuisine, and it is traditionally made with raw fish. This satisfying version is quick to prepare and requires minimal cooking. The citrus-based, tart Japanese ponzu sauce is used to marinate the tuna, infusing it with a great flavor. You can buy a jar at the store or use the recipe on page 215 to make your own. In addition to the avocado and the spicy sriracha sauce, black sesame seeds and chopped scallions make colorful garnishes for this dish. If you can't find it in the store, you can quickly make your own sriracha mayonnaise by mixing ½ cup of mayonnaise with 1 teaspoon of sriracha hot chili sauce.

........................................................................................

**1⅓ cups uncooked long-grain white rice**

**1 pound frozen ahi tuna steaks, thawed and patted dry**

**1 cup ponzu sauce**

1 tablespoon olive oil

**2 avocados, sliced**

**½ cup sriracha mayonnaise**

---

**Serves** 4
**Prep time:** 5 minutes
**Cook time:** 25 minutes

1. In a large saucepan, cook the rice according to the package instructions. (This should take 20 to 25 minutes.)

2. Meanwhile, place the ahi tuna steaks in a large bowl and coat the steaks with the ponzu sauce. Marinate for at least 10 minutes.

3. Heat a large nonstick skillet over medium-high heat. Pour in the oil and heat until shimmering, about 2 minutes. Remove the steaks from the bowl, shake off any excess marinade, and sear for 1 to 2 minutes per side for rare or 3 to 4 minutes per side for medium.

4. Transfer the steaks to a cutting board. Let them rest for 4 to 5 minutes before cutting them into ¼-inch slices.

5. Evenly divide the rice among four serving bowls. Arrange one-quarter of the sliced tuna and one-quarter of the avocado slices over the rice in each bowl. Drizzle the sriracha mayonnaise over the tuna and avocado.

**VARIATION TIP**: To save some time, try using pre-cooked and pre-portioned sticky rice bowls, like Annie Chun's restaurant-style sticky white rice (you will need four 7.4-ounce bowls).

**WASTE-NOT TIP:** Use leftover ponzu sauce as a dipping sauce for dumplings, a marinade for meats and seafood, or to stir-fry meats and vegetables. You can also use it to drizzle over rice. You can also substitute ponzu sauce for teriyaki sauce in the Pan-Seared Pork Chops with Sweet Teriyaki Sauce (page 173).

Per serving: Calories: 739; Total fat: 37g; Saturated fat: 5g; Protein: 31g; Carbohydrates: 71g; Sugar: 8g; Fiber: 7g; Sodium: 1,870mg

# Roasted Cajun Salmon with Remoulade Sauce

This spicy season-and-bake dish is inspired by the flavors of Louisiana's Cajun fare. Remoulade sauce is a French condiment similar to an aioli. You can buy a prepared jar of remoulade or try making your own using the recipe on page 214.

4 (6-ounce) fresh salmon
  fillets, skin off

1½ tablespoons olive oil

Salt

Freshly ground black pepper

1½ tablespoons Cajun
  seasoning

1 lemon, cut in half

½ cup bottled remoulade
  sauce, for topping

**Serves** 4
**Prep time:** 5 minutes
**Cook time:** 15 minutes,
plus 20 minutes to rest

1. Preheat the oven to 450°F. Line a baking sheet with foil.

2. Pat the salmon fillets dry with paper towels, and then place the salmon fillets on the lined baking sheet. Brush the fillets with oil on both sides, and then season both sides with salt, pepper, and the Cajun seasoning.

3. Roast for 8 to 10 minutes, then turn off the oven and let the fillets sit in the closed oven for an additional 3 to 4 minutes. The fillets are ready when they are opaque and flake gently when tested with a fork.

4. Remove the salmon from the oven, squeeze lemon juice over the top, and let it rest, covered, for 4 to 5 minutes before serving. Serve with remoulade sauce on top.

**STORAGE TIP:** Store cooked fish in an airtight container in the refrigerator for 2 to 3 days. Freeze for up to one month (without the sauce).

**WASTE-NOT TIP:** Use leftover remoulade sauce as a spread for sandwiches and on seafood, such as the Panfried Crispy Catfish (page 196).

Per serving: Calories: 380; Total fat: 25g; Saturated fat: 2g; Protein: 35g; Carbohydrates: 5g; Sugar: 0g; Fiber: 2g; Sodium: 990mg

*Spinach Pesto Sauce* **207**

# 9

## Sauces, Dressings, and Condiments

# Olive Tapenade

**DAIRY-FREE, GLUTEN-FREE, NUT-FREE, QUICK, VEGAN** ...............................................

This tangy topping is commonly used as a spread for bread, to brighten hors d'oeuvres, and as a stuffing for poultry. It can instantly upgrade the flavor profile of any sandwich and works great on top of grilled meats. High-quality olives are best for this dish since the olives are the star, but whatever you have on hand will still be delicious. You can make the dish even more flavorful by using mixed olives, but if you choose black olives, make sure to get kalamata.

**1 (7- to 8-ounce) jar
green olives, drained
(about 1 cup)**

1 garlic clove, minced

**2 tablespoons capers**

2 tablespoons olive oil

**3 fresh basil leaves**

1 tablespoon freshly
squeezed lemon juice

**Makes** about 1¼ cups
**Prep time:** 5 minutes

Put the olives, garlic, capers, oil, basil, and lemon juice into a food processor and process until the mixture has the consistency of a coarse paste, for 30 to 60 seconds. Stop once or twice to scrape down the sides of the food processor. Transfer the tapenade to a bowl and serve at room temperature.

**VARIATION TIP:** You may add 1 to 2 oil-packed anchovy fillets to the recipe, if desired.

**WASTE-NOT TIP:** Use leftover capers and basil in salads, pastas, and sandwiches as well as in dishes such as the Spaghetti with Roasted Bell Pepper Sauce and Basil (page 138) or the Pan-Seared Salmon with Lemon and Garlic Caper Sauce (page 199). Use any leftover olives in pastas and salads, or as a substitute for kalamata olives in Individual Pita Pizzas with Red Onion and Kalamata Olives (page 134).

Per ¼-cup serving: Calories: 118; Total fat: 12g; Saturated fat: 1g; Protein: <1g; Carbohydrates: 4g; Sugar: <1g; Fiber: <1g; Sodium: 512mg

# Spinach Pesto Sauce

**GLUTEN-FREE, NUT-FREE, QUICK** ................................................

Pesto is a basil-based Italian sauce, originally from Genoa. It means "to pound" or "to crush," because it was originally made with a mortar and pestle. Spinach Pesto Sauce is a modern variation of traditional pesto. This version is also nut-free and has a thicker consistency than the classic. It's herby, earthy, tasty, and nutritious. Definitely a clever way to get kids to eat greens in pastas and pizzas!

**4 cups packed spinach leaves**

**2 cups packed basil leaves**

⅔ cup olive oil

**¼ cup shredded Parmesan cheese**

3 garlic cloves, minced

Juice of 1 lemon

Salt

Freshly ground black pepper

**Makes** about 2 cups
**Prep time:** 5 minutes

1. Put the spinach, basil, oil, cheese, garlic, lemon juice, and a pinch each of salt and pepper into a blender or food processor and blend until smooth. You may have to stop the machine to scrape down the sides. Taste and adjust seasoning, if needed.

2. Use immediately or store in an airtight container in the refrigerator for up to 3 days.

**VARIATION TIP:** For a spicy version, stir in ¼ teaspoon of red pepper flakes after blending. You may replace spinach with cooked kale, collard greens, or arugula. For a dairy-free version, omit the cheese and add a bit more salt. For a nutty sauce, add about 1 tablespoon of toasted pine nuts.

**WASTE-NOT TIP:** Use spinach pesto in pastas, as a spread for sandwiches, or in any recipe that calls for traditional pesto, such as the Zucchini Noodles with Pesto Sauce and Shaved Parmesan (page 137) or One-Pan Roasted Chicken Thighs with Pesto and Cherry Tomatoes (page 155). You may use leftover Parmesan in Fried Garlic and Parmesan Pasta Chips with Marinara Sauce (page 82), No-Knead Brazilian Cheese Rolls (page 80), or the Buttery Sweet Potato Noodles with Garlic and Parmesan (page 136).

Per ¼-cup serving: Calories: 180; Total fat: 19g; Saturated fat: 3g; Protein: 2g; Carbohydrates: 2g; Sugar: <1g; Fiber: 1g; Sodium: 60mg

# Chimichurri Sauce

**DAIRY-FREE, GLUTEN-FREE, NUT-FREE, QUICK, VEGAN** ......................................

Chimichurri is the South American pesto. It originally comes from Argentina, but it's also common in Uruguay and Southern Brazil. This recipe is for *chimichurri verde*, or green chimichurri, which is marvelous as a marinade for grilled and roasted meats, like the One-Pan Roasted Chicken Thighs with Pesto and Cherry Tomatoes (page 155) or the Pan-Grilled Pork Chops with Pico de Gallo (page 170).

**1 bunch fresh parsley, roughly chopped**

½ cup olive oil

**3 to 4 tablespoons red wine vinegar**

4 garlic cloves, minced

**2 tablespoons fresh oregano leaves**

½ teaspoon salt

**⅛ teaspoon red pepper flakes**

**Makes** 1 cup
**Prep time:** 5 minutes

Put the parsley, oil, vinegar, garlic, oregano, and salt into a food processor. Blend until combined and chunky, for 20 to 30 seconds. Stir in the red pepper flakes. Use immediately, or transfer to an airtight container and refrigerate for up to 2 days. If you have refrigerated it, let it come to room temperature before serving.

Per ¼-cup serving: Calories: 254; Total fat: 27g; Saturated fat: 4g; Protein: 1g; Carbohydrates: 3g; Sugar: <1g; Fiber: 1g; Sodium: 308mg

# Spicy Cilantro Sauce

**DAIRY-FREE, GLUTEN-FREE, NUT-FREE, QUICK, VEGAN** ................................................

This sauce originated in Latin America and the ingredients can vary from one country to the next. Cuba, Puerto Rico, the Dominican Republic, and the Canary Islands all have their own versions. This recipe is the spicy version of *mojo de cilantro*, or cilantro sauce, which is usually served with fish. But it's actually an herby, multipurpose sauce that also works well as a dip, a spread for sandwiches, or as a condiment or sauce for seafood and grilled meats.

**1 bunch fresh cilantro, roughly chopped**

⅓ cup olive oil

**1 serrano pepper, sliced**

4 garlic cloves, minced

3 tablespoons lime juice

¼ teaspoon salt

**⅛ teaspoon cumin**

**Makes** ¾ cup
**Prep time:** 5 minutes

Put the cilantro, oil, serrano pepper, garlic, lime juice, salt, and cumin into a food processor. Blend until combined and chunky, for 20 to 30 seconds. Use immediately, or transfer to an airtight container and refrigerate for up to 3 days. If you have refrigerated it, let it come to room temperature before serving.

**VARIATION TIP:** If you are not a fan of cilantro, you may replace it with parsley. A jalapeño can substitute for the serrano pepper, or lemon juice for the lime juice.

**WASTE-NOT TIP:** Use this sauce to replace the pesto in One-Pan Roasted Chicken Thighs with Pesto and Cherry Tomatoes (page 155), to replace the pico de gallo in Pan-Grilled Pork Chops with Pico de Gallo (page 170), as an addition to Panfried Crispy Catfish (page 196), or as a spread on the Bacon and Avocado Grilled Cheese Sandwich (page 121).

Per ¼-cup serving: Calories: 237; Total fat: 24g; Saturated fat: 3g; Protein: 2g; Carbohydrates: 4g; Sugar: 1g; Fiber: 2g; Sodium: 218mg

# Pico de Gallo

**DAIRY-FREE, GLUTEN-FREE, NUT-FREE, QUICK, VEGAN** ...............................................

*Pico de gallo* (translation: "rooster's beak") is a traditional Mexican salsa, also known as *salsa fresca* (fresh sauce) or *salsa cruda* (raw sauce). It's usually served with tacos and fajitas, but it also is great as a sauce for meats, especially the Pan-Grilled Pork Chops with Pico de Gallo on page 170, or as a dip for tortilla chips. It can lend the "it" factor to many dishes!

**4 Roma tomatoes, seeded, cut into ¼-inch pieces**

½ white onion, diced small

**1 serrano pepper, seeded, finely chopped**

**12 cilantro leaves**

Juice of 2 limes

Salt

---

**Makes** about 1¼ cups
**Prep time:** 10 minutes

In a medium bowl, gently mix together the tomatoes, onion, pepper, cilantro, lime juice, and salt. Serve immediately, or transfer to an airtight container and refrigerate for up to 3 days.

**VARIATION TIP:** You may adapt this recipe to your liking by replacing cilantro with parsley. You may also substitute a jalapeño for the serrano pepper, or lemon juice for the lime juice. But keep in mind that the traditional pico de gallo is made with the ingredients listed above. Brazil, my home country, has its own version called *vinagrete* (vinaigrette). It's milder and is made with tomatoes, green bell peppers, onions, cilantro, lime juice or vinegar, and salt.

---

Per ¼-cup serving: Calories: 38; Total fat: 1g; Saturated fat: 0g; Protein: 1g; Carbohydrates: 7g; Sugar: 6g; Fiber: 1g; Sodium: 7mg

# Lime and Cilantro Aioli

**DAIRY-FREE, GLUTEN-FREE, NUT-FREE, QUICK, VEGETARIAN** .......................................

This aioli is not a traditional recipe, but is inspired by bright Latin flavors. It shines as a replacement for regular mayonnaise or as a mild alternative to Chipotle Sauce (page 213). It can be addictive in potato salad! To switch up the flavor profile, you can replace the lime juice with lemon juice and the cilantro with parsley or basil. Just don't skimp on the garlic—the garlic is what gives this recipe its kick.

½ **cup mayonnaise**

¼ **cup cilantro,**
   **roughly chopped**

2 garlic cloves, chopped

Juice of 1 large lime

Salt

Freshly ground black pepper

**Makes** about ¾ cup
**Prep time:** 5 minutes

Put the mayonnaise, cilantro, garlic, lime juice, and a pinch each of salt and pepper into a blender or food processor and blend until smooth. Serve immediately, or transfer to an airtight container and refrigerate for up to 3 days.

**WASTE-NOT TIP:** Use leftover aioli as a flavorful condiment for hot dogs and burgers or as a spread for toasts and sandwiches. Try using it as a replacement for the chipotle aioli in the Fresh Veggie Sandwich with Chipotle Aioli (page 118) or to replace the cream cheese in the Smoked Salmon Wrap with Capers and Cream Cheese (page 120).

Per ¼-cup serving: Calories: 248; Total fat: 27g; Saturated fat: 4g; Protein: 1g; Carbohydrates: 1g; Sugar: 4g; Fiber: <1g; Sodium: 190mg

# Chipotle Sauce

.............................................

This chipotle sauce is a spicy mayonnaise-based sauce inspired by Mexican cuisine. It's perfect for drizzling on sandwiches, tacos, fancy toasts, and grilled meats or stirring into potato or chicken salads. It's creamy and spicy and gives a nice kick to any dish. Try it as a replacement for the chipotle aioli in the Fresh Veggie Sandwich with Chipotle Aioli (page 118).

**1 small chipotle pepper in adobo sauce, plus 1 tablespoon of the sauce**

**¼ cup mayonnaise**

**¼ cup plain Greek yogurt**

**2 tablespoons chopped cilantro**

Salt

**Makes** ½ cup
**Prep time:** 5 minutes

1. Combine the pepper, mayonnaise, yogurt, cilantro, and a pinch of salt into a blender or food processor and blend until smooth. Taste and adjust the salt, if needed.

2. Pour the mixture into a clean airtight container and refrigerate for up to 2 weeks.

**WASTE-NOT TIP:** Use leftover chipotle peppers in Shrimp a la Diabla (page 186) or add them to any dish that could use an extra kick—for example, you can add one or two peppers to the Creamy Tomato Bisque (page 99).

Per ¼-cup serving: Calories: 219; Total fat: 22g; Saturated fat: 4g; Protein: 1g; Carbohydrates: 4g; Sugar: 6g; Fiber: 1g; Sodium: 261mg

# Remoulade Sauce

**DAIRY-FREE, GLUTEN-FREE, NUT-FREE, QUICK, VEGETARIAN** .....................................

Remoulade, a French condiment popular in several European countries, also plays a part in Louisiana Creole cuisine. There are numerous variations with different uses, but in general, remoulade makes a great sauce for French fries, hot dogs, roast beef, seafood, and even hard-boiled eggs. You can use whatever mustard you have on hand, but I love the spice Dijon lends.

½ **cup mayonnaise**

1 garlic clove, chopped

2 **tablespoons mustard**

1 **teaspoon sweet paprika**

1 **teaspoon horseradish**

1 **teaspoon hot sauce**

---

**Makes** about ¾ cup
**Prep time:** 5 minutes, plus 30 minutes to chill

Put the mayonnaise, garlic, mustard, paprika, horseradish, and hot sauce into a blender or food processor and blend until smooth. Transfer to an airtight container and refrigerate for at least 30 minutes. Serve chilled, or store refrigerated for up to 3 days.

**VARIATION TIP:** You may replace the hot sauce with ketchup and omit the horseradish for a milder version. If you enjoy a spicy version but you don't have horseradish at home, add one more garlic clove and one more teaspoon of hot sauce to this recipe.

**WASTE-NOT TIP:** Use leftover horseradish as a condiment for meats and dishes that call for potatoes, beets, broccoli, peas, or leeks. Just a teaspoon will noticeably spice up the Autumn Potato Salad with Apple and Golden Raisins (page 115) or the Pressure Cooker Broccoli and Cheddar Soup (page 98).

---

Per ¼-cup serving: Calories: 246; Total fat: 27g; Saturated fat: 4g; Protein: 1g; Carbohydrates: 1g; Sugar: 5g; Fiber: <1g; Sodium: 336mg

# Ponzu Sauce

DAIRY-FREE, NUT-FREE, QUICK, VEGAN ..........................................................

Ponzu (meaning "punch") is a tart Japanese sauce commonly used as a marinade, dressing, and dipping sauce. This recipe is an adaptation of the classic. Use it as a dipping sauce for dumplings and sushi, drizzle it over sticky rice, or as a sauce to stir-fry meats and vegetables. Although similar in appearance to soy sauce, it has a more complex flavor. For a gluten-free version of this sauce, use tamari or a gluten-free soy sauce.

..........................................................................................................

2 teaspoons sugar

2 tablespoons warm water

2 tablespoons fresh
lime juice

**2 tablespoons mirin**

**2 tablespoons low-sodium
soy sauce**

**2 tablespoons rice vinegar**

---

**Makes** about ⅔ cup
**Prep time:** 5 minutes

In a small bowl, stir the sugar and warm water together until the sugar dissolves. Then, mix in the lime juice, mirin, soy sauce, and vinegar. Store in the refrigerator for up to 3 days.

**VARIATION TIP:** You may replace mirin, a sweet Japanese rice wine, by mixing 2 tablespoons of white wine or dry sherry with a dash of sugar.

**WASTE-NOT TIP:** Use Ponzu Sauce as a marinade for meats, as a dipping sauce, and also to stir fry meats, fish, vegetables, or tofu, including the Pan-Seared Ahi Tuna Bowls (page 200).

---

Per ⅓-cup serving: Calories: 55; Total fat: 0g; Saturated fat: 0g; Protein: 1g; Carbohydrates: 12g; Sugar: 9g; Fiber: <1g; Sodium: 705mg

# Five-Spice Barbecue Sauce

**DAIRY-FREE, NUT-FREE, QUICK, VEGAN** ......................................................

Five-Spice Barbecue Sauce is infused with a Chinese five-spice blend. Although there are variations, a common mix for five-spice blend incorporates cloves, star anise, fennel, cinnamon, and Sichuan pepper. This sauce has a warm flavor that is deeper than Western-style barbecue sauce. It works like a charm for basting ribs. Surprise your friends and they'll beg you for the recipe!

........................................................................................................

½ cup sherry or red
  wine vinegar

½ **cup ketchup**

½ **cup low-sodium soy sauce**

⅓ cup sugar

4 garlic cloves, minced

½ **teaspoon Chinese
  five-spice powder**

_____

**Makes** about 2 cups
**Prep time:** 5 minutes
**Cook time:** 10 minutes

In a small nonstick saucepan, combine the sherry, ketchup, soy sauce, sugar, garlic, and five-spice powder. Cook over medium-low heat for about 10 minutes, or until the sugar dissolves and the sauce thickens. Stir occasionally. Use immediately on meats or let cool before refrigerating in an air-tight container for up to 7 days.

**WASTE-NOT TIP:** Use this as a replacement for regular barbecue sauce. Use it as a basting sauce for grilled meats or as a serving sauce for cooked meats. You may use it to replace the barbecue sauce and five-spice powder in Slow Cooker Falling-Off-the-Bone Five-Spice Barbecue Pork Ribs (page 169). You may also use it as a substitute in the Hawaiian-Inspired Turkey Meatballs (page 166) or the Sweet and Sour Pork Chops (page 174).

_____

Per ¼-cup serving: Calories: 68; Total fat: 0g; Saturated fat: 0g; Protein: 1g; Carbohydrates: 17g; Sugar: 8g; Fiber: <1g; Sodium: 735mg

# Peanut Sauce

**DAIRY-FREE, QUICK** ..................................................................................

This peanut sauce is adapted from Thai cuisine. It's creamy and savory with a light touch of sweetness. It's a multipurpose sauce since it pairs well with salads, noodles, grilled chicken or pork, and tofu. It especially shines as a dip for fresh spring rolls and celery sticks. If you love anything with peanut butter, you must definitely try this sauce—but it comes with a warning: it's addictive!

..................................................................................

½ cup creamy peanut butter
¼ cup low-sodium soy sauce
2 tablespoons rice vinegar
2 tablespoons honey
1 garlic clove, minced

**Makes** about 1 cup
**Prep time:** 5 minutes

Put the peanut butter, soy sauce, vinegar, honey, and garlic into a blender and blend until smooth. Use immediately or refrigerate in an airtight container for up to 4 days.

**VARIATION TIP:** You may replace the honey with brown sugar. For a gluten-free version, use tamari or a gluten-free soy sauce. For a spicy version, add ½ to 1 teaspoon of hot sauce.

**WASTE-NOT TIP:** Add 1 to 2 tablespoons of water to dilute the sauce if using it to drizzle on salads. You may use it in the Panfried Tofu with Peanut Sauce and Broccoli (page 129) or in the Pad Thai Noodle Salad with Peanut Sauce (page 117).

Per ¼-cup serving: Calories: 231; Total fat: 16g; Saturated fat: 3g; Protein: 9g; Carbohydrates: 17g; Sugar: 12g; Fiber: 2g; Sodium: 720mg

# Coconut Curry Sauce

DAIRY-FREE, GLUTEN-FREE, QUICK, VEGAN ...........................................................

This is a creamy and spicy sauce inspired by the bold flavors and ingredients of Thai cuisine. It requires no cooking, although it can be used for stewing meats and/or vegetables. It's a multipurpose sauce since it works well as an ingredient in soups, stews, and noodle dishes, and as a sauce to serve with meats. You may even use it as a dressing for salads.

..................................................................................................................................

**1 (13.5-ounce) can coconut milk**

**1 to 2 tablespoons red curry paste**

3 garlic cloves, minced

**1 teaspoon ground ginger**

1 teaspoon sugar

Salt

---

**Makes** about 2 cups
**Prep time:** 5 minutes

Put the coconut milk, curry paste, garlic, ginger, sugar, and a pinch of salt into a blender or food processor and blend until smooth. Use immediately or refrigerate for up to 5 days.

**WASTE-NOT TIP:** Use this sauce to stew meats and to toss with noodles, including as a replacement for peanut sauce in the Pad Thai Noodle Salad with Peanut Sauce (page 117). You may also use it to replace the coconut milk and red curry paste in Chickpea and Potato Curry (page 127). Leftover red curry paste can be used as an add-on ingredient to spice up soups and stews such as the Slow Cooker Southwestern Meatball Soup (page 107) or the Creamy Tomato Bisque (page 99).

---

Per ¼-cup serving: Calories: 94; Total fat: 9g; Saturated fat: 8g; Protein: 1g; Carbohydrates: 3g; Sugar: 1g; Fiber: <1g; Sodium: 47mg

# Lemon Vinaigrette

**DAIRY-FREE, GLUTEN-FREE, NUT-FREE, QUICK, VEGAN** ...........................................

This is a basic vinaigrette that goes well with most salads—especially in the summertime. Unlike dressings that have a mayonnaise, buttermilk, or yogurt base, vinaigrettes are oil-based and not as shelf-stable and should be used right away. The advantage of vinaigrettes over dressings is that they are lighter and fruitier. You can alternatively make vinaigrette by just shaking all the ingredients together in a mason jar and taking it along to your picnic.

................................................................

¼ cup olive oil

3 tablespoons freshly
   squeezed lemon juice

2 teaspoons sugar

**2 teaspoons Dijon mustard**

1 clove garlic, minced

Salt

Freshly ground black pepper

___

**Makes** about ½ cup
**Prep time:** 5 minutes

In a small bowl, whisk together the oil, lemon juice, sugar, mustard, and garlic, along with a pinch each of salt and pepper. Use immediately for best results, or store in an airtight container in the refrigerator for up to a day, letting it come to room temperature and whisking well before using.

**VARIATION TIP:** You may replace the lemon juice with any citrus juice, including orange, blood orange, or lime. You may also use honey instead of sugar.

**WASTE-NOT TIP:** Use leftover dressing in most types of salads, or as a replacement for the balsamic vinaigrette in the Very Berry Salad with Candied Walnuts (page 112) or the Pickled Beet and Crumbled Goat Cheese Salad (page 114).

___

Per 2-tablespoon serving: Calories: 133; Total fat: 14g; Saturated fat: 2g; Protein: <1g; Carbohydrates: 3g; Sugar: 2g; Fiber: <1g; Sodium: 63mg

# Orange Balsamic Dressing

DAIRY-FREE, GLUTEN-FREE, NUT-FREE, QUICK . . . . . . . . . . . . . . . . . . . . . . . . . . . . . . . . . . . . . . . . . . . . . . .

This is a creamy, citrus dressing that is best served chilled. It's perfect for salads or as a dip for fresh vegetables and even strawberries. The balsamic vinegar gives it a sweet and sour flavor that is balanced by the creaminess of the mayonnaise. You can make it sweeter by adding a little bit more honey.

2 tablespoons olive oil

**2 tablespoons balsamic vinegar**

**2 tablespoons mayonnaise**

1 tablespoon orange juice

1 garlic clove

**½ teaspoon Dijon mustard**

**1 teaspoon honey**

Salt

Freshly ground black pepper

**Makes** about ½ cup
**Prep time:** 5 minutes

Put the oil, vinegar, mayonnaise, orange juice, garlic, mustard, honey, and a pinch each of salt and pepper into a blender and blend until smooth. Use immediately or refrigerate in an airtight container for up to 3 days.

**VARIATION TIP:** You may replace the orange juice with any citrus juice. You may also use granulated or brown sugar instead of honey.

**WASTE-NOT TIP:** Use this dressing in salads or as a dip for vegetables such as baby carrots and celery sticks. It works well as a replacement for the balsamic vinaigrette in the Very Berry Salad with Candied Walnuts (page 112).

Per 2-tablespoon serving: Calories: 117; Total fat: 12g; Saturated fat: 2g; Protein: <1g; Carbohydrates: 3g; Sugar: 2g; Fiber: 0g; Sodium: 54mg

# Honey Dijon Dressing

**DAIRY-FREE, GLUTEN-FREE, NUT-FREE, QUICK, VEGETARIAN** ...................................

This is a creamy, sweet dressing ideal for drizzling over salads. It comes together in a snap and can likely be made with ingredients you already have at home. Not only will making your own dressing save some extra bucks, but you'll also have the opportunity to customize the spiciness from the Dijon, the sweetness from the honey, and the tang-iness from the vinegar, all according to your own tastes. Just scale these ingredients up or down to craft your own masterpiece.

⅓ cup mayonnaise

1½ tablespoons
   Dijon mustard

2½ tablespoons honey

1 teaspoon apple
   cider vinegar

⅛ teaspoon garlic powder

Salt

Freshly ground black pepper

**Makes** about ½ cup
**Prep time:** 5 minutes

In a small bowl, whisk together the mayonnaise, Dijon mustard, honey, vinegar, garlic powder, and a pinch each of salt and pepper. Use immediately or refrigerate in an airtight container for up to 2 weeks.

**WASTE-NOT TIP:** Use leftover Honey Dijon Dressing in salads, as a replacement for the balsamic vinaigrette in the Very Berry Salad with Candied Walnuts (page 112), or as a dip for crudités such as celery sticks and baby carrots.

Per 2-tablespoon serving: Calories: 165; Total fat: 13g; Saturated fat: 2g; Protein: <1g; Carbohydrates: 11g; Sugar: 13g; Fiber: 0g; Sodium: 243mg

*Mini Lemon Pavlovas with Lemon Curd* **228**

# 10

## *Sweets and Desserts*

# Coconut–Lime Macaroons

...........................................................

Coconut macaroons, also known in France as *congolais* or *rochers à la noix de coco*, are actually Italian cookies that were later modified by the French. They are naturally gluten-free and use eggs as their leavening agent. I added a bit of lime juice and lime zest to this version for a Latin twist. Be forewarned, you can't eat just one!

......................................................................................

**1 (14-ounce) can sweetened condensed milk**

**1 (14-ounce) bag sweetened coconut flakes**

5 teaspoons lime juice, divided

Zest of 1 lime

**2 large egg whites, at room temperature**

---

**Makes** 15 to 18 macaroons
**Prep time:** 10 minutes
**Cook time:** 35 minutes

1. Preheat the oven to 325°F. Line 2 baking sheets with parchment paper.
2. In a large bowl, combine the sweetened condensed milk, coconut flakes, 4½ teaspoons of lime juice, and the lime zest. Mix well.
3. Put the egg whites and the remaining ½ teaspoon of lime juice into another large bowl (or the bowl of a stand mixer). Using an electric mixer (or a stand mixer), beat the egg whites and lime juice on medium-high speed until firm peaks form, 3 to 5 minutes. Gently fold in the coconut mixture until combined.
4. Using a standard ice-cream scoop, scoop out batter and drop the scoops about 1 inch apart from one another on the lined baking sheets.
5. Bake for 25 to 35 minutes or until set and golden brown. Serve at room temperature.

**STORAGE TIP**: Store leftover macaroons in an airtight container at room temperature for up to 5 days. Freeze in sealable plastic bags for up to 3 months. Thaw in the refrigerator.

**WASTE-NOT TIP:** Use the egg yolks to make the Almond Queijadinhas (page 225).

---

Per serving: Calories: 210; Total fat: 11g; Saturated fat: 9g; Protein: 4g; Carbohydrates: 26g; Sugar: 24g; Fiber: 2g; Sodium: 103mg

# Almond Queijadinhas

**GLUTEN-FREE, QUICK, VEGETARIAN** ..............................................................

Queijadinhas are a Portuguese treat that is very popular in Brazil. Its name comes from *queijo* (cheese), which is one of its ingredients and serves to balance the sweetness of the treat. However, the addition of Parmesan cheese is optional in this recipe. Queijadinhas call to mind the filling of a crustless custard pie or tart. These delicious Almond Queijadinhas are gooey and sweet, with a predominant almond flavor. They are easy to transport, making them perfect for picnics or potlucks.

..............................................................................................................

1 (14-ounce) can sweetened condensed milk

1 cup sweetened coconut flakes

2 egg yolks, at room temperature

1 tablespoon grated Parmesan cheese (optional)

2 teaspoons almond extract

---

**Makes** 12 treats
**Prep time:** 5 minutes
**Cook time:** 20 minutes

1. Preheat the oven to 350°F. Line a 12-cup muffin tin with paper baking cups.
2. In a medium bowl, whisk together the sweetened condensed milk, coconut flakes, egg yolks, cheese (if using), and almond extract.
3. Fill the baking cups two-thirds full with batter. Clean off any stray drips from the baking pan with a wet paper towel.
4. Bake for 18 to 20 minutes, or until set and the top is golden. Remove from the oven.
5. Serve warm, at room temperature, or chilled.

**STORAGE TIP:** Store queijadinhas in an airtight container in the refrigerator for up to 4 days. Do not freeze.

**WASTE-NOT TIP:** Use the egg whites to make the Mini Lemon Pavlovas with Lemon Curd (page 228), and use the coconut flakes to prepare the Microwave Coconut Curry Popcorn (page 84).

---

Per serving: Calories: 165; Total fat: 7g; Saturated fat: 5g; Protein: 4g; Carbohydrates: 23g; Sugar: 23g; Fiber: 1g; Sodium: 61mg

# No-Bake Caramel-Pecan Cookie Balls

VEGETARIAN .................................................................................

This treat showcases the decadence of chocolate, the warmth of pecans, and the richness of gooey caramel. They make great edible gifts, as well as treats for holidays and parties. Store them in an airtight container in the refrigerator for 3 to 5 days.

.......................................................................................................................

**34 vanilla wafers**

**3 tablespoons chopped pecans, divided**

**4 ounces cream cheese, softened**

**1½ tablespoons caramel sauce**

**1⅓ cups bittersweet chocolate chips**

---

**Makes** 18 cookie balls
**Prep time:** 15 minutes
**Cook time:** 5 minutes, plus 45 minutes to chill

1. Line a baking sheet with parchment paper.
2. Put the wafer cookies and 1 tablespoon of chopped pecans in a food processor. Pulse until the cookies and nuts are finely ground crumbs, about 1 minute. Transfer to a large bowl and combine with the cream cheese and the caramel sauce. Mix well.
3. Using a tablespoon, scoop the dough and roll each scoop into a ball (about 18 balls total). Place onto the prepared baking sheet and freeze for 10 to 15 minutes.
4. In a medium microwave-safe bowl, melt the chocolate chips in 30 second increments, stirring between each increment, for 1 to 2 minutes. Stir well until smooth.
5. Using a fork, dip the cookie balls into the melted chocolate, then place them back on the baking sheet in a single layer.
6. Sprinkle the remaining 2 tablespoons of chopped pecans over the cookies and then refrigerate for at least 45 minutes, or until firm.

---

Per serving: Calories: 152; Total fat: 9g; Saturated fat: 4g; Protein: 2g; Carbohydrates: 18g; Sugar: 12g; Fiber: 1g; Sodium: 59mg

# Macadamia Cheesecake Cookie Bars with Chocolate Drizzle

**VEGETARIAN** ............................................................

You can store these decadent cookie bars in the refrigerator for up to 5 days or freeze them in a single layer for up to 3 months, making them a great make-ahead treat! Try different cookie dough flavors and experiment with different toppings.

............................................................

2 (16-ounce) packages refrigerated white chip macadamia nut cookie dough

1 (12-ounce) package cream cheese, softened

½ cup sugar

3 large eggs, at room temperature

¼ cup white chocolate chips

⅓ cup roasted and salted macadamia nuts

---

**Makes** 15 small bars
**Prep time:** 5 minutes
**Cook time:** 30 minutes, plus 2 hours to chill and 15 minutes to cool

1. Preheat the oven to 350°F. Grease a 9-by-13-inch baking pan and then line it with parchment paper. Spread one package of cookie dough in an even layer on the prepared baking pan.

2. Put the cream cheese and sugar in a large mixing bowl. Using an electric mixer, beat the cream cheese and sugar until smooth. Add the eggs and continue beating until smooth and slightly pale. Pour the batter over the cookie dough and distribute evenly.

3. Pinch off pieces of the remaining package of cookie dough, flatten them, and place the flattened pieces on top of the cheesecake filling here and there to create a patchwork pattern. Bake for 25 to 30 minutes, or until the cheesecake is set. Let cool for 10 to 15 minutes, then cut into 15 bars.

4. Place the chocolate chips in a small microwave-safe bowl and melt it in the microwave in 30-second intervals, stirring between each interval, until completely melted and smooth, for 60 to 90 seconds.

5. Drizzle the melted chocolate on top of the bars, and then top with chopped macadamia nuts. Chill in the refrigerator for at least 2 hours before serving.

Per serving: Calories: 429; Total fat: 24g; Saturated fat: 10g; Protein: 6g; Carbohydrates: 49g; Sugar: 32g; Fiber: 2g; Sodium: 277mg

# Mini Lemon Pavlovas with Lemon Curd

**DAIRY-FREE, GLUTEN-FREE, NUT-FREE, VEGETARIAN** .................................

A pavlova is a meringue-based dessert that is crisp on the outside and soft on the inside. It's usually flavored with vanilla extract and topped with whipped cream and fruit, especially berries. Unlike the more typical family-size pavlova, these are individual pavlovas, flavored with lemon juice and topped with store-bought lemon curd and fresh lemon rinds.

..............................................................................

**4 large egg whites, at room temperature**

2½ teaspoons lemon juice, divided

1¼ cups sugar

**1 teaspoon cornstarch**

**¾ cup lemon curd**

1 to 2 tablespoons thinly sliced fresh lemon peels, for garnish

---

**Makes** 12 mini pavlovas
**Prep time:** 15 minutes
**Cook time:** 40 minutes, plus 1 hour 10 minutes to cool

1. Position oven racks in the upper and lower thirds of the oven. Preheat the oven to 250°F.

2. Line 2 baking sheets with parchment paper. Then, using a 3-inch round cookie cutter, trace 6 circles in pencil on each of the sheets. Invert the parchment paper, or position the parchment sheets tracing-side down.

3. Before you begin, make sure that the mixing bowl for your stand mixer is very clean and dry, with no traces of grease; otherwise, the egg whites will not reach full volume.

4. Put the egg whites and ½ teaspoon of lemon juice into the mixing bowl and secure it on your stand mixer. Using the whisk attachment, beat the egg whites and lemon juice on medium-high speed until soft peaks form, 1 to 2 minutes. With the mixer still running, add the sugar, one tablespoon at a time, beating until the mixture becomes stiff and glossy, for 4 to 5 minutes. Sprinkle the cornstarch and remaining 2 teaspoons of lemon juice over the egg whites, then gently fold until combined.

5. Using an ice-cream scoop, scoop a mound of the meringue and place one mound in the center of each traced circle. Then, using the back of a spoon, make an indentation in the center of each mound.

6. Place the baking sheets on the racks at the upper and lower third of the oven and bake for 35 to 40 minutes, or until the pavlovas are firm and dry to the touch yet not brown.

7. Turn off oven and let the pavlovas cool for about 1 hour. Transfer to a wire rack and let cool completely, about 10 minutes more.

8. Top the pavlovas with enough lemon curd to fill their indentations, ½ to 1 tablespoon of curd. Scatter lemon peels on top and serve immediately.

**WASTE-NOT TIP:** Use leftover lemon curd as a filling for cakes and cupcakes, or to spread on cookies and toasts. You could even make a simple parfait of lemon curd, blueberries, and whipped cream for a quick and delicious dessert. Use the egg yolks to make Almond Queijadinhas (page 225).

Per serving: Calories: 146; Total fat: 1g; Saturated fat: 0g; Protein: 1g; Carbohydrates: 32g; Sugar: 32g; Fiber: 0g; Sodium: 28mg

# No-Churn Strawberry Ice Cream

GLUTEN-FREE, NUT-FREE, VEGETARIAN ..................................................

Do you love homemade ice cream but don't have an ice-cream maker handy? No worries! This recipe requires no churning, yet it's still very creamy and contains chunks of fresh strawberries. It's a summer favorite that my family and I have made many times using the same recipe, but with different types of fruit, such as peaches, other berries, cherries, or mango.

1 (16-ounce) container
   fresh strawberries, leaves
   removed, chopped
¼ cup sugar
Juice of 1 lemon
3 cups heavy cream
1 (14-ounce) can sweetened
   condensed milk

**Serves** 6 to 12
**Prep time:** 5 minutes
**Cook time:** 20 minutes,
plus 10 hours to chill

1. Put the strawberries into a food processor or blender and puree them.
2. Pour the pureed strawberries into a medium saucepan set over medium-high heat. Stir in the sugar and lemon juice and let the mixture come to a boil over medium-high heat, about 5 minutes. Reduce the heat to medium-low and simmer until slightly reduced, about 15 minutes. Transfer to a large bowl and refrigerate until chilled, 60 to 90 minutes.
3. Pour the heavy cream into a large mixing bowl (or the bowl of a stand mixer). Using an electric mixer (or a stand mixer), beat the cream just until stiff peaks form, 1 to 2 minutes.
4. Fold in the sweetened condensed milk until combined. Then, fold in the chilled strawberry mixture. Transfer to a standard (9-by-5-inch) loaf pan.
5. Firmly press a piece of plastic wrap directly against the surface of the ice cream to prevent the formation of ice crystals. Then wrap the entire pan in plastic wrap. Freeze for at least 8 hours or until firm.

Per serving: Calories: 684; Total fat: 49g; Saturated fat: 31g; Protein: 8g; Carbohydrates: 56g; Sugar: 54g; Fiber: 2g; Sodium: 113mg

# Avocado and Lime Mousse

....................................................

Mousse is a French dessert prepared by incorporating air bubbles into a sweet base. Depending on the ingredients and preparation, this can either produce a light and airy dessert (usually when made with whipped egg whites) or in a thick and creamy treat (when made with whipped cream). This Avocado and Lime Mousse has Latin-inspired flavors and a thick and creamy consistency, which is obtained by making whipped cream in the blender. It takes less than 5 minutes to prepare, and the real time spent is mostly for chilling. It's a versatile treat since it can be served as a mousse or even frozen to enjoy as an ice cream.

**1 (14-ounce) can sweetened condensed milk**

**3 small avocados**

3 tablespoons fresh lime juice

**2 tablespoons heavy cream**

---

**Serves** 4
**Prep time:** 5 minutes, plus 45 minutes to chill

1. Put the sweetened condensed milk, avocados, lime juice, and heavy cream into a blender and blend until smooth.

2. Pour the mousse into four ramekins and smooth the tops in an even layer.

3. Cover and place in the refrigerator for 45 minutes or until set and chilled. If desired, you may garnish the top of each mousse with fresh mint leaves, chopped pistachios, or any other garnish of your liking.

**MAKE-AHEAD TIP:** You can make this mousse ahead of time and keep it covered in the refrigerator for up to a day before serving. You can also freeze it and serve it as ice cream.

**WASTE-NOT TIP:** Use leftover heavy cream to make the Shrimp Scampi with Orzo (page 187) or the No-Churn Strawberry Ice Cream (page 230).

---

Per serving: Calories: 475; Total fat: 22g; Saturated fat: 8g; Protein: 9g; Carbohydrates: 65g; Sugar: 59g; Fiber: 5g; Sodium: 109mg

# Coconut Rice Pudding with Mangos

APPLIANCE, GLUTEN-FREE, NUT-FREE, QUICK, VEGETARIAN ...........................................

Rice pudding is a popular dessert worldwide, and almost every country has its own version. This one uses Arborio rice—an Italian short-grain, starchy rice—along with sweetened condensed milk and heavy cream to produce the best results: a thick and creamy dessert that is sure to please! Coconut milk is also used as a flavoring, and together with the mangos, that makes this dessert reminiscent of the popular Thai dish coconut sticky rice with mango. For a hands-off approach to the recipe, see the tip on how to make it in the slow cooker on the next page.

2 (13.5-ounce) cans full-fat
  coconut milk, divided

⅓ cup water

¾ cup dry Arborio rice

¼ cup sugar

1 (14-ounce) can sweetened
  condensed milk

½ cup heavy cream

3 to 4 ripe mangos, peeled
  and sliced

---

Serves 6 to 8
Prep time: 5 minutes
Cook time: 25 minutes

1. In a medium saucepan, bring 1½ cups of coconut milk and the water to a boil over medium-high heat. Stir in the rice and let it boil for 1 to 2 minutes. Then reduce the heat to medium-low and simmer, stirring often, until the rice has absorbed the liquid, 8 to 10 minutes.

2. Meanwhile, in a separate medium saucepan, heat the remaining coconut milk and the sugar over medium heat until warm, about 5 minutes.

3. Add this mixture and the sweetened condensed milk to the rice. Cook, stirring often, over medium-low heat until the rice absorbs the mixture, is cooked through, and gets creamy and thick, 10 to 12 minutes. Remove the pan from the heat.

4. Put the heavy cream in a small microwave-safe bowl and microwave for 60 to 90 seconds, or until warm. Stir the cream into the rice mixture.

5. Transfer the rice pudding to serving bowls. You can serve this dish warm, at room temperature, or chilled, with mango slices on top.

**STORAGE TIP:** Store leftover rice pudding in an airtight container in the refrigerator for up to 3 days. You may have to stir in extra heavy cream to loosen the pudding after chilling. To reheat in the microwave, stir in a little cream and then heat for 60 to 90 seconds. Do not freeze.

**APPLIANCE TIP:** To make rice pudding using a slow cooker, pour the coconut milk, water, and rice into the slow cooker and stir. Cover and cook on High for about 2 hours, or until the rice is fully cooked. Then, stir in the sugar and sweetened condensed milk. Cook on High for an additional 15 to 30 minutes, or until creamy. Heat the heavy cream in the microwave until warm, 60 to 90 seconds. Then, stir the cream into the rice mixture. Transfer to serving bowls and serve warm, at room temperature, or chilled, with mango slices on top.

Per serving: Calories: 699; Total fat: 36g; Saturated fat: 28g; Protein: 9g; Carbohydrates: 86g; Sugar: 63g; Fiber: 2g; Sodium: 110mg

# Amaretto Panna Cotta with Macerated Berries

**GLUTEN-FREE** ...................................................................

Panna cotta (or "cooked cream") is an Italian dessert made from boiling cream and sugar together, and then adding gelatin as a thickener. It's usually flavored with vanilla, coffee, or amaretto, among other possibilities. This panna cotta is smooth and silky, with an amazing almond flavor. The macerated berries, which have undergone a process of softening with sugar, make it beautiful and irresistible. It's the type of treat that you can make ahead and conveniently unmold and garnish before serving.

...................................................................

**2 cups heavy cream**

**1 cup half-and-half**

¾ cup sugar, divided

**2 teaspoons amaretto flavor extract or almond extract, divided**

2 tablespoons cold water

**1 (1-ounce) envelope unflavored gelatin**

**1 cup frozen mixed berries, thawed**

---

**Serves** 6 to 8
**Prep time:** 10 minutes, plus 35 minutes to macerate berries
**Cook time:** 10 minutes, plus 4 hours to chill and 10 minutes to cool

1. In a large saucepan, combine the heavy cream, half-and-half, and ½ cup of sugar. Bring to a boil over medium-high heat, stirring constantly, and cook for 5 to 8 minutes. Turn off the heat and stir in 1½ teaspoons of amaretto. Keep the pan on the burner.

2. Pour the cold water into a cup or ramekin and sprinkle the gelatin over the water. Let the gelatin mixture stand for 1 minute to soften; then microwave on High for 15 to 30 seconds until it is hot (but not boiling) and the gelatin is dissolved.

3. Stir the gelatin mixture into the warm sweetened cream. Then, pour the cream mixture into 6 to 8 ramekins and let it cool at room temperature for 5 to 10 minutes. Cover and refrigerate for at least 4 hours, or overnight.

4. About 40 minutes before serving, in a small bowl, mix the thawed berries with the remaining ¼ cup of sugar and the remaining ½ teaspoon of amaretto. Let the berries sit at room temperature for 25 to 35 minutes.

5. Right before serving, dip the bottoms of ramekins, one at a time, into a bowl of hot water for 3 to 5 seconds. Gently run a paring or table knife around the edges to loosen, then invert the ramekin onto the center of a small serving plate. Top each panna cotta with macerated berries.

**MAKE-AHEAD TIP:** You can complete steps 1 through 3 up to 3 days before serving. Keep the panna cotta, covered, in their ramekins in the refrigerator until ready to serve. Complete steps 4 and 5 just before serving.

**WASTE-NOT TIP:** Use leftover half-and-half as a replacement for heavy cream in soups such as the Creamy Tomato Bisque (page 99). The amaretto can be used to prepare the Cherry-Almond Cobbler (page 241).

Per serving: Calories: 436; Total fat: 34g; Saturated fat: 21g; Protein: 4g; Carbohydrates: 32g; Sugar: 31g; Fiber: 1g; Sodium: 46mg

# Mexican–Style Hot Chocolate Pudding

**GLUTEN-FREE, NUT-FREE, QUICK, VEGETARIAN** .....................................................

Traditional chocolate pudding is a custard dessert made with dairy and sugar, thickened with a starch, and flavored with chocolate. Sometimes egg yolks are also added. It's creamy, smooth, and velvety. The difference is, this version is eggless and also is flavored with cinnamon and cayenne pepper, which gives the pudding a warm and spicy tweak. For a mild version, skip the cayenne and whisk in 1 teaspoon of vanilla before pouring it into ramekins.

..................................................................................................................

½ cup granulated sugar

**6¾ teaspoons cornstarch**

**2 teaspoons ground cinnamon**

**⅛ teaspoon ground cayenne pepper**

**1¾ cups half-and-half**

**1⅓ cups bittersweet chocolate chips**

---

**Serves** 4 to 6
**Prep time:** 5 minutes
**Cook time:** 25 minutes

1. In a large stainless-steel saucepan, mix together the sugar, cornstarch, cinnamon, and cayenne. Then set the pan over medium heat, and pour in the half-and-half, whisking constantly, until it comes to a boil and thickens to the consistency of heavy cream, 5 to 8 minutes.

2. Turn off the heat, leaving the pan on the burner. Add the chocolate chips, cover, and wait 30 to 60 seconds. Remove the lid and whisk until the chocolate is fully melted and the pudding is smooth.

3. Pour into 4 to 6 ramekins. Let cool at room temperature until it sets, about 15 minutes. You may serve this immediately or cover and refrigerate for up to 3 days.

---

Per serving: Calories: 548; Total fat: 30g; Saturated fat: 19g; Protein: 5g; Carbohydrates: 74g; Sugar: 62g; Fiber: 4g; Sodium: 49mg

# No–Bake Mocha Pots de Crème

**DAIRY-FREE, GLUTEN-FREE, NUT-FREE, VEGAN** ......................................................

Pots de crème (or "pots of cream") is a French baked dessert made with egg yolks, sugar, cream, milk, and a flavoring ingredient such as vanilla or chocolate. They are creamy, sweet, and custardy. Unlike the classic, this recipe is dairy-free, eggless, and is not baked—but it's still creamy, with a bittersweet mocha flavor. It's made as a vegan dessert, but you don't have to be vegan to enjoy it. Take a look at the variation tip below for ingredient substitutions. If desired, garnish with fresh berries before serving.

......................................................

**1 (13.5-ounce) can full-fat coconut milk, divided**

**¼ teaspoon instant coffee**

**1 (12- to 16-ounce) container pitted Medjool dates**

**2 small avocados**

**2 (3- to 4-ounce) 90-percent chocolate bars, chopped**

---

**Serves** 4 to 6
**Prep time:** 5 minutes, plus 4 hours for chilling
**Cook time:** 5 minutes

1. Put ¼ cup of coconut milk in a small microwave-safe bowl and microwave for 30 to 60 seconds, or until hot. Whisk in the coffee just until dissolved. Transfer to a blender. Add the remaining coconut milk, the dates, and avocados. Blend on high until smooth.

2. In another microwave-safe bowl, melt the chocolate in 30-second intervals, stirring in between intervals, until completely melted, for 60 to 90 seconds. Stir well until smooth.

3. Add the blended ingredients to the melted chocolate, stirring until well combined and smooth.

4. Pour the mixture into ramekins, cover, and refrigerate for at least 4 hours, or up to 4 days.

**VARIATION TIP:** This recipe lends itself to substitutions. You can replace the coconut milk with half-and-half, the Medjool dates with ¼ to ½ cup of sugar, and the dark chocolate with bittersweet or milk chocolate.

---

Per serving: Calories: 773; Total fat: 42g; Saturated fat: 27g; Protein: 6g; Carbohydrates: 103g; Sugar: 84g; Fiber: 14g; Sodium: 49mg

# Brazilian Chocolate Bread Pudding Flan

...........................................................................

Bread pudding is a comfort food in many places across the globe. Brazil, my home country, has its own version. Unlike its American cousin, it's baked in a Bundt pan and has a smooth rather than chunky texture—more like a flan. Also similar to a flan, Brazilian bread pudding has a glaze of caramel sauce cascading from top to bottom once unmolded. This recipe is flavored with chocolate and has a balanced bittersweet flavor. It's pure indulgence!

...........................................................................

**5 cups stale baguette, chopped**

**3 cups whole milk, warmed**

3 cups sugar, divided

½ cup water

**4 large eggs, at room temperature**

**⅓ cup unsweetened cocoa powder**

---

**Serves** 8 to 12
**Prep time:** 10 minutes
**Cook time:** 50 minutes, plus 20 minutes to soak and 15 minutes to cool

1. Place an oven rack in the middle of the oven. Preheat the oven to 350°F. In a large bowl, soak the bread in the warm milk until softened, about 20 minutes.

2. Meanwhile, in a medium nonstick saucepan, combine 1 cup of sugar with the water over medium-high heat. Without stirring, let the sugar dissolve. If sugar crystals form on the sides of the pan, brush the sides with a pastry brush dipped in a little water. Every so often, gently swirl the pan around to lightly mix. The color will start to change in 8 to 10 minutes. Once it reaches an amber color, remove the pan from the heat and pour the caramel into a 10-inch ring baking pan or Bundt pan. Using oven mitts, swirl the pan to fully coat the bottom with the caramel. Set aside to cool and harden.

3. Put the soaked bread, remaining 2 cups of sugar, the eggs, and cocoa powder into a blender and blend until well combined, about 1 minute. Pour the bread pudding batter into the pan lined with caramel.

4. Bake on the middle rack, uncovered, for 35 to 40 minutes or until an inserted toothpick comes out clean.

5. Let the bread pudding cool on a rack for about 15 minutes, or until warm. Then, gently run a thin knife around the edges of the pan to loosen the bread pudding. Carefully invert it onto a large serving plate. Serve warm or cover and refrigerate until chilled to up to 3 days.

Per serving: Calories: 444; Total fat: 7g; Saturated fat: 3g; Protein: 9g; Carbohydrates: 92g; Sugar: 80g; Fiber: 2g; Sodium: 189mg

# Cherry–Almond Cobbler

.................................................................

Is there anything more American than cobbler? Bubbly, hot fruit filling topped with a batter, biscuits, or dumplings—yum! This cobbler is made from cherries flavored with almond extract and topped with store-bought biscuits. It's the perfect summer dessert and even more delicious when served with vanilla ice cream.

1 cup sugar, plus
  2 tablespoons
¼ **cup cornstarch**
**2 pounds frozen pitted**
  **cherries, thawed**
**2 teaspoons almond extract**
**Unsalted butter, for**
  **greasing**
**1 (16.3-ounce)**
  **can refrigerated biscuits,**
  **divided into fourths**

**Serves** 6 to 8
**Prep time:** 10 minutes
**Cook time:** 25 minutes

1. Preheat the oven to 400°F.
2. In a small bowl, combine 1 cup of sugar and the cornstarch.
3. Put the cherries with their juices in a large saucepan. Stir in the sugar and cornstarch mixture. Cook over medium heat, stirring often, until the sugar and cornstarch dissolve and the mixture thickens, 4 to 7 minutes. Stir in the almond extract.
4. Use the butter to grease a 9-by-13-inch baking dish, and then pour the filling into the baking dish and spread it in an even layer.
5. Put the remaining 2 tablespoons of sugar in a medium bowl. Add the biscuit pieces and toss to coat. Arrange the biscuit pieces on top of the cherry-almond filling. Bake for 12 to 15 minutes, or until the cherry filling is bubbly and the biscuits are golden brown. Serve warm.

**STORAGE TIP:** Store leftover cobbler in an airtight container in the refrigerator for up to 3 days. Reheat in the microwave on high for 30 to 90 seconds.

Per serving: Calories: 485; Total fat: 10g; Saturated fat: 2g; Protein: 6g; Carbohydrates: 98g; Sugar: 62g; Fiber: 5g; Sodium: 773mg

# Peach–Cardamom Crumble

DAIRY-FREE, VEGETARIAN ...................................................................

Sometimes confused with a cobbler, a crumble is deliciousness all its own. A crumble topping is usually made from granola or a mixture of butter, flour, and sugar. This recipe uses fresh peaches flavored with cardamom (an aromatic Indian seed) and topped with granola. It pairs perfectly with ice cream. If you can't find cardamom, simply replace it with an equal amount of ground cinnamon.

................................................................................................

**3 tablespoons unsalted butter, melted, plus more for greasing**

½ cup packed light brown sugar

**1 teaspoon cardamom powder**

**6 medium fresh peaches, pitted, skin-on, and cut into ⅓-inch slices**

**2 cups granola**

---

**Serves** 4 to 6
**Prep time:** 5 minutes
**Cook time:** 50 minutes

1. Preheat the oven to 375°F. Grease an 8-by-8-inch baking dish with butter.
2. In a large bowl, combine the sugar and cardamom, and then add the peaches and toss gently until the peaches are coated. Transfer the sugar-and-spice peaches to the greased baking dish. Bake for 30 to 40 minutes, or until bubbly and most of the fruit juices have evaporated.
3. Meanwhile, in a medium bowl, mix together the granola with the melted butter. Sprinkle the granola over the fruit and bake for an additional 5 to 10 minutes, or until the granola is golden brown.

**VARIATION TIP:** You can also make this crumble with frozen peaches. Thaw the peaches and drain them well before using. Also add 1 tablespoon of cornstarch to the sugar and carda-mom mixture in step 2. Complete the recipe as directed.

**WASTE-NOT TIP:** Use leftover cardamom to replace the ground cinnamon or chai latte powder in the Chai-Spiced Napoleons (page 244) or in the Chai Latte Waffles with Maple Syrup (page 59). Use leftover granola to make the Honey and Ricotta Dip with Figs and Granola (page 70).

---

Per serving: Calories: 443; Total fat: 12g; Saturated fat: 6g; Protein: 7g; Carbohydrates: 92g; Sugar: 50g; Fiber: 7g; Sodium: 12mg

# Spiced Skillet Cake with Caramelized Pears

NUT-FREE, VEGETARIAN .................................................................

This upside-down skillet cake is made from fresh pears and spice-cake mix. It's fragrant and comforting, perfect for a coffee break or served warm with ice cream as a decadent dessert. Although you may enjoy it all year round, it makes the perfect autumn treat.

.................................................................

**⅓ cup unsalted butter**

⅔ cup sugar

**2 teaspoons ground cinnamon**

**3 medium ripe yet firm D'Anjou pears, peeled, cored, and thinly sliced**

**1 (15.25-ounce) box spice-cake mix**

1 cup water

½ cup vegetable oil

**3 large eggs, at room temperature**

---

**Serves** 8 to 12
**Prep time:** 10 minutes
**Cook time:** 55 minutes, plus 5 minutes to cool

1. Preheat the oven to 325°F. Heat a 10-inch cast-iron skillet over medium heat. Put the butter, sugar, and cinnamon into the skillet and stir until the butter is melted and the mixture is smooth, about 2 minutes. Remove the pan from the heat and carefully arrange the pear slices on the bottom of the skillet.

2. In a large bowl (or the bowl of a stand mixer), combine the cake mix, water, oil, and eggs. Using an electric mixer (or a stand mixer), beat until combined, about 2 minutes. Then, pour the cake batter over the pears and smooth the top to form an even layer. Bake for 45 to 50 minutes or until a toothpick inserted into the center comes out clean.

3. Transfer the pan to a rack and let it cool for 5 minutes. Carefully run a thin knife around the edge of the pan to loosen the cake, and invert it onto a large, round serving plate.

**STORAGE TIP:** Store leftover cake tightly covered at room temperature for up to 2 days.

**VARIATION TIP:** You can also make this in a dark 10-inch round cake pan with 2-inch sides. If you don't have pears on hand, feel free to use apples instead.

---

Per serving: Calories: 578; Total fat: 28g; Saturated fat: 9g; Protein: 6g; Carbohydrates: 79g; Sugar: 53g; Fiber: 2g; Sodium: 448mg

# Chai-Spiced Napoleons

NUT-FREE, VEGETARIAN ..........................................................................

Are you throwing a tea party or having guests over for dinner? These napoleons are sure to impress, both for their classic elegance as well as their flavor. While they're super simple to prepare, you can bake the pastry ahead of time and assemble the dessert the day of serving, if you know you'll be busy. No matter how you get there, the result is layers of crispy pastry filled with fluffy clouds of spiced whipped cream.

..........................................................................................

½ **pound phyllo dough, thawed**

⅓ **cup unsalted butter, melted**

⅓ **cup heavy cream**

1 **teaspoon chai latte powder**

4 tablespoons powdered sugar, plus extra for dusting

---

**Makes** 4
**Prep time:** 20 minutes
**Cook time:** 20 minutes

1. Preheat the oven to 400°F. Freeze a medium mixing bowl and the beaters of an electric mixer for at least 20 minutes.

2. Meanwhile, lay out the phyllo dough on a flat surface and cover it first with a dry kitchen towel and, on top of that, a damp kitchen towel so that the pastry won't dry out.

3. Line a flat surface with a sheet of parchment paper, place one sheet of the phyllo dough on top of it, and lightly brush the phyllo with melted butter. Place another phyllo dough sheet on top and brush it with melted butter, repeating the process until there are 8 layers of phyllo dough. Brush the top with melted butter and then cut the stack of phyllo in half, crosswise, to make 2 rectangles. Next, equally divide each rectangle into 6 other smaller rectangles, totaling 12 rectangles.

4. Line a large baking sheet with parchment paper. Using a metal spatula, carefully transfer each rectangle to the lined baking sheet, leaving a small space between them.

5. Cover the phyllo rectangles with a sheet of parchment paper and place another baking sheet on top, pressing down on the rectangles. Bake for 12 to 16 minutes, or until browned. Transfer the stacked baking sheets to a rack and let them cool completely. Carefully remove the top baking sheet and parchment paper.

6. Meanwhile, prepare the chai whipped cream. Remove the mixing bowl and beaters from the freezer. Put the cream, chai latte powder, and sugar into the mixing bowl. Beat on high speed for about 1 minute, or until stiff peaks form. (Do not overbeat!)

7. To assemble the napoleons, lay four of the phyllo rectangles on a flat surface and either spoon on or pipe about one-eighth of the chai whipped cream on top of each rectangle (after you finish, you should still have half of the whipped cream left). Top each with another rectangle, then an even portion of the remaining whipped cream. Finish by topping each portion with one last layer of phyllo, so you have 4 (3-layer) rectangles, each with a double layer of whipped-cream filling. Generously dust the top of each napoleon with powdered sugar and serve immediately.

**MAKE-AHEAD TIP:** You can bake the phyllo rectangles 1 to 2 days ahead and store them in an airtight container at room temperature so that they will still be crispy. Assemble and fill them just before serving. To make the whipped cream more stable, add ½ teaspoon of cream of tartar with the other ingredients before beating.

**WASTE-NOT TIP:** Use leftover phyllo as a replacement for crescent dough in the Fig, Brie, and Pecan Bites (page 71), and use the remaining heavy cream to make Strawberries and Cream Panettone (page 252). Try leftover chai latte powder in the Chai Latte Waffles with Maple Syrup (page 59).

Per serving: Calories: 406; Total fat: 26g; Saturated fat: 15g; Protein: 5g; Carbohydrates: 39g; Sugar: 9g; Fiber: 1g; Sodium: 286mg

# Dulce de Leche and Banana Pie

**NUT-FREE, VEGETARIAN** .......................................................................

This decadent dessert was inspired by banoffee pie, an English dessert with a buttery cookie crust that's then filled with dulce de leche and topped with banana slices, whipped cream, and toffee. This version is a toffee-less take that's no less indulgent. It's buttery, sweet, and creamy—a treat for the eyes and the palate!

......................................................................................................

**14 graham crackers**
**⅓ cup unsalted butter**
**2 (13.4-ounce) cans dulce de leche**
**1½ cups heavy cream**
3 tablespoons sugar
**3 large bananas**

---

**Serves** 6 to 8
**Prep time:** 10 minutes
**Cook time:** 5 minutes, plus 4 hours to chill and 20 minutes to cool

1. Preheat the oven to 350°F.
2. Put the graham crackers in a food processor and pulse until they are finely ground. Transfer the crumbs to a large mixing bowl.
3. Put the butter in a small microwave-safe bowl and melt it in the microwave for about 1 minute. Pour the melted butter over the crumbs and mix until combined.
4. Pour the butter and crumb mixture into a 9-inch round pie pan. Using your hands or the back of a spoon, evenly spread and press the mixture along the bottom and up the sides of the pan to form an even crust.
5. Bake the cookie crust for 5 minutes, or until golden brown. Transfer it to a wire rack and let it cool, 15 to 20 minutes.
6. Once cooled, spread the dulce de leche over the bottom of the crust in an even layer. Cover and refrigerate for at least 4 hours, or overnight. About 20 minutes before serving, freeze a large mixing bowl and the beaters of an electric mixer.

7. Remove the mixing bowl and beaters from the freezer. Pour the cream and sugar into the mixing bowl. Beat on high speed for about 1 minute, or until stiff peaks form. (Do not overbeat!)

8. Remove the pie from the refrigerator. Slice the bananas and arrange them over the dulce de leche layer. Top with the whipped cream, spreading evenly to cover the bananas. Serve immediately.

**WASTE-NOT TIP:** Use leftover butter and graham crackers to make the No-Bake Dulce de Leche Chocolate Tart (page 248). The graham crackers can replace the sandwich cookies. Use the leftover heavy cream to make the Chai-Spiced Napoleons (page 244).

Per serving: Calories: 951; Total fat: 46g; Saturated fat: 27g; Protein: 14g; Carbohydrates: 126g; Sugar: 101g; Fiber: 3g; Sodium: 314mg

# No-Bake Dulce de Leche Chocolate Tart

**NUT-FREE, VEGETARIAN** ................................................................

Don't you love a no-bake scrumptious treat, especially in the hot summer? This dulce de leche chocolate tart is satisfying without being too rich. You can make this for entertaining, a weekend treat, or special occasions like indulging the sweet tooth of your Valentine.

1 (14.3-ounce) package
    chocolate sandwich
    cookies
½ cup unsalted butter, plus
    2 tablespoons
1 cup dulce de leche
8 ounces bittersweet
    chocolate chips
½ cup heavy cream

**Serves** 6 to 8
**Prep time:** 10 minutes
**Cook time:** 3 minutes,
plus 30 minutes to freeze

1. Put the cookies in a food processor and pulse until they are finely ground. Transfer the cookie crumbs to a large mixing bowl. Melt the butter in the microwave for about 1 minute. Pour the melted butter over the cookie crumbs and mix until well combined.

2. Pour the butter and crumb mixture into a 14-inch rectangular tart pan with a removable bottom. Using your hands or the back of a spoon, evenly spread and press the mixture into the bottom and up the sides of the pan to form an even crust. Make sure to make the edges a bit thicker so that it won't crumble once un-molded. Freeze for at least 15 minutes.

3. In a small microwave-safe bowl, heat the dulce de leche in the microwave until warm, 30 to 60 seconds.

4. Remove the tart pan from the freezer and spoon warm dulce de leche over the bottom crust and gently spread it to form an even layer. Place the pan back in the freezer.

5. Put the chocolate chips in a medium bowl. In a small microwave-safe bowl, heat the heavy cream in the microwave for 30 to 60 seconds or until warm. Pour the warm cream over the chocolate and whisk until the chocolate is fully melted and smooth.

6. Remove the tart pan from the freezer, pour the melted chocolate on top of the dulce de leche layer, and gently spread it to form an even layer. Place the pan back into the freezer for 15 minutes or until set. Serve immediately.

**STORAGE TIP:** Cover the tart and refrigerate for up to 3 days, or wrap in parchment paper, then tightly in plastic wrap, and freeze for up to 1 month. Make sure to thaw at room temperature 1 hour before serving.

**WASTE-NOT TIP:** Use leftover dulce de leche to make Dulce de Leche and Banana Pie (page 246), the chocolate chips to prepare Dark Chocolate Bark with Dried Raspberries and Pistachios (page 250), and the heavy cream to make No-Bake Mocha Pots de Crème (page 237).

Per serving: Calories: 879; Total fat: 52g; Saturated fat: 28g; Protein: 8g; Carbohydrates: 105g; Sugar: 80g; Fiber: 4g; Sodium: 387mg

# Dark Chocolate Bark with Dried Raspberries and Pistachios

**GLUTEN-FREE, QUICK, VEGAN** .......................................................................................

I love dried raspberries and pistachios in this recipe, but customize the chocolate bark to your preferences. Add a touch of heat by stirring a dash of cayenne pepper into the melted chocolate. It'll taste exquisite!

..........................................................................................................................

2 (3- to 4-ounce) dark
    chocolate bars, chopped
⅓ cup freeze-dried
    raspberries,
    roughly chopped
2 to 3 tablespoons
    roasted and salted
    pistachios, chopped

---

**Makes** about 12 pieces
**Prep time:** 5 minutes
**Cook time:** 5 minutes,
plus 10 minutes to chill

1. Line a baking sheet with parchment paper.
2. Put the chocolate in a medium microwave-safe bowl. Heat in the microwave in 30-second intervals, stirring between intervals, until the chocolate is melted and smooth, 1 to 2 minutes.
3. Spread the chocolate onto the lined baking sheet in a ¼-inch layer. Then quickly and evenly sprinkle the raspberries and the pistachios over the top. Very gently press the berries and nuts down into the melted chocolate.
4. Place the baking sheet in the refrigerator for about 10 minutes, or until the chocolate has hardened.
5. Gently invert the bark onto a flat surface. Remove the parchment paper and break the bark into about 12 pieces.

**STORAGE TIP:** Wrap leftover pieces individually in parchment paper and refrigerate in an airtight container for up to 7 days. Let it come to room temperature before unwrapping.

**WASTE-NOT TIP:** Use leftover freeze-dried raspberries as a snack on the go, to replace the berries in the Strawberries and Cream Panettone (page 252), or as a garnish for desserts.

---

Per serving: Calories: 97; Total fat: 6g; Saturated fat: 4g; Protein: 1g; Carbohydrates: 13g; Sugar: 10g; Fiber: 2g; Sodium: 14mg

# Almond–Flour Brownies

**GLUTEN-FREE, VEGETARIAN** ..........................................................

These almond-flour brownies are fudgy, nutty, and gluten-free. "Blanched" almond flour just means that it's almond flour that has had the skins removed from the nuts before being processed. If you don't have almond flour at home, no worries! Replace it with the same amount of all-purpose flour. To make this recipe low carb or keto, just substitute monk fruit for the sugar.

..........................................................

1 cup unsalted
   butter, melted

2 cups sugar

3 large eggs, at room
   temperature

1 cup blanched almond flour

⅔ cup unsweetened
   cocoa powder

---

**Makes** 9 to 12 brownies
**Prep time:** 5 minutes
**Cook time:** 35 minutes,
plus 30 minutes to cool

1. Preheat the oven to 350°F. Line an 8-by-8-inch baking pan with parchment paper and set aside.

2. Put the melted butter and the sugar into a large bowl (or the bowl of a stand mixer). Using an electric mixer (or a stand mixer), beat the butter and sugar until just combined. Beat in the eggs, one at a time, until just combined. Add the flour and cocoa powder and beat until the batter is smooth.

3. Pour the batter into the lined baking pan and shake the pan from side to side to even out the batter.

4. Bake for 25 to 35 minutes, or until the top is set and a toothpick inserted into the center comes out with moist crumbs.

5. Transfer the pan to a rack and let it cool for about 30 minutes before lifting out the parchment paper and cutting into 9 to 12 brownie bars.

**STORAGE TIP:** Store leftovers in an airtight container in the refrigerator for up to 5 days. Freeze for up to 3 months.

---

Nutritional information (per serving 1 of 9 total): Calories: 460; Total fat: 29g; Saturated fat: 14g; Protein: 6g; Carbohydrates: 51g; Sugar: 45g; Fiber: 3g; Sodium: 28mg

# Strawberries and Cream Panettone

..................................................................................................

Panettone is an Italian sweet bread very popular in Latin American, especially Brazil, which has a large number of descendants of Italian immigrants. This panettone resembles a strawberry shortcake yet requires no cooking. It's easy to assemble and perfect for holidays such as Easter and Christmas, not only for its lovely presentation, but also for its quick preparation. To make it more festive, garnish with fresh mint leaves or chocolate ribbons.

.............................................................................................................

**1 (17.5-ounce) panettone, such as Bauducco brand**

**1 pound fresh strawberries**

**2 cups heavy cream**

½ cup powdered sugar

**1 teaspoon pure vanilla extract**

---

**Serves** 6
**Prep time:** 25 minutes

1. Freeze a large mixing bowl and the beaters of an electric mixer for at least 20 minutes.
2. Meanwhile, remove the panettone from its box and plastic bag. Place it on a cutting board and slice it horizontally into 3 layers, using a large serrated knife.
3. Cut the berries into quarters.
4. Remove the mixing bowl and beaters from the freezer. Pour the cream, sugar, and vanilla into the mixing bowl. Beat on high speed for about 1 minute, or until stiff peaks form. (Do not overbeat!)
5. To assemble, place the bottom panettone round on a serving plate and spoon or pipe about one-third of the whipped cream onto it. Top with one-third of the strawberries. Top this with the middle panettone round and spoon or pipe on another one-third of the whipped cream, and then add another one-third of the berries. Top with the top panettone round and spoon or pipe the remaining whipped cream on top. Garnish with the remaining strawberries. Serve immediately or refrigerate for up to 4 hours.

Per serving: Calories: 1,237; Total fat: 60g; Saturated fat: 39g; Protein: 20g; Carbohydrates: 153g; Sugar: 100g; Fiber: 5g; Sodium: 571mg

# MEASUREMENT CONVERSIONS

|  | US STANDARD | US STANDARD (OUNCES) | METRIC (APPROXIMATE) |
|---|---|---|---|
| **VOLUME EQUIVALENTS (LIQUID)** | 2 tablespoons | 1 fl. oz. | 30 mL |
|  | ¼ cup | 2 fl. oz. | 60 mL |
|  | ½ cup | 4 fl. oz. | 120 mL |
|  | 1 cup | 8 fl. oz. | 240 mL |
|  | 1½ cups | 12 fl. oz. | 355 mL |
|  | 2 cups or 1 pint | 16 fl. oz. | 475 mL |
|  | 4 cups or 1 quart | 32 fl. oz. | 1 L |
|  | 1 gallon | 128 fl. oz. | 4 L |
| **VOLUME EQUIVALENTS (DRY)** | ⅛ teaspoon | —— | 0.5 mL |
|  | ¼ teaspoon | —— | 1 mL |
|  | ½ teaspoon | —— | 2 mL |
|  | ¾ teaspoon | —— | 4 mL |
|  | 1 teaspoon | —— | 5 mL |
|  | 1 tablespoon | —— | 15 mL |
|  | ¼ cup | —— | 59 mL |
|  | ⅓ cup | —— | 79 mL |
|  | ½ cup | —— | 118 mL |
|  | ⅔ cup | —— | 156 mL |
|  | ¾ cup | —— | 177 mL |
|  | 1 cup | —— | 235 mL |
|  | 2 cups or 1 pint | —— | 475 mL |
|  | 3 cups | —— | 700 mL |
|  | 4 cups or 1 quart | —— | 1 L |
|  | ½ gallon | —— | 2 L |
|  | 1 gallon | —— | 4 L |
| **WEIGHT EQUIVALENTS** | ½ ounce | —— | 15 g |
|  | 1 ounce | —— | 30 g |
|  | 2 ounces | —— | 60 g |
|  | 4 ounces | —— | 115 g |
|  | 8 ounces | —— | 225 g |
|  | 12 ounces | —— | 340 g |
|  | 16 ounces or 1 pound | —— | 455 g |

|  | FAHRENHEIT (F) | CELSIUS (C) (APPROXIMATE) |
|---|---|---|
| **OVEN TEMPERATURES** | 250°F | 120°C |
|  | 300°F | 150°C |
|  | 325°F | 180°C |
|  | 375°F | 190°C |
|  | 400°F | 200°C |
|  | 425°F | 220°C |
|  | 450°F | 230°C |

# INDEX

# ACKNOWLEDGMENTS

There are so many people to be thankful for when it comes to this cookbook.

My grandma Socorro, who made me fall in love with food at an early age and cooked for us the simplest yet most delicious dishes ever.

My dad, Clóvis, who taught me the value of discipline and perseverance, and who passed on without seeing my dreams come true. And also to my mom, Dorotéa, who made cooking messy and fun—it took away my fear of failure so that I could learn from my mistakes and succeed the next time.

Dedé, who made magic out of leftovers at my parents' home for more than 40 years. You taught me so much without even knowing it.

Katie Parr, who approached me for this amazing project.

Gleni Bartels, my editor, who believed in me and stretched my writing and cooking muscles. I have learned so much from you! And to Erika Sloan, who made sure the book was as detailed as possible.

All the stay-at-home parents and full-time professionals who hustle every day and still strive to provide good meals for their families. You are all heroes!

Last but not least, to my followers and readers who support my work and invite me to be a part of their lives in the kitchen. You make me smile every day!

# ABOUT THE AUTHOR

 Denise Browning was born and raised in Brazil, where she worked for many years as a lawyer before marrying an American and immigrating to the United States in 2002. Subsequently, she has become a Le Cordon Bleu–trained chef, cooking instructor, recipe and menu developer, and food writer with special expertise in global cuisine, including Brazilian cuisine.

Denise also founded the former blog *From Brazil to You*, which grew to be one of the most successful English-language blogs dedicated to Brazilian cuisine. It featured Brazilian recipes, stories, and photography of Brazil. Later she broadened her focus to encompass cuisines from around the world, transforming her site into *Easy and Delish*, with an emphasis on easy and healthy meals on a budget.

She believes that cooking should be approachable and affordable, and that food should nourish both the body and soul.

Her recipes have appeared on influential sites such as Food Network Canada, Food52, the Daily Meal, Parade, *Country Living*, *Smithsonian Magazine*, and many others. She is happy to count among her previous clients several famous national and international food brands, and even a critically acclaimed restaurant in Brazil.

Denise lives in Texas with her husband and two children, juggling motherhood and a full-time career—and embracing every bit of it!

CPSIA information can be obtained
at www.ICGtesting.com
Printed in the USA
JSHW030246260620
6363JS00003B/71